The Man Who Saw the Face of God

George Craig McMillian
(Kirantana)

C.T.P

Collins Trust Publications

Published by:

    RJ Communications
    51 East 42nd Street Suite 1202
    New York, New York 10017

In Cooperation with:

    Collins Trust Publishing
    Charleston, South Carolina

Design and Layout:

    HSA Design
    4 West 43rd Street
    New York, New York 10036

Cover Art:

    Jane Nussbaum
    www.artofvisionarylight.com

For my Father, Colonel Robert M. McMillian… a gentle man who became a warrior in WW II, then again in the Korean conflict, so I could grow up to become a different kind of warrior…

And

My mother, Rosemarie Klucznik… a nurse who danced with the soldiers at the USO.
She gave her life in healing service to others, so I could grow up to be a different kind of healer and server.

And

To my stepfather, Warren Collins… master Freemason, aeronautical engineer… a man whose kindness and generosity reaches his family and friends from beyond death. He showed me the unbreakable power and warmth of optimism.

And

To my spiritual mentor, Dr. Wanah T. Arnold…a blind physician who never knew the concept of 'giving up'. He taught me to pray till I got an answer.

And

To my many colleagues and friends, peace workers all over the world…who daily risk their lives in dirty little places…the people who make it happen behind the headlines.

TABLE OF CONTENTS

Preface vii

Generation Stage*

Chapter 1   I Came with a Sword 1

Chapter 2   Trial by Fire 35

Chapter 3   Dark Night of the Soul 59

Chapter 4   Goddesses & Witches 77

Chapter 5   Grace: The Vision 99

Chapter 6   The Test 119

Completion Stage*

Chapter 7   The Return 141

Chapter 8   Service 159

Chapter 9   Love 183

Chapter 10 Meditations from the Front Line 193

Epilogue 207

*Generation Stage, completion stage refers to the Tantrik Buddhist system of spirituality. In the Generation stage the student learns the scriptures and old stories of the lineage. Devotion and discipline are "generated", sometimes for a specific deity, or archetypal ideal.

In the Completion stage the student has absorbed the discipline and devotion and now actually becomes the embodiment of the deity or ideal. Whereas the first stage is very formal, following set learning schedules and practices, the second stage cannot be taught in a formal and set way. The becoming of the deity is an inner process that only the practioner discovers how to do as they move through life. The key word for this part of the journey is "imperceptibly." The process is imperceptible to the practioner as well as anyone else.

As applied to western spirituality it could be stated like this. First there is the learning of devotion for or to God, then in latter stages, one must give up God as an "object" in order to know God subjectively.

*All italicized sentences are meant to denote inner events, spontaneous prayers, or the author in dialogue with himself.

Preface

One morning in 1995, while living and teaching in Amsterdam, I felt a wave of deep depression and hopelessness pass though me as I sat in morning meditation. Later that day I visited one of my students, who told me how she had burst into tears for no apparent reason about the same time I was feeling this pain. We subsequently found out that it was the day that the French President, Jacques Chirac, had exploded the first of his atomic bombs deep in the earth, opening the way for a series of tests to follow. It was also a bloody summer in the last years of the Bosnian war. The news of the atrocities and slaughter in Sarajevo had been pumped into our minds for the past four years, and now the bomb was back. In one moment I felt the hopes and dreams of peace for the future shattered in the hearts of people all over the globe. It was not hard to read the thoughts of the world as we rushed toward the year 2000. A few weeks later I stood in the center of Sarajevo, feeling scared for all Humanity.

The western news had censored the true extent of the devastation and atrocities, and had spoon-fed it to us as just another bloody TV event, among the hundreds of murders and the violence seen daily on any TV station or movie theater. The world watched as all our famous spiritual leaders prayed, and national leaders practiced their politically correct rhetoric, and no one lifted a finger to stop the slaughter and rape of thousands of civilians in a modern European city, home of the 1984 Winter Olympics. 'Ethnic cleansing' became the correct word for television. The 'civilized' European feigned shock at the war in their backyard, and worked hard at negotiating, cutting deals, and planning for the future of their Euro dollar; big profits can be made in wartime. But when hundreds of thousands of refugees came pouring in, they were hit hard by the same reality they had seen just fifty years earlier, the nationalist hatreds, prejudice and competition, now surfacing again out of the fog of TV-controlled, happy consumer utopia. Sarajevo became a flashing neon sign for the whole world to see— "Money and politics— both political and religious— come before integrity and the sacredness of life."

Now that it is in the open, let us not shirk from the rest of this more accurate picture; let us give a truer definition to the word 'civilization.' We are survivors in a sea of thousands of years of human carnage, sheepishly and hypnotically chained to this self-perpetuating habit of pain. How could it be otherwise, as civilizations are built upon the backs of slaves. So slaves are what are needed in abundance. Religions, learning institutions, mega-business, and governments, unknowingly, and also many times knowingly, act in complicity to make sure that the supply is not slowed down in the feeding of this ravenous god.

So now, where do we turn for truth, for sanity, when we have seen that the very institutions in which we want to turn for help, are used by and have become the 'principalities' that St. Paul speaks of, to actually enslave us?

There is, and always has been, a shining beacon of light— like the Lotus flower that gently floats on the darkest brackish swamp— one power still stands unbroken, the power of the 'individual.'

Modern men and women, pushed and pulled by common need, drowning in images and words, painstakingly and carefully created to hypnotize obedient consumers into a life of cheap glamour and contrived significance, have little time to consider what an individual might be. As Emerson said, "civilization everywhere is in conspiracy against the individuality of all its members." This overwhelming immensity of today's outward allure, and the confusion it causes, slowly destroys the ability to find the individual in the integrity, strength, peace and beauty of our own souls. By soul, I mean, who we are in our original innocence, prior to all the programming: the mythological and cultural, and the way our personal biological family interprets and teaches us these filters hiding a more universal perception.

For two thousand years we have prayed, "Thy kingdom come, Thy will be done, on earth as it is in heaven." Yet as we look around us we can see humanity in worse perils then ever; a runaway train of pollution, crime, political corruption, starvation, caste hatred, and now the ability to blow ourselves out of existence in a matter of moments. Is this 'Thy will be done?' Is this really God's will for us?

It seems that Christianity has failed in its promise to bring 'peace on earth, good will toward all beings.' I personally feel that all the past religions have failed in this, or have not yet evolved enough to lead humanity to a better future, but I focus on Christianity because it is my native religion and the first religion to make the promise of peace. Could it be that they failed in the promise because they missed that the message of Christ was about God's honoring and trust for the individual, not suppression of the individual?

There are endless interpretations and arguments about what

Christ really taught or did not teach, none of which satisfies our whole being. For there can be only one understanding of Christ that ends all arguments, and that is to commune spiritually, mentally and viscerally with the fount of life itself. "I and my Father are one." This union was not just the accomplishment of one individual 2000 years ago; it is every human's birthright. But instead, Christianity has thrown down the 'Golden Calf' and placed Jesus in its stead. They have turned Him into a pagan icon to be worshipped, rather than to practice what he tried to teach us and asked us to do, and that is to find the Kingdom of Heaven within ourselves, and love each other as though it were Christ himself in each being.

The simple teachings of Jesus were made difficult to grasp with the coerced emphasis laid upon His divinity, an emphasis that He Himself never made. It was made to appear that he alone, and no one else, could possibly do His same works. Theologians have forgotten that He stated, ... "Greater works than these shall you do, because I go unto my Father." There are those that will argue he was talking only to his apostles. Don't believe them. Christ spoke to all peoples through all time, and most importantly, he spoke directly to You. So while the numerical growth of followers and theological interpretation has increased over the centuries, world peace has escaped us. Because of the distortion of His teachings and the remote relation to his human-ness, thus the blessing and empowerment of our own, we as a species, have yet to do these 'greater things.' I do not wish to belittle the great humanitarian works practiced by Christians around the world, for the coming of Peace is largely dependent upon creating right and charita-ble human relations. But in the Church's goal to convert all people to Christianity, the gospel according to Jesus has been badly trampled upon. It has emphasized theological doctrine and dogma, not the lov-ing understanding as exemplified by Jesus. It has preached the fiery Saul of Tarsus, and not the gentle carpenter of Galilee.

True Communion with Christ, turns millions of years of robotic biological behavior and thinking, into a new luminous biology and Universal thought, thus empowering us with the ability to give healing and 'life in abundance' to those around us. But instead, we meekly set-tle for a comparison of ourselves with scripture, written and edited by the Church hundreds of years ago, and of course, always find ourselves falling short. Harboring under this chronic sense of inadequacy, or what the Church calls sin, is the very mechanism for creating slaves.

But alas, we cannot be discouraged and fall under the spell of the past, and human victim mentality. If duality, confusion and the suffer-ing of history now force us to a genuine realization of our Selves, and our powers to co-create in this world, then indeed it has been the most precious of gifts. Disappointment is a profound sign of intelligence; it forces us into a choice, which is the fundamental requirement for a life of spirited power. In this day and age, when we are so fascinated by glamour and materialism, by empty rhetoric, medicine that doesn't heal and technology that doesn't bring peace, Jesus words to "seek the kingdom first before all things", where all our needs are met, will soon be a matter of survival, and not just an occasionally practiced Biblical quote. Faith is no longer enough, we call out for experience. The gestation period comes to an end, and the Second Coming is here and now, in our own hearts and bodies, if we truly hear the message of our own deepest individual Selves.

But how does modern mankind practice this seemingly impossible task? How do we practice putting God first above all things, when we are so goaded into focusing on more 'practical' things to attend to? This is by no means a purely Christian problem. Today, people of all religions around the world are faced with distractions and decisions that could not have been imagined in the simple times when the great world religions were founded. Before worldwide communication, the different faiths and philosophies grew in little pockets of the world, relatively undisturbed. Of course, they would be different according to the times, customs and needs of the people in the region. But today's technology of worldwide communication, has amplified and thrown back into our face, our lack of commitment to understand each other and create harmony, and this has created grave danger for us all; we are truly at a turning point in our evolution— Does this run away train of habitual behavior continue, or are we mature enough to step up and become co-creators of our planetary reality?

It was my own questions about violence in the world, and how it infiltrated my own person, that started me on my spiritual quest for answers. As the middle child born into a Roman Catholic family, I toyed with the idea of the priesthood. But while beginning pre-seminary studies with the priests of Notre Dame, my mother and father divorced. My mother was unfairly shunned by the Church, which caused our whole family to leave the faith. The Vietnam War was starting to engulf the attention of the world; millions of us watched in disbelief as the body counts rose. My father, a life long military man, told me that the reason he had fought in World War II was because they said it was the last war, the war to end all wars. His silence and disgust at the continuance of this 'sickness' only served to fuel my fervor at understanding the world I lived in. Having always been an introspective person, I began to ask questions about how I might be programmed to passively accept violence as being normal. Fighting came easy to me and I became suspect, because I knew that it was not my true inner nature, even though current evolutionary science said it was. I needed answers, and so I continued my early search and questions in eastern religions and meditation. After almost twenty years of authentic Tantrik practice, my whole life changed, when one morning I received a vision of the Universal Christ. This was a Christ unlike any I had heard or read of before. This was a Christ of today. A Christ that honored all people, cultures, religions and philosophies that search for truth, justice and harmony. A Christ for the artist, the sensualist, with a little effort even the atheist could grasp this vision. I saw the way of peace by seeing that we all came from one common origin, as all boundaries were dissolved and I merged into the infinite, called God in the language of our time. Now standing scared in Sarajevo, some thirty years after my search began, I felt an urgency to write this story.

In my early years of trying to share this vision I was met with skepticism and consternation; I naively thought I should first reach the ministers and clergy. Sadly, I saw that most of these well meaning people had unknowingly become the Pharisees and Sadducees of our day, or worse, they shake their Ph.D.'s at you like old witch doctors shake their bones. By what authority do I say these things? An age-old question. The people who always ask this question, have their own ancient lineage of being caught in the historical rut of preference for conceptual knowledge. Religion and education have become constrained in a language-based understanding of Life, rather than trusting Life Itself at the very core of our reality. But conceptual systems, which rely upon our belief for their existence, shut out both our natural awareness and new evolutionary information that brings loving-kindness and better conditions into the world. A belief must be defended, whereas 'knowing' stands on it's own and need never be defended. Without this restful 'knowing', we become so preoccupied with defending the concepts of our imaginations, that we become virtual prisoners of our own projections. In contrast, the full visceral experience of 'knowing' Christ, takes courage and responsibility. One must be willing to accept the magnificent power and erotic reality of human design, as ones bio-circuitry interfaces with the living, joyful intelligence that keeps every molecule of the Universal landscape and mindscape, moving in absolute Harmony. And there is responsibility, for the lineage of Jesus is one of service and healing in this world. No belief system requires such a complete surrender and participation. On the contrary, static systems vend a sweet hidden poison offering to assume responsibility for us, short-circuiting us from our own innately intelligent I Am, shrouding us under thousands of years of dogmatic fear. Our own inner guidance by a truly 'wholly' spirit, of which human language can describe only the smallest tip of the ice berg, embodies a deeper, and more ancient sense of intelligence, and is the only authority we need. No more 'middlemen'— we need direct hook-up.

So, in order to answer the question— "By what authority do I say these things?"— I felt it would be helpful to tell the whole story of my spiritual search leading up to this vision of Christ. And because revelation is so much more than just an event or flash, I have also written of my life for many years following. The sincere seeker of spiritual life needs, and has the right to know, what is true and possible. Because of this I have given great effort in recording the stories as they happened. Memory at best is still a plastic phenomenon, but a life in God is beyond memory; it is a stability in Now— the vision lives in me today as fresh as the Now moment in which it unfolded. I have chosen only the stories about which I have an accurate recollection. These are clearer to me because I feel they were the turning points that moved me along the whole journey, and best explain my efforts at trying to bring the vision into my everyday life.

I am by nature, what most people would consider an ascetic and private person, so it has not been easy to open my private life to public scrutiny, and before Sarajevo I would have been embarrassed at how many times I used the word 'I' in this book. But I felt that I must give my all to honor this vision, and do my best to give it its destiny to stand on its own merit as a true and further revelation of the living gospel, and our mysterious unfoldment as humans. For when the faceless "principalities" allow for the spread of hatred and murder in God's name, all hesitation must be put aside, surely sane men and women must stand forth and speak out.

For those readers of more mainstream and conservative sensibilities, I do not wish to lose you, so I give pre-warning, you may not like the young man in the early chapters of this book. The earliest working title of this book had a sub-title... "The Secret Confessions of a New Millennium Man." I assure you I am not condoning or recommending the way in which he searched for answers. My intent in presenting his many indulgences is to show the great contrast in how his life changes after a true encounter with God, chapter 5 "the Vision", the turning point of his biography, especially in how he changes toward the feminine.

Some may think that I have had an extraordinary life. I feel that we all have extraordinary lives, if we pay attention. My life has only had more 'miraculous' occurrences than most, because I have lived outside of society for almost thirty years, and because they were the natural by-product of my particular craft in the world; much more is possible when one lives outside the psychic boundaries of society's agreed upon reality. But revelation is the same for all, no matter where or how we live. It is created by an urgency, a cry deep in the soul of collective humanity; we all feel the pain of growth, we all know light when we see it, though many pretend they don't. Anyone can say they are telling you some great truth, but I have been struck by how many have thanked me for writing the words that described their own revelations and inner triumphs, learned in their own many different ways. And that is one of the great miracles of Christ, that each person can have an absolutely unique and personal relationship with this sacred mystery, if we are willing to leave all our concepts behind— that is the price of the ticket. So read with your spiritual organs, and I have no doubt you will find all this familiar. If revelation is true, it will feel that way to all of us, it will give power to all of us. It has been said that absolute power corrupts absolutely. But it is only so when the few have it. This vision of Christ gives absolute power to all, if understood correctly, for it will take this kind of grass roots power to change "Thy will be done, on earth..." from a fading, wishful, storybook dream—to an actual golden reality for all.

Generation Stage

Chapter 1

I Came With A Sword

Heat Pressure

Surfaced into awareness from some inscrutable stupor of cosmic drowse. Not the words, but the infant sensations of the first shadow of what I later came to know as Self. A millionth of a second by millionth of a second, a recognition incessantly, yet aimlessly focused the kaleidoscope of sounds, colors, and smells dancing before me. And whatever it was that came from the temple across the street, I knew that It was the 'Pied Piper.'

Temple? Street? The question, "Where am I?" And it all started again. Around and around, repeating forever some unconscious act. Dissolution, - Nothingness, - Peace. - Heat, - Pressure, - Breath, - Self, - Dissolution, on and on.

I had been laying in a pool of my own sweat for weeks, helplessly burning and delirious, unable to communicate with anyone to let them know I was ok, I was right where I was supposed to be.

Whenever I could hold together a Self long enough to put a few thought sentences together, I wondered at how the will to live and the will to die had become one in the same adventure. And I loved adventure. The sense of alertness and curiosity, confronting the viewless dangers of the unknown. I was bored with my predictable California life. There wasn't much more to explore in the world. But this was India, and there is no frame of reference for a Westerner no matter how many books you read, or films you see. India really happens under the surface, one big subliminal explosion.

The three doctors stood around me, concerned and baffled as I melted away over the weeks. I could read their minds so easily. It didn't look good. What if the young white master were to die here in our care. They did their best, but nothing seemed to work. But I felt safe and knew there was a sense of grace to this. It was the way I was gently lifted from my body every time the pain became too much. The temple across the street had around the clock, nonstop chanting to God, which had continued unbroken for hundreds of years. One had only to focus on the music, and you were projected into uncharted interior territories, some more blissful than others, but always glorious release from the pressure and heat.

But then there was that doorway I was so curiously uncurious about; an opaque doorway that I stood in front of for days, fascinated by the feelings that called through my forced laziness. I knew what was behind that door, and that is why I took my time. Natural curiosity always propelled me into the unknown, but this was not so unknown. I knew exactly what was there, but had spent so many years pretending I didn't know, all I could do was stand paralyzed unable to enter, unable to turn back. I could have stood there for thousands of years not knowing what to do. Then he would come.

That is what grace has always meant to me. When you are out there alone, stretched beyond your limits, there is always something more that we in our limits could never have thought of. Something unexpected, factor X. It is said, "Ask and you shall receive," and sometimes it comes when you forget to ask. He was a skinny little man, with a kind whimsical face, comfortably resting behind a cloud of white beard. He could have been right off some Hollywood set, except for the life that oozed from his gaze. As he came into focus, I saw he wore only a diaper, covering his privates, and a starched white turban over his tanned face. He walked regally on his bird-like legs up to my bed, as the doctors sheepishly moved to the side. No words did he ever speak, and I wondered who this might be that everyone in the room so passively moved aside for him. A small rock pendulum was reverently pulled from his diaper, and he began to swing it over my navel. And in his eyes I saw *knowing*. He knew everything that a being could possibly know at this time in earthly evolution; and I knew with my whole being that he knew. As my body began to relax, I felt myself come back from my formless perch, and begin to spread through the fibers and sinews of what was now my completely changed unfamiliar body. The little pendulum seemed to smooth out all the reverberations and resistance in me, until I was a deep pool of calm. And now I knew I could enter that doorway.

I was fifteen years old in my old house in Los Angeles, my father sitting in front of me. "Don't cry. Be strong, these things happen. Your mother and I just don't get along anymore, and I'm going to move out. It happens all the time, so there is no reason to feel bad." A rip in the fabric of my reality had just happened, and through that crack, the words implanted themselves in me, "Don't feel, — don't cry." In that moment I became a split person, suddenly self conscious and ashamed of my normal intense emotions. It was as if a demon under a large black cloud had been waiting just outside my aura, a turbulent whirl of dark thoughts and feelings, and a susceptibility I had never known before. As soon as the crack opened, I was pounced upon and became enveloped in a new universe of pain, a prison that would now be my home for many years.

I had always been a natural athlete, chosen for the all-star teams: football, baseball, track, etc. But this year the fun was gone. As if the sap had run out of my every pore, I became a hollowed-out tree, looking strong and solid on the outside, but cold and empty on the inside. I started to get into fights, and if there was no one to fight, I cut myself with glass just to see if I could take the pain, smell the blood. After all, wasn't this world about the blood?

All this flashed in front of me as if I was living it, but also at the same time, I was standing outside myself observing. I could feel the pendulum gently swinging over my belly, and those droll knowing eyes. Always, when the emotional pain seemed like it was too much, I could feel him pulling me back to the center, smoothing me out and preparing me for what would come next. Then swoosh! —I was somewhere else.

Doctors again! An intense false light! I could see them around me; all through the room, the men of authority stretching back to antiquity, the old Jewish priests and doctors, learned men, temple sages, and Catholic priests with stern faces. No word was spoken by them at my birth. I was taken from my mother and laid out on a table—the very act, a symbol. They all gathered around. In their minds, I could hear their unspoken words reaching back into the ancient history of this new place I had come.

"Welcome to our tribe."

"Here are the rules."

"Do as you are told."

"Don't make trouble."

"Don't rock the boat or make waves."

"You have no boundaries."

"You belong to us."

"Think what we teach you to think, and if you don't, we are going to hurt you."

"Here is the proof."

Hot searing pain, shot through my nervous system; I screamed in terror and revulsion as they cut the skin from my penis! I awoke in this world with the smell of my own blood on my loins, a fear burned into the core of my body. This was a world of blood and pain.

Flashes of light! Swoosh! Eighteen years later! I was standing on the football field of Notre Dame's Catholic Preparatory School, in full 'armor.' The blood was all over my hands and streaming down my face from a cut over my eye. I had learned to be proud of it. It meant I was playing good, with no thought for my body. Just one pure intention; crush my opponent. This disregard for our bodies had been indoctrinated into us for years. "You only get hurt when you fear getting hurt," the coach drilled into us. Since being cut to the second team for 'attitude' problems, my emotions swung like a hinged door, from total indifference to pure rage and abandon. Taught to think what I was told, I never associated the trauma of my parents' divorce with my dramatic nosedive in my studies and athletics. My brother, sister and mother, were too much into their own pain to notice very much, we never talked about it. Mother worked hard to keep us all together, but in our souls we all went our own ways. To me there was no trauma. My father said, "It was nothing," so I took that to be true. My life had just changed for the worse for no apparent reason. I had 'attitude' problems. This was the Notre Dame football machine, bigger than all of us, and nothing else could be considered.

One of the coaches was a sadistic little Mexican man with big aspirations to coach college football. He always seemed to know when I was at my most neurotic high. The coach ran his offense through my position in the defensive line, over and over again, smiling as I became increasingly more violent. I was driven into a frenzy of hate and rage, until I was either too hurt to continue, or I had hurt too many other players. The minutes of hate turned into hours, days, weeks, months and years, and through the rip in my being poured the world's mindless shapes and forms of violence.

One day, my friend who had the position next to me on the line, called me over to his car. He pulled out a rolled cigarette, lit it up, and told me it was marijuana. The only thing I knew about marijuana, was many years earlier, seeing George Putnam on the Channel Five News make the first live TV drug bust. George was self righteous and indignant, but I remembered the strange smiles of disbelief on the faces of the people as the cameramen broke into the house. I tried it, and after a few coughs and sputters, noticed I was smiling like those people on TV, and didn't know why. Suddenly we were both laughing. For better or worse, my life was about to change.

It was toward the end of the football season in my senior year, the team in third place with no chance of progressing. My friend and I decided it was time to try getting stoned before going to practice. After laughing our way through warm-ups, we started to scrimmage. The coach was in one of his sadistic moods, which he fell into often these days. With a third place team, his college aspirations were becoming more and more remote. He ran his running backs at me six plays in a row, to see if he could get a rise out of me. But by the end of the season in my senior year, it had become just another boring day. With the effects of some very good grass, I was actually having fun. Coach became furious as I destroyed and beat up his backs. He was screaming to them, "Grind that big sissy into a hole." I didn't react. Then, something very peculiar started to take place. I began to feel as if, now I was controlling him in my calmness. He became like a yo-yo to me; I could make him angry with the slightest change in my attitude and body language. I remembered all the times over the years that the coaches had told us to try and injure opponents, to get them out of the game. Every insult this man had given me was echoing in my head, and I felt a force of violence in me that went way beyond my understanding. It was not red-hot anger; it was a motionless white-hot anger. This force of violence was all around me; pushing me, pulling me, yet inside I was a perfectly calm observer. The ball was snapped. Everyone moved in slow motion. The coach's favorite player was going for an end-run. Normally you take it easy on your star running backs; but like a foul wind, the wrath of the coach pervaded the field. I knew the runner's every move before he made it, before he even thought it. He was following my will like a cat hypnotizing a bird; he headed right for my jaws. The two opposing linemen were supposed to take me out, but I jumped to the outside, moving with the running back. I could sense my own outside line-backer moving behind me, and knew that he was moving to cut the runner off from going around the end, forcing him to cut back to the middle of the field. In a perfect flow of thought and movement, I hesitated so the runner's attention would shift to the linebackers moving behind me. I was in the action, but also observing the whole play, seeing the micro-movements, hearing the sounds of his breath. I turned on all my speed and anger just as the running back was shifting his weight to cut back to the center. I caught him at full-speed while he was standing on one leg — 225 pounds of trained violence smashed into him. I heard cracks in his ribs, the air rush from his body. He hit the ground and started to convulse. As the coach ran to him, I stood in silence and noticed two things. One, I didn't care what had happened to him. The part of me that had been trained to do violence had done its job. Even though I thought that I might have killed him, I was coldly detached and my revenge was complete against the coach. The other thing I noticed was that I was also a very peaceful observer watching all of this. A being that was completely separate from the violent person standing there, from the action, the contrived purpose and meaning of football, school spirit, violence, my whole culture. Lights! Heat! Swirling in my belly!

* * *

The smiling little man stood over me with his pendulum. As soon as I was focused in the room, he stood up, politely bowed to everyone and shuffled away on his little bird legs. At other times in my life I would have had a thousand questions. What was happening to me? How? Who is this little man? But the part of me that always needs to know everything was lost somewhere in the weeks of fever. Outside the big cities, everyone in India seems to act like this. Strange occurrences are part of this culture, so there is an attitude of acceptance of things the way they are, and not much curiosity of why. Though the people around me treated me, and the whole event of my 'sickness' with reverence, they could not know the enlightenments constantly exploding in me during the fever. From my outer actions and appearance they knew that something special was happening. The fever would burn in me all through the day and then mysteriously subside just before midnight. Midnight is when the men were allowed, by themselves, into the temple to clean the entire interior and grounds. Pushing aside everyone's concern, I dressed in my best whites and crossed the street to the temple. Though I had been sick all day, I still seemed to have the strength to clean from midnight until about three thirty in the morning. To me this all seemed quite normal, but to others I was an object of curiosity, as they watched me literally change day to day. I dropped from 215 pounds to 155 pounds during a forty-day period.

The temple was magic! It sat by itself in the middle of a huge pool of water, with only one walkway across. At night it glowed like a jewel in a sea of black. The top half was made of gold, the bottom of marble. We entered the temple and stood on the bottom floor to say the prescribed prayers after all the carpets had been taken up. After prayer, some of the men threw buckets of milk and water onto the marble floors. On our knees, we scrubbed every inch, upstairs and downstairs with our towels. This happened every night until about 3:30 a.m. when the first worshiper would appear. If I finished early, before the temple opened, I was allowed to go sit by myself on the second floor and listen to the chanters reading from the scriptures; beautiful songs and poems from the greatest spiritual poets of India, creating a sound current that filled the temple. These were sacred and precious moments of ecstasy, in union with these poets in their worship. All other times of the day the temple was packed with people, but this time was for the committed. There were small alcoves with open windows looking out over the water that one could sit in. Staring into the dark pool outside, the sound of all the chanters moved through my body; opening, caressing, bathing me in peace; changing the structure of my senses. Around five a.m., I would go back to my room and sleep until about eight a.m. then awaken again with the fever.

In the long hours lying on my back, I had plenty of time to consider the pictures that surfaced in the most intense periods of fever. Things that had happened to me earlier in my life that I could not understand, now I saw from an overview. Not hindsight, but rather as an over-viewer; observing, making connections to all 'events' in my life, seeing the decisions I had made in those earlier times, hidden from my conscious mind at the time of their happenings. It was easy to go back to that moment on the football field and view the momentous questions that were just beginning to form in my suppressed, but sincere consciousness. Why was I so violent? Why is this world so violent? These were my first questions on the long journey I was about to embark upon. From my perspective in India, I could watch my young thoughts form. The peaceful observer on the football field on that day, and the observer here in India, were now one in the same. "But if this peaceful center is what I am, then how and why was I acting so violent, competitive, and uncaring?" I saw this 225-pound young man as a programmed robot, with almost no free will at all, *conditioned* to act on cue to hypnotic words — God, love, religion, women, war, sex, money; the images on TV and magazines, carefully created over the years to have hypnotic effect; a certain look of women, used to sell us clothes, cars, liquor, and just about everything. I was truly expected to give up my own Will and go 'gaga' on cue. In times before, it was called sorcery, the craft of capturing another's attention. Today, high paid experts of the art, control whole countries. And if I didn't want to be part of it, then what? Who was I then? And there was that insidious underlying feeling, the invisible "they" that would hurt me if I didn't obey. These were *my* first questions, *Me*— the first crying out from my painful prison. I raged against the manipulation. And that was the real sorcery of how I was kept in my place in the scheme, the endless knot: rage fighting against rage.

The running back recovered, but didn't play the rest of the season. Neither did I. That next Friday my father was coming to watch me play. I hadn't seen him in months. The coach had me sit on the bench the whole game, and I became smaller and smaller. He never came again. I watched the painful thoughts form in my young mind, "He left because I wasn't good enough." Not a good thing to decide when so young and starting to get stoned, which seems to amplify every thought. I watched as my fate became set for many coming years. I was locked into a one-lane track of seeking attention, endlessly trying to prove myself, pushing everything I did to the extreme, goaded by my culture, and always ending with, "I wasn't good enough."

Lying on my back, I watching the hopelessly sad movies of my life as the fever burned them from my cells, and for the first time, wept with no holding back. The stories paraded in front of me for days on end. New connections in my brain were being forged, new understandings were born and old ones were burned away. Memory was nothing but a chemical chain in a certain sequence, locked in the body. Everything moved and shifted in the heat, as the marbled pathways of pain turned to liquid. The little 'bird man', as I affectionately called him, came every few days, always at the right moment in my reverie. Feeling his pendulum swinging over my belly, I would return from my mental wanderings to a silent calm, the place of *knowing*. I began to sense that I had known that peace before, in some other place, and the easy longing to see it again, told me I was not yet through with the fever.

Fearlessness is discovered when one rises above the world's sea of thought forms. After many weeks of fever, I had disassociated myself from any concern of death and began to see that everything happening to me, interiorly and at the temple, had a beautifully orchestrated pattern and coherence. The Indians called it the Mother Kundalini. I didn't know, but whatever "it" was, "it" had earned my trust. Even urgency surfaced so gently, as the slightest shift in my thinking or questioning whisked me off to new interior wanderings that would last for days.

* * *

I loved to see my father in his uniform. He was a Quartermaster and officer, sent to Alaska to ship supplies into the Korean conflict. He had fought in the worst Naval battles of WWII on board a destroyer warship, and then transferred to the Army Officer's School after the war ended. Fighting, war, discipline — the aura was always around me. We awoke early in the morning to the sound of bugles and cannon blast.

Alaska was a young boy's paradise and I spent many hours alone, walking in the woods behind the school; the trees, snow, animals, and myself. I never met any other children in the woods, but to me it just seemed right to be here. If you were quiet long enough, some wild animal would always show up; deer, elk, giant moose, and occasionally a bear. There was always a silent communication with them, a feeling I had not yet learned to question. One day, a giant Bull Moose appeared behind our school. We could look out the windows and see him standing alone on the small plateau overlooking our playground. He came day after day and would stand perfectly still in majestic silence for about an hour, then leisurely walk off into the woods. On the days he didn't show, I was sad and would return to school the next day in anticipation of seeing him again. I noticed the days he didn't come were the days on which the Army Ski Patrols would be out on maneuvers near the school. They could show up at any time, but he always knew.

This was our sledding hill, and when the recess bell rang, we all dashed for the plateau with our brightly colored sleds. The Moose would quietly walk to the edge of the woods and watch us as we played, then return when our play period was over. I loved this old bull. He was so majestic standing up there alone, steam spouting from his nostrils in the cold Alaskan air.

So as young boys will do, one day we made a dare to see how close one of us could get to him. Four others and myself, started to crawl up the hill until we reached the ledge. The bull was standing in the middle of the plateau, about thirty yards from us. The plan was to quietly move over the ledge and walk towards him. Whoever got the closest, without chickening out and running back, was the winner. If he charged, we would turn and run, leaping over the ledge into the soft snow below. In all the weeks we had seen him, he never got too close to the ledge, so we felt safe that he wouldn't follow us. I knew a moose couldn't see very well. My father had told me that sometimes they would attack the supply trains, thinking it was another moose on their territory. It is hard to imagine how big they are until actually getting close to one — ten to fifteen feet tall, with antlers that stretch out as big as tree limbs. And this old bull was big! We waited until the wind shifted toward us. Inching our way over the ledge, we slowly stood up to find our footing in the loose snow. Quietly, we inched our way across the plateau until reaching about half the distance between the ledge and the Bull. He stood silent! Suddenly, his head dropped and his eyes looked right at us, he stomped his front foot and charged. We turned and raced for the ledge. I felt my foot sink into a snow pocket, and the next thing I knew I was sliding on my belly, raising my head up just in time to see my friends vanish over the ledge. I turned in terror, only to see that he hadn't charged at all, but instead was casually walking towards me and stopped about five yards away. He stood like he always did, staring off into space. I suppose it was because I had seen him so often and had grown to love him, that my fear left me. And also the awesome wonder at how big he was! He didn't move, which made me think, "What is he looking at?" I turned to look in the direction he was staring, and it happened, a timeless moment of peace, as I sensed the world as he did. The purple and orange sky was alive with movement and *sound that I could see*; the mountains in the distance, the smells of the pine, the oneness of breathe. We breathed in as the trees breathed out. We breathed out as the trees breathed in; a slow powerful tide moving back and forth. There was no separation between me and what was outside me, as my senses were pushed beyond human range. No separation between the old Bull and myself, as we communed with everything over, under and around us. I felt his joy and wonder at life, unburdened by human thoughts and complication. The cold, the wind, the colors, the feelings, and comradeship, all blended together in ecstatic living intelligence; information; ancient stories, transmitted prior to human language.

I don't know how long I was there when he stomped his foot and let out a long sigh. I turned as his head dropped and I looked into his eyes, and from my perspective in India, I saw wisdom. He was my first and best teacher. I turned and took a running leap over the ledge, yelling in joy. By that time the teachers had arrived and were heading up the hill. To see me flying over the ledge laughing must have startled everyone. I didn't recall what I said to all the questions, I guess nothing, but I remembered feeling differently after that. Many years passed before I realized that not everyone communicated with the animals. It was a sad and confusing day when I first understood that intelligence in this world was measured by who had the biggest gun, and the biggest mouth. So few understood what could happen in silence.

* * *

The Korean War came to a close and we moved back to Los Angeles. It wasn't too much of a shock because we lived near the beach. I always found nature, and it always found me wherever we went. The images raced through my head. Pretty normal childhood. Little league baseball, surfing, Catholic school, discovering sex in the back of my Volkswagen bug. Then suddenly there I was standing on the Notre Dame football field again, covered in blood, and silent. But the "I" that stood in silent peaceful observation connected with the "I" in Alaska, and they connected with the "I" in India. In a flashes of neuronic light and power, the painful memories of what stood between the three burned away and they now became one. And as it burned, I watched it all. I wanted to watch it all. It was my life, the hard-earned grinding of manure that was the foundation for the garden to come.

* * *

As a young man, the Catholic faith really meant very little to me. I could not see what their sorrowful story had to do with my life: God creates the world, all powerful God who never makes mistakes; but we are created with a defect, we are sinners; so He sends his Son to be hor-ribly tortured to save us from sin. What did any of this have to do with what I felt, communing with the ocean, racing down the face of a six foot wave, or standing silent in a primeval forest? It just never made sense to me. After my mother divorced, her friends, many of them Catholic nuns, easily turned their back on her, even though it was my father who had run off. The whole aura of these priests and nuns seemed to be about pain and sorrow, a heavy sense of guilt because we were responsible for getting this guy crucified. And now, when my mother needed help, all she was given was rebuke. There was nothing ever really said in the family, we just stopped going to church, and each of us went off into our own private lives. Being too young to know how to help my mother, I absorbed my parents' sense of failure, lack of trust in life or happiness, and subconsciously decided that this was life. Because my father told me that this was normal and not to cry, I took all the feelings and put them in a little ball, tucked them away somewhere inside me, and carried on.

Years earlier, my grandfather had shown me his guitar, and I immediately fell in love with it. I was told that I could have it if I learned the ukulele first. I bought a chord book and learned it in two weeks. I never *practiced* the guitar. Each time I picked it up, there was always the joy of new discovery, sounds and textures, which I seemed to instinctively understand. It was the energy of Nature and the playful ways of organizing the energy in music, which kept me insulated from the brooding Nuns and Priest, and whatever they were selling. The Church remained big confusion to me. I'd had many years of its programming by now, but because of my own experiences of God, though I never named it that, I never bought into the guilt and the obvious methods of trying to control one by fear.

The Beatles started to happen, along with the psychedelic drug scene. After high school I went to work at MGM Film Laboratory, following in my father's and older brother's footsteps, but also lifted weights everyday, thinking I would go back to college and play more football. One day, one of the members of my band gave me some LSD. I immediately found it was a great escape from my home life, which was sad and confusing. Mother worked hard to keep the family together physically, but working as a nurse all day, left no time to be a therapist too. My older brother left home and moved to the beach, very near to where she worked. She sometimes would go to his apartment and share her pain with him, while my father would call my younger sister and share his pain with her. So they slowly mourned and worked out the grief in at least some way. But I was the middle child, and though I was always taken care of on the physical plane, on the mental plane I felt alone and adrift. Seeing no one to respect or look up to, I retreated to the interior world.

I don't know what everybody else was doing with LSD, but I saw its potential right away. I sat for long hours by myself, exploring all the interesting new things I could do with my mind, except for the time I went to a football game after ingesting a good dose. I was appalled with these people running up and down the field chasing a ball, trying to beat each other up as scantily clad girls on the sidelines, with no idea of what was going on, jumped up and down while screaming. It all looked pretty silly. With the tragedy of Vietnam starting to happen and having seen some of my friends go off to war, I was in no mood for any violence, especially with the associations I had in my mind with the 'game' of football. With the images on TV of dead young soldiers lined up on the ground like a meat market, the abhorrent body counts of the enemy, like that was supposed to make us happy, the forced draft to feed this insanity, I and thousands of other people were forced to wake up from society's stupor. Not really knowing the politics of the situation, something inside of me, an intuition, a soul voice awoke in me, and I knew I was to have nothing to do with this. As I became aware of my humanness slowly turning to numb apathy at the images on TV, and the horrific realization that I belonged to a culture that tried to keep me happy by body counts of the enemy, my first puerile questions about violence suddenly became a burning desire for answers.

Although the LSD was interesting, it did not answer my questions, and after coming down from my excursions, I again found myself in the same confused world. It's only purpose was to overly sensitize me, which quickly made me aware that the world operated as a knee-jerk reaction, and somehow I had to find out who "I" was in the middle of all this. More and more, it started to seem like a self-indulgent escape as I lost three friends in one year to drug overdose, including the lead singer of my band. But I didn't know how to cry or even what to say. I acted like this was normal life, just as my father had said; I kept walking. Even the strongest doses of LSD never touched that place where I had stuck all the pain. I was in control. No one was allowed to see that pain. Not even me.

Because of allergies, which had plagued me for many years, and the help of my mother, I was able to stay out of the draft. The focused effort to stay out of the war was increasingly hard to maintain while getting high, and many times I suspected that the confusion caused by getting stoned was exactly what "they" were hoping for; a weakening of my will. I did not care at this time to put effort into serious research about who "they" were, even though subconsciously I was on a journey that would require me to define "they" in a very exacting way. For now, it was enough to act on my feelings about the wrongness of this war by not participating. Through reading some books on self-hypnosis, I could bring on and exaggerate all the symptoms of my allergies. My mother found the right doctors to get the documentation from, which we then sent to the head Army surgeon, and I was out. I felt no guilt about this once the sense of wrong of this war had settled in me, and decisively acted on my feelings about Vietnam, though consciously not knowing at the this time what a momentous turning point in my personal evolution it would become. When one has been taught one's whole life to shut up, follow orders and feel guilty and scared when one doesn't, the voice of Soul which comes in emergencies is clearly heard; the decision to not listen to the voices of outside *authority*, contrast so sharply with the years of conditioned self-doubt. When societal conditioning goes against your own deepest voice, then you are forced into choice between the "you" which is created by society, and the "you" that is unique and outside of all conditioning. When our first 'choices' are presented to us, if a decision is not made, the muscle atrophies and it becomes easier to feebly follow along with the current milieu, even when you know it is wrong. It wasn't until much later that I found out I had not made that choice alone. A whole generation was standing on a node in human evolution.

* * *

My family was of the working class, and I was expected to fall in line. I played my part for a few years, then one day, decided to leave. Everyone was shocked when I told them I was quitting work and taking off to Europe. Seniority was how you advanced through the studio system, and once you left you had to start from the bottom again. But one choice leads to another, as the muscle developed, and I was compelled to keep following through.

"Why are you going to Europe?"

"I don't know"

"How will you live?"

"Don't worry about it."

There wasn't much I could say as I didn't know why I was going myself. I saved what money I could, but was so desperate to leave I didn't even consider it was the middle of winter. Winter in Southern California is a lot different than in Northern Europe. I was slowly being talked out of the move, and my new sense of confidence was beginning to abrade. I had sold everything but my motorcycle, even though knowing it had become a feckless symbol for freedom. It never worked well, but I spent lots of money fixing it up and needed to hold on to it till the very end. But fate, consciously chosen, will always find ingenious ways of kicking you when you get off the path.

One night a friend from the studio called and asked me to accompany he and his new girlfriend to a party at the beach. I put on my biker clothes, took a mild dose of LSD, and rode to the party. Everything was going fine until six "Straight Satan's" walked in; they were a brother group to the "Hell's Angels." I was quite stoned when they came up to me and decided they wanted my leather jacket. I started to laugh at these funny-looking clowns, which was the way they appeared to me while stoned. Suddenly, the front guy took a swing at me. I saw it coming and easily stepped out of the way. He smashed the wall with his hand and screamed in pain. That woke me up! The other five jumped in, but because there were so many of them, no one could get a good shot at me. They kept getting in each other's way as I danced around the room and covered up. This was nothing compared to football! I saw many openings to seriously injure a few of them, but just couldn't get mad enough. It ended when one of them jumped on my back and pulled my jacket down as I was kicking at the other five. Once they had the jacket, they felt they could save face and made it to their bikes. I rode home, still stoned, and checked for cuts and bruises. I had come out of the fight with no serious damage, but when I sat down on a chair I felt the soft wet feeling, and noticed a bad smell. I had shit in my pants. There it was again! My body was scared and moving like a trained fighter, but "I", like the eye in the middle of a hurricane, was calm and centered during the whole episode. That week I sold my motorcycle, and the following week left for Europe.

✸ ✸ ✸

It is always delightful surprise how Life will throw so many interesting new ingredients in the pot, once there is commitment. The first of these was a last minute decision by my older brother to come along with me. This was a big blow to the family. He was the oldest, and expected to carry on the tradition. He would be giving up many years of seniority in his job, but decided to throw it all to the wind. Always a very responsible, hard-working person, this was going to be his big fling. Because it was winter, we decided to head south into Spain. A friend, who had taken this path before, told us to go to the train station and get on Train #9 to Barcelona, but during the flight we were both asleep when they announced that Luxembourg was fogged in and we would be landing in Frankfort, Germany. After landing we celebrated with many tankards of beer and proceeded to the train station. We stumbled unto Train #9, and after a few hours arrived at our destination. Never having studied any languages but Greek and Latin, and under the influence of large amounts of beer, I was not sure, but it didn't seem that these people were speaking Spanish, and I received many indignant looks of disgust when trying out what little Spanish I knew. It took many hours, and many beers later, to find out that somehow we had arrived in Paris. After more beer and pondering, we wandered into a small charming hotel run by a very beautiful middle-aged French woman, who took one look at us and started to laugh. She made some

comment about Americans, then took us upstairs to a room with a bed
that seemed to sink to the basement when laid in. I tried to grab her,
but she had obviously had experience with the likes of me and pushed
me onto the bed, and into a black coma — sleep. The next morning this
happy and handsome woman brought us breakfast and got us all
straightened out; I was sheepishly charmed, but for now that was to be
my French adventure.

This incident seemed to set the tone for the whole trip; lost most
of the time, and meeting many wonderful people on the way. And, of
course, we wouldn't have met Stuart if we had landed in Luxembourg.
On the train to Barcelona, sitting across from us, was a tall, impeccably
dressed young man with blonde, bushy, Jimi Hendrix-style hair. I
watched as he tried to pick up on two amused French girls, bumbling his
way through the French language, but with so much sincerity and style
that I immediately liked him. Later, we talked and were quickly locked
in a rampage of bawdy stories and laughter. We decided to travel together, and upon arriving in Spain, purchased an old VW bug with dubious
papers, which caused numerous incidences at the border crossings. But
Stuart with his proper British accent and style, seemed to be able to talk
us out of anything. He took care of the border police, I took care of the
VW, and my brother did maps and food; a great team. By the time we
reached North Africa we had been thrown out of many fine museums,
chased by gypsies, condemned by a Spanish priest for kissing girls in
public, ran screaming on battlements of old castles, fighting imaginary
warriors, laughed at El Greco's and Dali's paintings, all while stoned on
LSD. After sneaking across the Moroccan border and finding out that
the hashish was not that good, we decided to make an expeditious dash
for India. Under the influence of wine and hashish, the map agreeably
shrunk for us; it didn't seem as though it was half way across the World.
We raced up Spain, across France, tried to take along a French hooker,
got in a fight with French Police, absconded to Italy, and almost froze
to death in the mountains of Yugoslavia. The carburetor kept freezing
in the snowy mountains, so I kept jugs of water in the car, which we had
to keep drinking, then take turns getting out and urinating on the carburetor until it unfroze. With many bowlfuls of Hashish, numerous
ingenious 'divine interventions' were granted to us for keeping the old
VW running. We made it across Bulgaria and into Turkey, where the car
decided it had found it's resting place, and finally blew up. Not having
reached our goal of India, the decision was made to hitchhike to Ankara
where we would find a Turkish bath, which we sorely needed, and consider our next move. Wrong! Instead, we were promptly arrested by the

Turkish police for having left our junk car by the side of the road. I had no patience with third-world bureaucrats, and almost got us into serious trouble, but Stuart always saved the day. But dealing with Turkish authorities took the wind out of our sails. My brother didn't want to go further, Stuart met an American girl studying in Ankara, and I decided to go see Greece. Before parting ways, Stuart took me aside, and asked to speak with me alone. I became very curious as he changed from the 'old charmer comedian' to deadpan serious.

"Go to Thera."

"There is something waiting for you there."

"You must go."

His words seemed to reverberate in me. Then, he simply said goodbye and we parted ways. I was fascinated by what Stuart had said to me. It was so out of character for him to be so serious, I felt a little scared, his words resounding in me for many days. My brother and I found a boat to Greece, where we explored Athens for a few days, then he decided it was time for him to go back home. We said goodbye in Piraeus, he went on to Italy, and finally back to California; I went on to face my destiny alone.

✳ ✳ ✳

Arriving from the 20th Century with our modern ways and conveniences, I never stopped to consider that the people on this mysterious little island of Thera lived in an entirely different century. Very few had electricity or running water, and there were only three cars on the island, all taxi cabs. They certainly were not ready for a surfer, biker, rock and roller from Southern California, on a quest for truth, and I promptly found myself in trouble. I walked to the little village Stuart had told me to go to, at the very tip of the island. As I entered the town, guitar and backpack in tow, a friendly man standing by the side of the road met me. I had an eerie feeling that he had been waiting for me. He was one of the two people in the village who spoke English. No greeting, he just smiled and asked me to follow him. "You need a place to stay," he said pleasantly. It was not a question, but rather a statement. Leading me to the side of the village, overlooking another big island, we climbed down many steps, past ruins of houses that had been carved out of the side of the mountain. When about half way down to the ocean, he turned onto another smaller pathway winding around the side of the mountain, until we arrived at a small white domed church, and a partially ruined house standing next to it. He said, "You can stay

here," then turned and walked away. That was all he said! I thought it
a bit strange, but entered the house and looked around. It was really a
cave with three rooms that went straight back into the mountain, as if
they had built only the front of a house, and stuck it on the opening of
a cave. From the front door, you could see straight back into the last
room. I chose the middle room and set up my little camp. It was dirty
and half ruined, but had a well of fresh water and a view that was spectacular. I looked out over the blue Aegean Sea, and I had the whole side
of the mountain to myself. So I thought!

So that I could quickly merge into the ambiance of this new place
I had come to, I decided to drop some acid, which was carefully hidden
in the lining of my pants. In about a half an hour the whole cave was
moving and breathing, and I was engulfed in a bodily thrill to be in
Greece. Through all my schooling, I had loved the old Greek stories of
the gods, the Iliad and the story of Odysseus being my favorites. This
was the only tale of a spiritual guest that I knew, and had read it many
times. And here I was, standing on the very dirt where it had all happened! I had even passed the Island of the Cyclops on the boat ride
here! I stepped outside, walked up to the church, and stood on the small
landing overlooking the sea. The wind was blowing through my long
hair, and my black cape, a gift from Morocco, floated on the currents,
while awaiting Ulysses' ship to come sailing into view in any moment.
I was 'into it', as they say in Southern California, stoned, surfer talk.
Suddenly, I heard footsteps on the maze of stairs above me. I turned
and focused psychedelized orbs on a young boy of about ten years, happily skipping down the stairs. Just out for a young boy's walk. He had-
n't seen me yet, but I watched him as he progressed slowly down the
mountain. He disappeared behind a wall, then a few moments later I
heard him come around the corner of the church behind me. And there
I was! Long hair and cape in the wind, standing alone with storm clouds
over my head! He had probably made this walk a hundred times, but
never expected this. He stopped dead, staring at me in awe. Slowly he
backed away, and in an instant, before I could say a thing, turned and
was running furiously up the stairs. He reached the top, took one last
look down at me, and ran off. Ah, but the clouds forming overhead
were magnificent, and the ocean a deep violet-blue, so I quickly forgot
the boy, and after awhile, walked back to my cave house.

It seemed like an hour had gone by; sitting, breathing slowly, feeling at one with my environment, when there was a knock on the door.
Quite stoned by this time, and without thinking much about it, I found
my best cordial voice and called out, "Come in! Come in!" Happy to

have a visitor come see me in my ruins, I was all smiles. In steps a policeman! Shock ran through my system! This was the last person on earth I wanted to talk to while seriously tripping out on acid, and to make things worse, I could see he was terrified. He definitely didn't want to be here anymore than I wanted him to be here, but it was his job to check things out. Weeks later I got to know him, and although he was a very nice man, he had the intelligence of a stick. He stood at the door, trying to see me through the rock archway in the gloomy second room. I was huddled in the middle of the floor, wrapped in my black cape with eyes as big as beach balls, I'm sure. He spoke no English; I spoke no Greek. The walls had already been dancing, and started to move in rhythm with his breath; the colors of the cave were marvelous; and this was definitely a bad time for a cop to show up! But seeing he was scared, I took pity, and took control of the situation, saying a few words in English, waving to him, and literally 'thinking' him out of the cave. He slowly backed out, and without saying a word, shut the door.

The mind under the influence of a powerful psychic energizer can run away from you very fast. One thought can explode into a thousand thoughts in a moment. So if it is not the right first thought, you are in big trouble. Knowing the potential danger, I immediately took control and reasoned that since I hadn't been arrested, everything was OK. It took about half an hour to calm down, but just as I was feeling settled, there was another knock on the door. "Come in! Come in!" " I'm a nice guy," I reasoned to my self. "What do I have to be afraid of?" The door opened, and another terrified man entered! He was smoking a cigarette, dragging on it like some kind of machine stuck on repeat. I didn't like the smoke and stood up to talk to him. At six feet three inches tall, I towered over him and his eyes became saucers as he backed up. I was still too stoned, or 'in the moment', to put the three events together— the boy, the policeman, now him. I had no idea who he was or what he wanted. Days later, I found out it was the boy's father. Trying to understand why he was so scared, I focused my mental powers and silently 'probed' him. I could see that it had something to do with the cape, and all at once I grasped the situation. How strange I must have looked, suddenly appearing in this village. He obviously thought I was some kind of bad guy, so all I had to do was explain to him who I was, and that the cape was a gift from Morocco; no problem! I picked up my guitar case, which had stickers of all the places I had played. I pointed to the Moroccan sticker, then to my cape. "Come on buddy, you can get this," I'm thinking to myself. But much to my alarm, he started to become more frightened. I was watching his face turn white, and could not even imagine why he was doing this! Then I looked at the symbol of Morocco that I was pointing at. It was a big black pentacle, the sign of the devil in this part of the world! There I was pointing back and forth to my black cape and pentacle! When I realized what had happened, I gasped and let out an urgent, "Oh shit!" He turned and ran out of the house. The wrong first thought boldly took control, and in a moment I had visions of the whole village at my door trying to run a stake through my heart, or burn me to death. I rolled a rock up against the door and spent the whole night listening to every sound, readying myself for a life or death struggle. And this was my first night! Thank you, Stuart!

By the time the sun came up, I was seriously pumped with adrenaline and ready to hit the road. Then, from the other side of the door I heard footsteps, and then "Who's in there?" An English voice! Opening the door, I came face to face with Stephen, a tall, slender American with short hair and a scraggly beard. His sardonic eyes peered through thick glasses. "Some people from the village came to me all shook up, talking about Varikalyke, and asked if I would come down here to see what was going on." "What's Varikalyke?" "It means Vampire," he laughed. My mind began to spin again. "Oh, that's just great; great start here." So I told Stephen my story, all except the part about dropping acid. "So come over to my house, the people will see you with me and it'll be OK." That's all he said!

We became quick friends, he being the only person I could really speak with, and he also seemed lonesome. He knew the local people, and told me about their customs and superstitions so I could keep out of trouble. The people on this island were very superstitious, believing in vampires, ghost, devils, you name it, they had a story. And of course, there was the opposite polarity to all that, their savior the Christ. Those stories were under the control of the Greek Orthodox Church, a group of grim-looking, bearded priests who made it obvious they didn't like me at all. It wasn't too bad. The only thing I had to be cautious about was when I walked in the late night, which I did often. With very few lights on the island, and hundreds of miles from any large metropolis, the night sky was major entertainment. My only restrictions were to be quiet and stay away from the more populated parts of the village. These people shut their houses down when the sun set, and if anyone saw me walking around at midnight, it was sure to cause trouble. So I slowly settled in and became comfortable in my cave, and had long nightly visits with Stephen.

Stephen had a brilliant mind and could converse about anything concerning religion, philosophy, and psychology. He told me he was a psychologist from New York City, and for all kinds of reasons having to do with his childhood, he had a mental breakdown, and had spent some time in an asylum for the mentally disturbed. He had come to this island to 'think' and get himself back together. His only method seemed to be smoking hashish, of which he had a huge block, and drawing nonsensical pictures. Some he posted on the wall, others he threw away. I had never met anyone from New York City, or a psychologist, or anyone who had spent time in a mental institution, so I was fascinated with his strange world. One night I told him the story of how I had come to this curious island. When I mentioned Stuart, he suddenly became very focused and quiet.

"Yes, I know Stuart."

When I probed him for more information, he became peculiarly silent and said nothing more than "Stuart had once been on this island." Because of Stephen's willingness to talk about anything and everything but this, I naturally became very curious, and was slowly becoming more enmeshed in this seductive little mystery.

Almost a month went by and not much happened. I took no more psychedelics after that first day, and didn't like hashish because it made me so sleepy. But Stephen always asked me to smoke with him, even though I had told him many times that I didn't want any; but on this night I acceded to his increasing banter. After a good bowlful, Stephen launched into his memory, and one particular incident when he had chicken pox and his mother became so angry, she locked him in the closet for a few hours. I knew nothing about psychology or childhood trauma, so I had no idea how damaged Stephen might be. To me he was just a peculiar person, and my only friend on the island. As he continued to remember this incident, his face suddenly broke out with chicken pox; big red spots and welts appeared and disappeared all over his face and hands. I was in a state of innocent openness and wonder about what I was seeing, when suddenly I began to feel a very dark and powerful presence surface in Stephen. It seemed to fill the room, and I can only describe this person as malicious, and intelligent. Not a dumb maliciousness like sometimes seen in war, people doing terrible things, hypnotized, following the pack. This was the presence of an intentional, calculating force. He looked straight into me and said,

"Chicken pox is infectious, I wonder if mental illness is to?"

Then silence. I felt this thought form enter me like some slow detonation bomb. Stephen stared in silence. I had just seen him break out in chicken pox. Yes chicken pox *is* infectious, he had spent time in a mental institution, but I don't know how much time, or for what. My thoughts whirled. The presence I felt was like nothing I had experienced before. Maybe I *was* catching his mental illness. Suddenly, I was very scared. Physical threats didn't mean much to me, but this was out of my league and had no idea what to do. I kept thinking; "don't let him see how scared you are." I stood up and said,

"Stephen, I think it is time that I go."

He didn't say a word. I walked out of his house about one a.m., forgetting my flashlight. Finding my way through the maze of stairways and passages was not going to be easy in the dark, but there was no way I was going back. With his *thought form* trying to implant itself in me, and the task of finding my way back in the dark, I became lost, took a wrong turn, and almost stepped off a 500-foot cliff. Very scared, I sat down in the dark and began to pull myself together. I knew how to deal with unwanted thoughts from my experiences with psychedelics. It was just a matter of getting off one track and onto another. I looked up at the stars, and the beautiful night sky filled me with calmness, wonder, and peace. I was safe; it was nature again, always my savior. I easily found my way home, and the thoughts were gone.

About a week went by before I saw Stephen again. He came over to my cave as if nothing had happened, and having no real understanding myself of what happened, I let it pass. By this time, the Greeks had discovered I was a musician, and I received many invitations from the two bars in the village to come play with the local Bazooki players. They drank huge amounts of homemade brew, and would play until people started throwing plates around the room. I always thought this was great fun, but this was the time of the Colonel's dictatorship in Greece, and they had enacted laws to stop this practice. I felt strange feelings when the plates went flying, and couldn't tell if people were happy or angry. One night the head policeman came to the bar. I drank with the Greeks that night, and we played furiously for about an hour, but the room was silent. Suddenly the police officer stood up, grabbed his plate and smashed it against the wall. The room went wild, plates and glasses everywhere. The policeman stayed and drank way past closing time, when together, we all stumbled out and fell into the street. After that, the people accepted me, as the story was passed around the island. They all knew about the crazy American who loved to go walking at midnight.

As I started to make more friends, I noticed that Stephen was speaking more negatively about the villagers. He pointed out all of the negative things about them, and became more and more vehement about it. I had never experienced this before, so I politely listened, but inside I was becoming bored with him. He sensed this, but it only made him increase his negative attacks on the people, although to their faces he was charming and pleasant. I would have stayed away from him except for one thing that endeared him to me, Stephen liked animals. Because of my great love of all animals, I felt close to people who also liked them. I wanted to totally surrender to my love for the Greeks on the island, but they treated animals horribly, and this always made me feel uncomfortable with them. I had come across adults, old enough to know better, throwing rocks at the donkeys, or kicking cats, trying to kill them. I found out that many people believed that these animals were reincarnations of evil people who now had to live as beasts as punishment. This was so repulsive to me that it left me in a state of confusion as to how to be with these people, and caused me to overlook Stephen's negative attacks. Stephen often fed the wild cats in the village when they came near his house. This caused me to drop my guard with him, and soon I had forgotten the first incident I'd had with him.

One evening, he invited me for spaghetti dinner and some new wine grown by the villagers. As the evening progressed, Stephen pulled out his giant piece of hash and proceeded to smoke up the small room. With the combination of wine and hashish smoke, in about an hour I was feeling pretty good. Stephen started in again about smoking some hash with him and as the evening progressed, my defenses and caution were drowned in the delicious local wine. After taking two lung fulls of the hash, Stephen began his negative bashing of the villagers, and talking about his horrible childhood. He was just beginning to really get wound up, when I decided I'd had enough. I knew him well enough now, to know that this could go on for hours, and I also knew him well enough not to worry about being polite. I told him I was going into the kitchen to make some tea so I could come down a little and go home; also, I wasn't in the mood to listen to his complaining. He became very quiet as I stood up to walk into the small kitchen. Suddenly, I felt that same dark intelligence enter the room. Stephen spoke,

"OK, but be careful, don't burn yourself."

The words seemed to move through me like a wave, and without even stopping to think about it, I proceeded to the kitchen to boil the water. After lighting the small gas stove and filling the pan with water, I stood back and watched it boil, then placed some tea in a cup. While trying to pick up the pan, my hand slipped; it spilled it all over my arms, hands, and legs. Falling back against the wall, I screamed in agony;

dropping to the floor, I rolled up into a ball, letting out another cry as my arms touched the ground. I reached around for the cold-water bucket, but had left it up on the sink, so I picked myself up and looked at the stove. What I saw shocked and ran shivers through me! I hadn't even boiled the water! There it was, still sitting on the unlit stove. I walked into the other room. Stephen said nothing; his eyes were dull and empty. I didn't know what to say or feel. Had he done this? Did he even know anything had happened? Did it really happen? My mind was spinning, and I knew that was dangerous. I walked out and headed for my cave as fast as I could go. Remembering what had happened before, I walked cautiously, but by this time I knew the route perfectly, even in the dark. That night alone in the cave is when the real attack started. His previous statement about mental illness being contagious, was spinning through my head. It had a sound like a buzz and I began to understand the mechanism of mental illness. The mind turns against itself, asking questions that it can't possibly answer. Then, in a panic, adrenaline amplifies the whole experience, and in only a few moments, any center or sense of reasoning self is dragged into a spinning-wheel momentum. If you are by yourself, without any outside distractions, it is almost impossible to stop the process. Only a heavy sedative to knock you into sleep can work at his point, otherwise the internal heat is so intense it can cut a permanent groove into the thinking process, a perpetual "Catch 22." The fear was so powerful that I felt myself start to go into a paralysis. Fear of death was never an issue with me, for how can you fear the unknown. But the fear of going mad, alone on a little island, was a fertile pit of horrible images, and I was sinking. Then came one sane thought. One thought of self-reliance. The thought was just a simple one: "I am alone, there is no one to help; I'm just going to have to ride this out." As soon as the thought "I" came into focus, that little "I" became an island of calm in a stormy sea. In the calm, the next thought surfaced, "Go out and see the stars." The effect was instantaneous. The stars, my friends were like old wise and kind ancestors that blanketed me. I was surrounded by family. I watched for hours as the constellations moved around the North Star.

The rest of the night was one of peace. I awoke the next morning with a healthy curiosity, and the fire of a warrior. "I don't know who this guy is, but he's not going to get away with that kind of shit." Not really knowing what I was up against, but deciding I was up against something, I went back to Stephen's the next day, acting like nothing had happened. Stephen was in a friendly mood. We walked down by the ocean, talking to the men mending their fishing nets. I didn't know if he even knew something had happened to me the night before, but as long as he wasn't saying anything, neither was I. This went on for many weeks. It was during this time, that I first began to read books on yoga and meditation, including a curious book that Stephen gave me called "Freedom From the Known", by Krishnamurti. With no TV, radios, or other distractions, my mind hungrily drank up these new Eastern thoughts. It seemed very familiar to me, even though I had never read any eastern philosophy, and I took to yoga with ease. Having always been an athlete, and knowing the power and pleasure locked in the human body, I immediately saw the potential for these new ideas and postures. I now began to spend more time by myself, practicing meditation and thinking about all these new ideas. Then one day, Biazo came to the island.

✷ ✷ ✷

It was Easter vacation time, and Biazo was one of the local boys who came home from his studies at a University in Italy. He was a tall, handsome lad with black curly hair, and a wonderful sense of humor, filled with fun and mischief. He seemed to know Stephen from before. I could never get a straight answer from Stephen about how long he had been on the island, but they seemed like old friends. Stephen would always cheer up when Biazo was around; I noticed he never talked about his past, as if he was on his best behavior in front of him. Biazo was always pulling hilarious tricks on his village friends. In Italy, he bought a battery operated laughing box that he hid in his shirt, and was able to push the button by flexing his chest muscles. As the old women came up the stairs from the market place, Biazo would sit still and expressionless as the hideous laugh came out of him. The old women would cross themselves and run off as fast as they could, spreading stories throughout the village that Biazo had become possessed. He told me he always liked to give the old women something to gossip about because it made them happy. Then he looked at me very seriously and said,

"Always think good of these women because they love you."

"What do you mean they love me?"

"Never mind", he answered, "It is probably best that you don't know."

I thought this was curious, but didn't give it much thought considering all the other things that had happened to me in this place. I knew there was something special about Biazo, though I could not put my finger on it, having never seen it before. One evening, while out walking together, he stopped me and said,

"Look at my hand."

I looked, and ashes appeared in the palm of his hand. He smiled, and in a most comical way said,

"You can do anything with your mind, but you have to use it and not let it use you, nor let anybody else use you either."

Biazo had planted a seed in me. But it was Biazo himself that touched me, not his power or un-pretentious wisdom. He had a heart of gold and seemed to be all over the village, helping people fix houses, carrying wood for the old women, helping the fisherman with the nets, and I loved him like a brother.

Easter was fast approaching. One day Biazo came to me and asked if I would go to the Easter Sunday celebration with him in the Orthodox Church. I was surprised how happy I was at his asking me. It had been many years since I had been in a church, and though I never thought much about the mysteries concerning Christ, I did give thanks every day to the great Force that had created the sea, the sky and beautiful earth all around me. This was a way I could be in a place of worship with my friend. Stephen was also invited, but cordially declined. On Easter morning about an hour before the service, Biazo came to me with a deep look of sadness and concern.

"Please forgive me my friend, but I have come to ask you not to come to the mass."

He was genuinely upset about it.

"OK Biazo, I won't, but why?"

I tried to hide my disappointment to make him feel better.

"The priest came to me and asked me to tell you not to come, because the old women of the village believe you to be like their Christ; the priests are afraid you will cause a disturbance by your presence."

This caught me off guard! In my wildest dreams, I could never imagine an answer like that. I stood dumbfounded, having no idea what to say. I had seen these bearded priests only a few times in the village. They didn't seem very friendly, but I thought that maybe they were silent monks who rarely come out of their monastery. But seeing that Biazo was now very sad, I acted as though it meant nothing to me, and told him not to worry. I would join him after the service, and we would pray on the hillside together. Biazo immediately cheered up and invited me to his parent's home for a party after the service, and then we would go to the hillside together.

Disappointed, I walked toward my cave. Before reaching home,

Stephen appeared from around the corner, and I told him what had happened. He gave me a pained "I told you so" look, and laughed.

"Assholes, stupid assholes."

I said nothing, but inside I was in agreement. Through my mind raced many images of my Catholic days; the nuns turning against my mother, her sadness; the angry scary priests; the endless times I was slapped, or beaten with wooden rulers on my hands and knuckles, all because I had a sense of humor. "A sick bunch of people," I thought. But then Biazo's words came back to me, and I saw what my mind was doing, and was able to catch it. I didn't have to forgive anyone, as no one had asked me for forgiveness. I could merely put it out of my mind or jump tracks, and the joy of life would always be there to meet me. At that moment, I saw the difference between Stephen and myself. He just couldn't stop the endless obsession with his past, and at a certain point, made a choice to stay there; it worked for him. He built his life around those stories, and his weakness was that he *needed* others to join him there. A sly look surfaced on Steven's face.

"Come on, I know a place we can watch from."

He led me through the stairways and passages until we came to the side of the courtyard surrounding the central village church. We hid behind the wall until all the people had entered, then climbed up and sat upon it. Only 20 yards away, we could see the front row pews through an open door in the side of the church. Biazo was in the front row with his family. No one seemed to notice us, so Stephen chatted away while the mass went on. Then, I heard the tinkle of small bells coming from inside the church; and there was Biazo, in a state of ecstatic communion with his God. His hands were raised; eyes looking upwards, his mouth wide open. He gently swayed back and forth, and I could see a faint gold and white hue all around him. "I haven't been stoned in months," I thought to myself. "This is something else." And that became my last sensible thought as I began to merge with Biazo in his worship. I was tumbling through open space! Just then, Stephen hit me on the arm.

"Look at that asshole in there." "They're all assholes."

At that moment, appearing out of a clear blue sky, a white bird flew down, and hit Stephen on the neck. I only saw it out of the corner of my eye, like a white streak suddenly appearing, then gone. Stephen grabbed his neck.

"Did you see that?" "It was a bat."

"It wasn't a bat, Stephen. Bats aren't white."

"How do you know, did you see it?"

I answered dryly, seriously perturbed at having been knocked out of my reverie.

"Not really, but it was white, whatever it was."

"No, it was a bat."

I stood up.

"OK! Fuck off, Stephen."

I knew him well enough now, to know what was going to happen next. He was starting to wind himself up. I could sense his powerful mind starting to churn, and knew that in moments it would be a run-away train.

"No, it was a vampire bat, I just know it."

He stopped talking and a look of horror came across his face. He was obviously stoned and starting to go into his paranoia. It might have been comical had I not seen him break out in chicken pox; there was no telling what he might do with this idea.

What's a Southern California surfer/biker/rockin-roller, who has just been knocked out of communion with God by someone screaming about bats, going to do? Stephen was just about to scream, when I slammed my fist into his chest knocking him backwards off the wall. I jumped off the wall with him, and picked him up out of the dirt. He just stared at me with a look of disbelief on his face, then turned and walked off. This was turning into a bad day. But I knew if I hadn't hit him, he would be running around the island trying to bite people by nightfall. I had also seen him get freaked out over spiders one evening when he was stoned; soon he was seeing spiders everywhere. I climbed back up the wall and looked into the church, but could no longer see Biazo. Confused and saddened, I no longer felt welcome on this island, and walked home without going to Biazo's parents. That night I thought about what Biazo had said about the old women. I had sort of long hair and a beard, and I knew that sometimes the villagers saw me sitting alone in meditation, looking out at the sea. I really didn't know enough about Christ to give it much thought. I did know I was tired of being alone. What girls there were on the island were afraid of me, Biazo was leaving for school, and the only one I could really converse with was Stephen. I liked Stephen, but whatever took him over scared the hell out of me. I thought of Stuart and how I had gotten here. "Whatever you wanted me to see Stuart, I've had enough." I decided it was time to leave. Two days later I said goodbye to Biazo, and told Stephen my plans. I could feel the dark presence in him when I told him I was leaving. He said,

"We'll have to have a party, won't we?"

It felt more like a command, and I knew I could refuse, but instead, decided to see this through to the end.

✳ ✳ ✳

The evening passed pleasantly, sipping local wine, talking about yoga and the Krishnamurti book that I was reading. Later, we sat at the table by candlelight, and Stephen picked up the book and started to read aloud. I immediately noticed that his voice didn't sound as usual, and as he continued, I felt myself becoming weighted down; but at the same time, my mind became hyper-alert. Slowly, very slowly, his voice, phrase by phrase began to sound like an echo being projected from a long tube. But this time I was ready for him. We were not stoned, so I was able to watch him in careful observance. I felt the dark presence start to fill the room, surrounding me, looking for an opening. But nothing happened, he just kept reading very slowly, pronouncing each sound carefully. I was becoming more and more interested in the subject matter, and was slowly being pulled in. Krishnamurti's books are transcripts from live, spoken lectures. He has the habit of saying, "Now go very slowly, pay careful attention here," as he leads you through long passages, giving the reader an *experience* of how the mind forms it's realities. There is never any judgment of what is seen, it is purely passive observation. Stephen was reading from a chapter called "The Observer is the Observed." Previous to reading this book, I had never heard of this philosophy. I was slowly being led into a passive state of observation, seeing that the *judgments* we make about all phenomena that we see and experience outside of ourselves, are really just pictures of ourselves, are own prejudices and psychological makeup. The famous psychologist Carl Jung, a student of Eastern philosophy, called it "the seeing of your own shadow." This was the crux of the chapter Stephen was reading.

As I became more enmeshed in Krishnamurti's brilliant prose, I began to notice Stephen's face was starting to change. Because of the previous chicken pox event, my curiosity sharpened the focus of each moment, even more than I had already decided I would try to execute for this last hoopla of Steven's tricks. His ears and chin started to elongate; the complexion darkened, his eyes grew dark. As I watched, I was becoming more alarmed, but too fascinated to move. Then, two small bumps appeared on the top of his head, like the beginning of horns. Suddenly, I realized what I was seeing was a devil, or the classic Christian picture of what the devil was supposed to look like. I was amazed by what I was seeing, mostly because I had no belief in devils or Satan, but I could not move. He continued reading slowly. I had never read this chapter in the book before, so I didn't know what was coming, but a sense of grave danger started to envelope me. Not a physical danger, but rather an incomprehensible horror that I had never felt before. Word by word, as he continued to read, I felt a deep inner awareness arise, that my soul was about to be extinguished, that something so powerful was about to pounce on me, that "I" would no longer be; "It" only, would remain. Some supreme effort welled up inside me. I slammed my hand on the table, breaking the spell, grabbed the book from his hands, and ran out the door all the way to my cave. But I could still see his face in my mind's eye. Nothing I thought or did could make him go away. He had somehow pierced the walls of my own private mental world, his face sneering at me, surrounding me with the fiercest anger I had ever experienced.

About a month earlier, Stephen had given me a magazine on the occult: astrology, palmistry, and such things. I now noticed that it was open to the page on Tarot, and there was the picture of the devil card, the classic goat head image. My eyes fixed on the eyes in the image, and I fell back into the trance. In my mind's eye, flashed scenes of castles and mansions, riches, beautiful women, jewels, all the 'temptations' of the world. I had no belief in "devils" or "temptation," and I felt that part of myself separate from what was happening to me. I was the calm center again, the eye of the hurricane. From this view I calmly discerned what was happening. I had power; I am power. How do I want to use it? It was not that all these things I was seeing were bad. The question was, "Am I going to use my power to accumulate these things?" Was this going to be my focus in life, or was there something more about myself that I hadn't yet seen, another value, another gradation. All these "things" may or may not come into my life, but the question was "what were my priorities, where should the gift of my attention fall?" But from the calm center, I slowly became aware that it was the "choice" that was the most subtle and dangerous trap of all. The allure to the "things" of the world was intense and erotic; I felt the heat and pressure of it in my nervous system. The allure of what most would see as the opposite of that, a selfless caring for humanity over the desire for "things", was a story implanted in me by the Church: Jesus' triumph over the temptations of the Devil. I became suspicious when I felt myself rush to this choice with more enthusiasm than I had for the former choice. It would have been too easy to go for being a 'good boy', thus winning the approval of an absent father and a society desperately wanting to believe itself altruistic. I knew that Catholics, conveniently forgetting the Inquisition, the decimation of millions of indigenous people while colonizing the America's, and many other excesses, was just a microcosm of the behavior of all systems that set themselves up as 'authority.' The price of seeing the 'Emperor without his cloths' was a deep, terrifying fear in my body, implanted in me at circumcision. But the calm center runs deeper than the nervous system, and from this clarity of observation, the two choices became an incestuous pun, no matter where I looked in history. The more I contemplated a choice, the more I felt agitated and pulled out of my center of peace. After many hours of this agony, the two choices finally burned themselves up in the heat of their own battle; the last desperate onslaught being a screaming voice at me, that I was a coward for making no choice. But for now, the "I" outside all conditioning of the world, had won. "I" had made a choice, to make no choice!

If I had made a choice for either side of the images shown to me, "I" would have been locked into, and fixed by their momentum. They would act as a filter, short-circuiting me from the spontaneous intelligence and life force of the Living Universe. What the old Bull Moose had taught me so long ago, was that without the thousands of years of arrogant, human dogma, that joyful intelligence kept me in absolute harmony. And now with yoga, I was beginning to realize in the most visceral way, the magnificent and erotic reality of Human design. Without the artificially created conflict in our nervous systems, the human bio-circuitry was designed to interface with that joyful, living intelligence and power. So, by not making a choice between society's images of good and evil, the choice of *Peace as my essence* finally surfaced, and was shown to have been made long ago.

The images collapsed in front of me; I sat in stillness for a long while. Finally I stood up, closed the magazine, and walked outside. Seeing which constellation now draped me, I knew that many hours had past since my hasty exit from Stephen. I silently watched the movement of the stars until the first rays of the sun peaked on the horizon, then went back to my cave and picked up my guitar. I strummed one chord, and the grace filled epiphany enveloped me. I could see the whole galaxy, and experienced it as a gigantic musical chord. The Earth, and a few other small localities, were like musical notes, slightly out of tune with the rest of the major chord, the galaxy itself. As I continued to play, the earth changed frequencies and went into resonance with the rest of the galaxy. Suddenly, there was instant flash of 'knowing', reverberating through the whole system, a sense of family, connected by a resonance of unfathomable beauty and mystery. I played and sang for hours, melting into the vision, knowing it was my life's purpose. Through the *sounds* that came from me, and keeping my body as an open conduit, the re-tuning of the Earth and the creatures that rode on her, would in some mysterious way be accomplished. The sour note would merge into the galactic chord, this being the direction of our further evolution; but only, if I could keep my mind and body open as a doorway for the necessary adjustments to come through. I had no idea how big an "if" that was going to become. Ah! Such is the exuberance of youth; always wanting power before maturity; always the erroneous interpretation of the word humility; and always thinking that winning one battle, was the winning of the whole war.

Later that day I picked up the Krishnamurti book and opened to the page Stephen had been reading. I noticed that I had slammed my hand down just before he was about to say, "and now we can see that the observer is the observed." If I had given Stephen time to say those words as I watched him transform into a devil, I knew I would have lost my soul, probably committed suicide; for I would have become him. I shuddered at the subtlety of the trap.

A few days later I went to Stephen and spoke my last goodbye; he acted as if nothing had happened, in character to the end. But I could feel the seething, forced cordiality. In my mind, I blessed Stuart, and with the new fire of a Bible prophet, started on my way back to America. Or was it just cockiness?

* * *

From my view in India, still, I could not answer that question. Though by now I was considered an accomplished yogi in the system in which I studied, I saw that it was not giving me the knowledge and confidence I needed to be what I had seen in my vision in Greece. But I did understand the significance and danger of the choice to make no choice. The path of wanting to know Truth with a capitol "T" is different than the path of wanting to be Good and found worthy before some Almighty Being. If one is not even sure there is an Almighty Being, then why waste time groveling in front of it. But if the seeker has yet no light of their own, it is preferable to govern oneself by the best light available, principals and standards of civil society, and this was the choice I would have made had I not been true to my own nature. From my omni view in India, I was pleasantly amused and appreciative of the young man I was watching in Greece. His mind was still too young to reason all this out; his decision to make no decision had come purely from his street punk distaste of authority. This was one tough, stubborn kid, and no one was going to push him around. If he was going to choose a way of life that society considered "spiritual", it was because he wanted to, not because he was afraid of what might happen if he didn't, punishment from an angry God and His ministers of justice. And yet, in spite of this tough attitude that most of society would consider negative, especially the group to which I now belonged, he still made the right choices and took care of himself very well. Now I could see, and appreciate, and integrate the "devilish" parts of myself as just one color in the bigger painting of Self. Had the young man in Greece allowed himself to see only that one piece before understanding that it was just an interesting stroke and not the whole picture, he would have reactively committed spiritual suicide by stopping any further inquiry, or gone insane. This I knew. From India, I saw that any wisdom outside oneself could be used to destroy, as well as enlighten. For the first time, I began to appreciate that there was some kind of unfailing guidance in my life, and felt a new buoyant delight at looking at my own self with almost a fatherly love and pride. No outside authority, sense of duty, or standards of behavior can be imposed upon a being that seeks liberation. To love or have compassion, to obey the highest truth of our being, to follow the command of Divine Providence are not duties; these things are the action of nature as it rises towards the heights of humanness, sometimes called the Divine. This action comes to one, or out of one, as a natural result of ones spiritual union with Truth, not from any edifying construction of mental thought or will, or practical reason, or social sense. Somehow, this young man in Greece knew this, and chose it as his way. And now, watching him in admiration from my view in India, I saw that his wisdom exceeded that of the teacher and group to which I was now in service. I had imperceptibly fallen off my own path and ended up in a personality cult. There are times when a conscious choice should be made, and perhaps this was one of those times. But the young man in Greece was teaching me something. He had no great philosophical reasons for making his choices; it was quite simply that he needed more information before setting off in any life direction. That was his wisdom. After seven weeks of fever, my mind splattered all over Time, I was not ready to act upon what I saw; I needed more information. But a seed was planted, and though I could still feel parts of myself that were not perfect in self-trust, I did know the seed would blossom in its own way.

Chapter 2

Trial by Fire

I returned to Los Angeles full of enthusiasm, interpreting my vision as meaning I should get a recording contract and flood the world with my music. I walked into recording companies, pulled out my guitar, and said, "Hey, listen to this." After being thrown out of a half dozen places and some ego bruising, someone was kind enough to tell me I needed to make a tape to present my music. Instead, I started my own company, and pushed till my music was on the radio. But slowly I was beginning to see the backstabbing, corruption, lying to your face, heart-breaking side of the music industry, and after a year of flagrant self-promotion, became thoroughly disillusioned. Playing music was one matter, having to deal with the kind of people that are drawn to fast money, was another matter entirely. I had no frame of reference for interacting with this kind of deception, except for Stephen, and I really didn't know what to make of my adventures with him. Yoga had stuck to me, but without a serious daily practice, the plethora of dark stimulation that a big city can supply was beginning to seep through the cracks of my dwindling interest, and I began to seriously look for a teacher, and a little peace of mind. I traveled around meeting all the yoga masters, Swamis, and Gurus, then making their exodus from India into the more fertile money field of the United States, and finally settled on a Tantrik master, solely because he was a little wilder and tougher then the rest. I needed someone with an edge, some fire, someone who was not intimidated by the fierce appetite for the answers I sought. The 'icky-sweet' persona of most of these Eastern teachers just didn't seem real to me. I made my decision after watching him get into a heated argument with another Indian teacher at a conference. He didn't care who was watching, or what people thought of him. After experiencing the hypocrisy of many record and film people that I hung out with, I appreciated the honesty of telling someone to their face you thought they were an idiot. Once deciding, I launched into the yogi world with the same gusto as when starting the record company, and after a few weeks of beginning classes from a student teacher at the local college, I asked to meet the Master. I told him I wanted to study with him, how I had first become exposed to yoga, why I wanted to continue, blabbering on as I had successfully done many times before in record pitch meetings, when suddenly he put his hand up and stopped me cold. What followed was a real wake up call, literally. I was to get up at 3:30 a.m., take a cold shower and practice a very powerful breathing - chanting technique, two and a half hours each day, for forty consecutive days, then he would talk to me. He stood up and walked out of the room!

The only time I had seen 3:30 a.m. was when staying up all night, usually playing music. But after bandaging my ego, I quickly understood the genius of this task. This was going to be a big cramp in my life style; in one fell swoop, everything in my life had to change in order to complete the forty days. I was living in a rehearsal studio in Venice Beach with a group of jazz musicians; we didn't even have a shower. But I told my friends what my intentions were; not only was I going to chant at 4:00 a.m., I was going to run it through the sound system with a big room echo chamber effect. This was going to be a forty-day experiment, not only for my good, but the good of the band, and the whole damned world. The consensus among the musicians was that this was a very cool thing to do, and they agreeably moved into the next garage for the next six weeks. Not knowing what might come from this, the motivation for making this supreme effort was simple and very practical. The Yogi told me I would get everything I wanted: new recording contracts, my girlfriend who had left me because her mother wanted her to be with someone who had more money, a new car, a better place to live, etc. The walls of boyish rectitude had defiantly thinned since the vision in Greece, warning me about using one's power solely for material gain. I rationalized that I didn't even have the essentials, after all I was living in Los Angeles, and if I didn't have a lot of money, at least I could look like I did. So at 3:30 in the morning I stripped naked, rolled up and down the cold sidewalk to simulate the effects of a cold shower, turned on the echo machine, and my yoga adventure began. I was told that the words I was chanting were Sanskrit words for many different names of God, and that this was the magic formula that made everything happen. My interpretation was a little different; through sleep deprivation and super oxygenation, I was getting high as a kite, forgetting everything I had previously wanted, and it was great fun so I continued. By the 37th day I had caught a bad cold. The 38th day I barely made it through two and a half hours. The 39th day I did two hours, the 40th day I did two hours and ten minutes. A few days after my completion, I went to see the Yogi. I complained that my girlfriend hadn't come back, and still no new recording contract. He looked at me carefully.

"Did you do the technique perfectly, like I told you?"

I told him I had missed 30 minutes on the 39th day, and about 20 minutes on the 40th day. He considered this for a few moments, and then with a big smile on his face, he said,

"See what happens when you don't follow instructions. Nothing happens. Do it again."

I loved this man's humor, and the technique really had worked in an interesting way. Somewhere along the journey, I had imperceptibly lost my interest in the girl and the contracts. Even though I had been tricked into it, seduced by my own greed, I quickly saw the results of my hard work; I was happier, very healthy, and on another adventure into the unknown.

A few weeks later I moved into my first ashram, where the discipline of getting up at 3:30 a.m. was a daily way of life. It was much easier to awaken at that hour when there were others around you to be supportive, and I quickly excelled. Time past un-noticed, and soon I was walking around in a God intoxicated state, a peace and fulfillment, with no need of anything other than what *appeared* in front of me in the moment — not exactly the Western ideal of a productive life. I even felt no need to talk. But as time moved on without me, I noticed that the more intoxicated and silent I became, the more trouble I drew. The women seemed to grow more attracted to me, the teachers grew jealous, because they were not as absorbed, others were concerned that I didn't eat very much, still others warned me that I would get too big an ego, because I was becoming too popular in the organization as a singer. Before long I was the hot topic of controversy, and the elder teachers complained to the Yogi. He found endless humor in this situation, and said that in fact, this was what was supposed to happen in an ashram. People's subconscious fears surface, because of the powerful techniques, then we are forced to deal with them and work them out by all the interchanges of group living. He told me I was doing a fine job, would be made a teacher myself, and I would soon be sent to the larger ashram in Northern California.

My relationship with the Yogi was not the typical sweet Guru—

obedient disciple relationship. I had many questions and wanted answers, and became angered by any spiritual rhetoric evasion. The senior teachers, trying to live out the stories they had read in spiritual literature, considered this an egotistical attitude. But the Yogi liked my honesty, and that I wasn't afraid to argue with him. Indeed, he loved a good argument, and the last heated discussion we had, before being sent to Northern California, was to change my life. If I was going to teach, I had to wear the costume of this yoga group and lineage, which made you stick out like a neon sign. I told him a story of how the old milkman brought good milk, but the son now had a motorized truck, while the father was still trying to use a horse drawn wagon; the son could give more milk out, and faster. He looked at me with much love and said, "But first the son must learn how to bow." It was truth! I had never bowed to anyone, or anything in my whole life. I could bow in rituals and make it look good, but inside I had never bowed to a teacher or religion, giving over to them my life to mold. This was the traditional way of the Eastern methods of realization, and if the student didn't comply, eventually they were made to feel left out, or not as committed as those who did bow. With the disillusionment of the Vietnam War, the blatant self-serving of the more traditional western religions, and the advent of powerful psychedelics, thousands of young Westerners were primed and ready to turn to the exotic eastern master/disciple traditions. All religious literature espoused a higher love and state of existence far above what a mere human, attached to their families and country could attain, and the breaking down of old loyalties was treated as an urgent, methodical process. The Yogi constantly stressed that this was our *real* family, and that America was a spiritually bankrupt country whose Mecca was Las Vegas. The ideas took hold as thousands of estranged and stoned kids seeked out a "spiritual" world, that to me, sounded suspiciously like the psychedelic experiences we were already having. As one way of dropping out and getting stoned transformed itself into a healthier way, many bought the eastern package, hook, line and sinker. The Yogi was beginning to know me. By turning the question of bowing or not bowing into a challenge, he had cleverly implanted a seed thought-form in me that took on obsessive dimensions, for I always rose to a challenge. The pressure of soul-searching consideration forced one to turn inside out, and that is what a teacher is supposed to do. But still, the 'choice to make no choice' was able to prevail a while longer. I needed more information, and if I were to bow, it would be a real bow.

The Northern California center was a beautiful, four-story mansion surrounded by bushes, greenery and large trees. There were thirty to fifty people in the house at different times, both married couples and single people. I was sent to the single men's dorm on the top floor. This was the second single men's dorm in the house, and actually considered the 'Macho Men's' dorm. Hard core fanatic yogis, we competed with each other in feats of strength, and spent many hours telling stories of how useless and silly women were to yogis like *us*. Indeed, why did they even have women in the house? I loved the comradeship and many jokes we played on each other, and there was a good-natured, but fierce fanatic passion for trying to out-do all the other 'soft' yogis in the ashram. If they took cold showers in the morning, we would jump into the freezing cold pool while biting on raw garlic. If they chanted an hour, we chanted three hours, if they went on a fruit and vegetable fast, we did water. It was a fearsome collection of men with many varied and colorful pasts: ex drug dealers, musicians, bikers, lumberjacks, carpenters, mechanics, you name it and we had one. On the floor below us was the single women's dorm. At night, we sometimes made lewd sexual moans and cries, humping on the floor to simulate the sounds of orgies, much to the horror of the young women below us. They often complained to the head teachers, and we were made to promise our conversion to more yogic-like behavior, but always found another way to torment the women below.

One of the jobs of the young women was to wake everyone in the house, starting at 3:15 a.m. Usually they would walk through the entire house singing or chanting, starting at the bottom floors and working their way up to the top floor, the dreaded 'den of wild beast', as we became known. It was actually a very lovely way to awaken, as the girls were told to chant softly and sweetly, knowing that no one really liked to get up that early. It wasn't until the cold water hit you that one really woke up. We could hear the young girls moving up the floors below us, as people woke and hit the showers. The girl slowly walked up the long stairs while singing, but when opening our door, she was met with catcalls, boos, banana peals, dirty underwear and socks. We were reprimanded many times for this behavior, but after awhile it was just accepted as an initiation for the new women, and a hormonal problem of celibate young men pumped up on Tantrik yoga.

One fateful morning, a new girl appeared at the door. My sleeping pad placed nearest the door, I was the first to see her as she entered, holding her candle and singing in the sweetest voice. She was tall and slim, long blond hair, beautiful eyes, and I saw on her face a look of terror. Her large blue eyes reminded me of a deer frozen in the headlights of an on coming car. She was met with the usual greeting, and fled down the stairs in tears. I limply sat on my pad with my mouth open, and felt terrible. I hurried through the morning rituals and found her downstairs in the meditation room, trying to find a spot near her as we started our daily, grueling three-hour yoga and chanting practice. She moved with the grace of a dancer, and I found out later, that she had been a ballerina. I could not keep my eyes from her, even though I was supposed to be concentrating on my prayers; it was useless! Damn! She came back the next day to awaken us, only to be met by the same brutish behavior; in contrast to her porcelain delicacy, I was painfully and embarrassingly seeing that I was nothing but a common thug. Again she ran down the stairs in tears. This went on for another week, but each day down in the practice room, I sat as close to her as I could. I knew I was beginning to fall in love, and started to feel protective toward her, looking for a way to stop the shenanigans in the 'den of wild beast'. I reasoned that it was my pay back for having pulled all those dirty tricks on so many of the other girls sent to awaken us. But she seemed to take her task as some sacred duty to save the other girls, and was determined to convert the barbarians. Finally, I decided to do something. After a few years of this daily yoga practice, I would naturally awaken by myself. As soon as I heard her on the lower floors, I was up, into the shower, and dressed before she reached the upper level. I met her at the top of the stairs in my best white clothes, and announced,

"It's OK, everybody is awake in here."

She stared at me wide eyed, but at least didn't cry, as she backed down the stairs. When I could see she had disappeared into the dark, I turned back to my room, opened the door and screamed,

"Get the fuck out of bed, assholes!"

I was met with garbage and underwear, but they got it right back this time. After a week of this, the boys didn't find it fun anymore, and we woke ourselves up. I found out her name was Leila, and though very shy, I saw that she had lots of spirit and a sense of fun. I manipulated the housework schedule so that we had morning kitchen duty together, and we slowly became friends. We talked for hours on the days when there was not much work. Other days we never spoke a word, but sat side by side in morning meditation. I hadn't even kissed her, and yet felt a merging with her I had never experienced before. The idea that there was some kind of "higher spiritual love" became a limp platitude in a matter of weeks. I became sort of a yogi hero to the women of the ashram, after they found out what I had done with the macho men, and

Leila was proud of me. But to me she was the hero; she had converted the barbarians.

* * *

After three years of intense daily practice, I was beginning to have many strange experiences. After meditation I would lay out flat on the floor, and could easily exit out of my body and float, sometimes willing myself to leave the house and go up into the stars. This was the only place I ever wanted to go, though I had been taught I could go anywhere. At this time I also started to develop a strange dull pain in my spine, behind my heart. It was not really pain, but it was uncomfortable, and would always be the first thing to draw my attention back to my body. This dull pain began to become an obsession, trying to figure out what it was, and how to get rid of it. Rather then something restful and uplifting, I found my yoga practice turning into a way to escape this pain. I knew almost nothing about my emotional world, and most eastern practices just teach you to ignore them, or 'turn your emotions to devotion', was our motto. But while sitting still and going into the pain, it felt like a deep sadness in me, something I could not grasp or understand. I talked with the teachers and finally spoke with the Yogi about it; they had nothing to say except 'keep going'. I increased my meditation practice and fasting, to try and escape, but became very thin, uncommunicative, and even more sad. I was becoming more and more tense, instead of relaxed. Leila didn't know what to do for me, and became sad to the point of tears while in my presence.

It was the day before Christmas, and I had been eating nothing but beets for the last fourteen days. I practiced my usual morning meditation, and then lay down under my blanket. After a short while I stood up and walked to the kitchen to begin my work. I said hello to everyone, but no one answered. I knew that I was out of my body! This did not disturb me as it had happened many times before, so I calmly walked back into the meditation room and back into my body. I stood up again and went into the kitchen; again no one saw me. I walked back to my body, remembering the instructions to concentrate in the navelpoint when something like this happens. Following the prescribed instructions, I stood up again. I looked down and saw my body, and decided I must be dead. I was surprised at how calmly I accepted this. It was just another fact, and that's all. Immediately, I felt a sense of adventure well up in me. I flew up through the ceiling of the house, and headed to my beloved stars, and I was free; I had never been this far from earth before. Looking upwards, a shooting star came into focus and I and decided to chase it. As I flew closer, I saw that it was huge, hundreds of miles long, and moving closer still, saw it wasn't a comet at all. It was an Angel! The most beautiful creature I had ever seen. Her long flowing robes were what I had thought to be the tail of the comet. She looked just like the classic pictures of the Christmas Angel, shimmering blue, gold, and white. I caught up with her, and touched her robes. A sense of joy and peace came over me, and then an even greater astonishment at the realization that I was touching a real Christmas Angel. All the years of growing up with Christmas, and I had never felt this joy. The angel kept moving, but I began to feel a stalling in my motion and gently began to float back to Earth, and I awoke in my body. This time I made it to the kitchen with my body. Leila stared at me like I was a ghost.

"What has happened to you?"

I could barely speak, and softly told her I was going to go walking in the hills behind the ashram. I felt I should have been joyous, but I was not. Having touched something so sublime, then having to come back to Earth, and my painful body, was too much of a shock for me. Gut survival instincts told me that this was a dangerous moment in my life. My life on earth had become sad, for whatever reason I didn't know, but I did know I was using my spiritual practices just to escape. I wanted out. Seeing how easily I accepted my death let me know that I must have some serious emotional problems to want to leave so badly, but I couldn't feel them or know what was wrong. I was taught to by-pass my emotions. Since I was doing everything I had been taught, I had no ideas of what was wrong with me. Again I asked the senior teachers and the Yogi, and received the same answer, "keep going."

The tendency to think and feel "what is wrong with me" is planted deep into the western Judeo-Christian mind set. But the Kundalini forces always worked correctly, and were bringing to the surface my subconscious feelings and emotions. The subconscious knots that we don't want to look at, translate themselves into physical tensions and strange spasms to get our attention. I probably could have gone on for many decades and not known that I had buried pain and dis-empowering prompters, but now with the use of powerful Tantrik techniques, I was turning my own sexual energy back into my nervous system, trying to smash my way though the gates of heaven, without first clearing the reasons for the blockages. Without free flow or outlet, the energy had no choice but to cramp and dissipate in fruitless 'Catch 22', worry and thinking. The harder I pushed, the worse off I became, losing my peace. The more I lost my peace, the harder I pushed. This was a true hell realm, but served the purpose of a self-protecting, safety- valve, dissipating energy when one's will and power exceeded their wisdom. The teachers were dangerously ignorant of the side effects of these practices. Again I was told to "turn emotion to devotion", and that was the only technique given to us to deal with emotions. With my strong will power and stubbornness, I kept increasing my practice, and occasionally could leave my body, but it was becoming increasingly harder as my body developed the strange cramping symptoms. I became increasingly restless and agitated. With nowhere left to turn, I consulted the 'great sages' in the 'den of wild beast'.

"Man, you just need to get laid."

It had been years since having sex. There was no particular rule about sex in the ashram, but we all knew that the techniques worked by saving and using the sexual energy for meditation, so there was not a lot of promiscuity going on. On occasion I would masturbate, but this was a dangerous thing for a Tantrik yogi. After a few years of practice, the sexual forces had become so powerful, it was like walking on the razors edge. One slip and you could spin off into weeks of daily masturbation, four or five times a day until exhaustion, and this happened to me on many occasions in the early years of training. One could build the sexual force up again in about a month, but masturbation had another effect to anyone sensitive enough to feel the movement of energy in the body. Physical stimulation in the sexual glands pulled the energy and cerebral spinal fluid down to the genitals; active imagination, in the minds eye, pulled the energy and fluids up into the head. The eventual result was a separation of energy at the center of the spine, in other words, a *cold heart*. People who masturbated excessively, developed weak and pain filled spines, eventually losing the ability to have successful relationships, as fantasies became more real to them. In Tantrik Yoga, it is not a question of morals, as in some Christian sects, but rather a question of economy of energy. The dedicated yogi employs the sexual energy to move up the spine, eventually kick-starting some very knarley higher brain functions. Visualization required a certain kind of refined energy that had been created in the heat of long practice, and if that energy was not continuously fed into the brain, the eventual effect was very much like running an engine without oil; the brain burns out, loses its circulatory powers, and meaningless images are hallucinated in later years. Even successful mating relationships were considered a function of magnetism and not chance. In yoga practice, the western virtue of Temperance was turned into an exact science. Semen, the most highly concentrated energetic substance in the body, was irradiated in the brain by the pressure of long concentration. Though the west looked at these practices as 'esoteric', they were simple common physics. Meditation was a way of closing down the leakage of bio-energy through the five senses. One became a container in which the energy was 'cooked'. Pressure creates heat; heat contained long enough, creates light. After the semen absorbs this radiation, it is given the name *Ojas* to signify that it has been infused with whatever qualities of light the yogi is able to capture. Mantra is then employed. These words are spoken with an exaggeration of the jaw movements, acting as a pump, pushing the refined *Ojas* into the higher cavities of the brain. This leads to the ability to sense, and sometimes internally see, the inner pathways of the body, called *nadis* in India, or *meridians*, in the Far East. The *Ojas* is then mechanically circulated through the whole body by a series of postures and rhythmical movements. When the body is filled, the *Ojas* having no more room to flow, again heats and refines even further, eventually seeping out of the whole body, spherically; and this is called *Aura*. We have seen this light represented in paintings and images of the Saints. This *Aura* is magnetic, and if cultivated, one can magnetize to themselves, what ever is needed to fulfill one's 'consciously chosen' destiny, eventually leading to complete union with God.

We all supposed the Master had achieved this union, and that compelled many to blindly give up their will and follow; because of course, he was all knowing. But I was in serious pain, and he had no answers. I thought that if he was all knowing, then he was a *&^%%$#$ for putting me through this. After three years of dedicated daily practice, I felt deserving of something better than this, and started to give serious thought to the wisdom of the 'den of wild beast'. The senior teachers began to take a more fanatic stance, and told me I was deserving of nothing, that pain was a great builder of character and I should happily surrender to God's will. My reaction was astonishment that I had some how ended up as a Catholic again! It was now only my love for Leila kept me going. I didn't want to leave her, but the thought of having sex with her for the first time, because I needed to release my tension, was never an option, even in thought. I prayed for an answer.

A week later, Leila left for Los Angeles to participate in a special training. Her radiance caught the Yogi's eye, and he wanted her as a secretary on his personal staff. We said, all the things people say when they have to part: we would meet again, it would be better the next time, etc. I didn't believe any of it, and felt worse as the days went on without her. Had I been surer of myself, I would have put more effort into making sure we stayed together, but I felt I had no right to subject her to my troubles. When I meditated about this situation, my only answer was, "If it is meant to be, it will be." One hears that a lot around 'spiritual' types, but I was never convinced that this wasn't just a cop-out. Action seemed the way to get what you wanted in this world, but then one had to be clear on what one wanted, and I wasn't. A feeling of shame at my own impotence to help myself increased the pain of losing Leila. It was time to leave.

I had been teaching yoga classes outside the ashram, to a wild group of singers and musicians who had started a rock and roll choir. They were a vast and happy family of groupies, girlfriends, 'old ladies', as they were called, tour personnel, children, family members, and many other young people all connected with the big rock bands in Marin County: Grateful Dead, Big Brother and the Holding Company, Sons of Chaplin, Quick Silver Messenger Service, Moby Grape, and a few other smaller bands. These people decided to form their own group but were usually too stoned to organize even a practice. So I was asked to teach them breathing and vocal exercises, which really just calmed them down so they could actually sing a few songs. In a few weeks I was involved with, not one, but two wild young ladies, having sex with both of them in various hippie havens all over Marin County, an honored guest of their huge family. In spite of what history says of this time, these people were generous, loving, and full of fun. I met many genuine spiritual beings from other lineages, actually living what Christ had proposed in the Sermon on the Mount.

I was introduced to a woman who was the manager for a popular female singer who had just recorded her first album on Colombia Records. She loved my songs, and saw that I had a big enough follow-ing, so she took me to Colombia Records, and I was back in the music industry. Music had always been a natural spiritual and calming force for me, meaning that I never had to force my attention, it was always fun, and an exploration; I could work for days in a recording studio, los-ing all track of time, and it was always effortless creation. Colombia Records decided to give me a chance; they would pay for half a record-ed album of my own songs, then they would consider what to do from there. My manager was confidant and pumping my excitement by assuring me that this is how they handled their other singers, I was not to worry, and the contract was assured. Needless-to-say, I was flying with the new direction of my attention. In the meantime, the other singer had just come out with her second album, and it wasn't very good. My manager got into a fight with the head of A&R about the new album. She called him a faggot and stomped out. In order to get his revenge, he took my finished master tape and threw it in the trash, never to be seen again. That was it for me! I was done with the world! My emotions were so intensified, and out of balance, that I easily caved in and fell back into deep depression. I couldn't go back to the ashram, and I didn't want to be around people for a while, so I decided to go live by myself in the mountains, a solitary yogi. My friends, feeling badly at how Colombia Records had treated me, pitched in and bought me a ticket to Hawaii.

* * *

For days I gleefully wandered through the rain forest of Kauai, until reaching the uninhabited backside of the island, and the beautiful old Hawaiian villages and healing grounds. Here I made home with my lover and friend, Nature. The days were long, slow and blissful, swimming in deep pools, meditating under waterfalls, and body surfing with a pod of dolphins that came to my beach each morning. My shelter was a large cave on the beach, and always having had some deep feeling and love for caves, I spent many hours absorbed in the colors and patterns of rock. Outside there was plenty of guava, mango, and fresh water. I never wore a shred of clothes and in weeks, lost my membership in the 'white butt' tribe, as the island hippies labeled them, but I gave up the idea of being alone when discovering groups of these hippie tribes living in some of the near-by valleys. The word got out there was a yogi around, and soon I was teaching classes on the beach to wonderfully happy naked people. My meditation practice became fruitful, my body lean and strong. I could swim for miles to the next valley, teach classes and feast overnight with good food and nice people, next day jump in the water and swim to the next valley. Water is the most natural healer of deranged emotions, and I spent many hours of the day surfing or just leisurely floating down the coast. Alone, out of the mind-fields of any conditioned beings, bobbing up and down in a primordial rhythm for hours at a time, allowed the knots to unravel as large gestalts of images surfaced in my mind's eye. Every image was sifted through, in glorious leisure...

This style of yoga was purported to be a "spiritual" path, but really just acted as an amplifier of whatever state of mind one was in—a powerful amplifier and tool if one had a clear mind and inten-tions, a loaded weapon if one had a tormented mind.

The Yogi considers himself a Saturn teacher… hard teaching… as opposed to a Jupiter teacher… softer, more joyous, and light— Heck! In Buddhist schools I'd have to go through years of meditation practice and self analysis before being given any of the power tech-niques which we practiced daily—What the hell was I thinking pick-ing this guy?… we're playing with the primal forces of the Universe…What a scam… you develop the powers— geeez-!!!!! — then you see your subconscious demons and have to stick around to do the real work of cleaning out your garbage…or now with all that power you can really screw your life up…WHAT THE!!!! —man are you ready for this shit!…all because he wants to make money off American's need for speed —

(The next wave caught me— treating me like it's long lost child)

— Now you have to deal with the—what did he call them?… "Five Demons": Lust, anger, greed, pride, attachment, in all their forms and levels of unconscious manipulation—Man!—he doesn't even know this shit himself…bastard!…tricked us huh!…just throw us in the water… sink or swim —

(I let myself sink below the water, my body becoming warm rub-ber in the currents…laughing like a mad man…..wondering if the fish could hear me…..they can see the bubbles!)

—But why did we all look the other way when we saw people burn out— Duh!… people who ask to many questions, or heaven for-bid, be "emotional,"— or had "big egos" they couldn't surrender,… were the "negative ones" — ya get the cold shoulder— all smiles on the surface but a big Fuck You underneath the sugar…Yuck!…I hate sugar! — Guess they "Pure Ones" didn't want to be polluted— no incriminating physical abuse — they were too smart for that — but the mental pressures and judgments from people practicing these pow-ers — Oh my God!

(a pod of dolphins thirty yards to the south, jumping, spinning, merrily squawking….. their joy feels like an electric current charging the aqua-blue water with vitality)

— so many cowering to their feelings… didn't want to be brand-ed as having— God forbid— AN EGO — don't want that mortal

sin, no way — oldest control technique in the world — undermine a child's self-trust by convincing them something is wrong with them — born defective — sinners from the get go —get em young, easier to control that way — Hey—Hey—Hey — wanna be saved — join the group—the religion—the organization —and don't forget to give a nice fat donation—

(Hey, are those seagulls laughing at me.)
"Hey punks! Get away from my car!"
(bob and roll—bob and roll in the waves)

— Yea— the Yogi was getting pretty rich — and all those chumps poorer and poorer— captured for years by there own material and spiritual greed — desire for money, powers, liberation — It's all the same game — desire for anything is still just desire — desire leads to more desire — but HAVING leads to more HAVING —

(The clouds over head were having an orgiastic symphony — a flying saucer rolled into a pyramid, silver golden light illuminating it from behind — a jagged cube — the Oscar Meyer wiener-mobile — giant floating penis — my torso undulated with HAVING as I drifted for miles down the jagged coast line—surrendering to the warm currents caressing me)

—Those poor chumps?—hell— look at me! —Original Sin — demons and devils — what the fuck man—I'm only in first grade — got to eat the body — drink the blood...yuck— or I'll burn forever in Hell? — Ya mean if I miss mass on Sunday and go surfing instead— and get killed in a car accident—hopefully after surfing— I'm going to go to Hell and burn forever?!!! — What's that man! — Damned sickos! — Perverted bastards! — Man if Jesus is right when he said "whoever corrupts a child should have a stone tied to their neck, and be thrown in the ocean", you idiots have a lot to answer for — but geeeez almighty—don't throw em in this ocean! — AND YOU —you whinny fat-ass gurus — you take the so-called lower classes, tell them if they serve the Brahmins, they will earn good karma and come back next time in better circumstances — I mean—what the hell is the difference between all you religious perverts — ya think your soooooo bad-ass — let me tell you something — the only way your whole trip works is by taking a little kid and scaring them — what a scam you guys have — you get em coming and going — you brainwash them

when they are defenseless — telling them they are sinners or lost in Maya — whatever dudes —then tell them YOU have the key to get them out of the mess that YOU just made up in the first place — what the fuck!

(The rage rolled out in unhurried, languid catharsis and was lovingly dissolved in the mellifluous, feminine liquid enveloping me. Below, seeing me through the crystal clear water, the fish watched in curiosity as I glided into the shallows just before sunset)

— Obedient, programmed "sheep" don't ask questions like, "Is original sin or bad karma real?" ....Hey man!...is that the way it really is...or did you just make it up in your sicko head? ...do we trash the world and kill each other in our wars because we are evil... or do we do it because you brainwashed us to think we are evil?...Junk in, Junk out man!!!! —Then you lie about history to make us think we need you to help us be good...a handful of people on the payroll, writing about a handful of people...hey man... there were lots of people having a damned good time all through history...they never even knew about your bloody damn wars...you want us to think everybody is a damned, flipped-out killer so YOU can save us...What a scam!...geeeez...Get a job!

(I dove beneath the shoreline waves and screamed out my last venom, then rolled onto the beach with a peaceful vacuous mind and a gloriously erotic body. The horizon was ablaze as the first blinking of my brothers' and sisters' eyes began to appear in the violet dome above me.)

* * *

After a year of this, (*can you imagine*) I began to feel I had absorbed paradise, and the inner voices softly gave me clues that it was time to consider moving elsewhere. Maybe just down to the next beach, but naaaa—I knew that wasn't it! But what can you do after absorbing paradise and it isn't enough? And it wasn't. I knew this was just a speed bump on the road; there was more for me than living out my life like this. Damn! I watched this thought deposit its residue of wanderlust in my mind, but received it as a gentle message from Wisdom, rather then an egotistical dissatisfaction.

One evening, I walked down the beach to my favorite meditation cave, and swam across the small lake to the passage of the deeper caves. With a small candle I crawled deep into the earth, further then I had ever explored in this cave, and inched along until reaching a very tight and long wormhole, which eventually opened into a large round room. After blowing out the candle I sat in silence for many hours, practicing my breathing tricks until becoming un-aware of my body. "I" expanded into the black void, feeling immense and electric, not knowing where "I" left off and the Universe began. I basked in this enigma for eons, until the immaturity of my assuredness was revealed to me by a wave of sadness welling up in me from I knew not where; then, the simple realization; I was alone. What did it matter, this power, this immensity; I had no equal exchange of love in my life; and what difference did it make if I had everything, but no love? The realizations turned to liquid and I began to weep, the tears being the first sensations recalling me to my human flesh, that and the damp chill of the pitch-dark cave that I now became aware of. After another eon of this agony, I reached for the candle but it was nowhere to be found. I sat in the dark silence. Was this the true nature of human existence, had I found the final core behind the peeling away of all the layers to hide it? Was all the contrived significance that human culture generated, just so it would not have to face this; do enquiring minds really want to know? Exasperated, I released a cry, "God, what now?" Suddenly, a small pearl colored light appeared in front of me! It pulsed slowly, and then began to expand and come into a focus simultaneously. It was the face of the Yogi! All the thoughts and feelings I had been chewing on over the past year, flashed through my head, and I saw the choice right then and there. The ups and downs, whining, complaining, the joy and sorrow, the Ah Ha's!!! — and the confusion, the whole plethora of what a human could go through, it was all just Life, and there were only two choices: Yes or No. At the exact same moment I spoke, the Yogi also spoke; one word coming from both of us resounded through the cave as we peered into each other's face: "YES".

His face dissolved into the small pearl light and began to move. I followed it to the small opening leading back into the passageways from which I had entered. Crawling on my belly, it led me through the wormholes into the larger tubes, and then disappeared as I entered the main room of the small underground lake. Then, the smell of danger!

While in the cave, four Hawaiian goat hunters had come into the valley, and proceeded to drink themselves into mindless behavior. As I crawled closer to the lake, I heard gunshots. Exiting the small tube, I stood up and inched my way to the shore of the lake. From their perspective, I had all of a sudden appeared deep in the cave, across the lake from them. The hunters saw me and slowly turned their guns in my direction. The very next instant, I was back in the low passageways deep into the cave. There was no sense of movement, or sequence of time; in one moment I was in one place, the next moment I was in another, without the slightest jot of alarm. After a short while I crawled back out of the tubes; seeing the hunters had departed, I swam across the lake to the gapping main entrance. A very anxious friend met me! He said the hunters had come into the valley about an hour ago, already drunk and shooting guns at the rocks. The tribes had safely hidden themselves, but he, an ex-Marine scout, had followed them at a safe distance. He laughed while describing to me; after he heard a few rifle shots, the hunters had come running out of the cave in terror. From what he could understand of their excited talk, they had seen a man appear on the other side of the lake, then in a flash of light, he had disappeared right before their eyes. I listened with amusement, recalling that the Hawaiians had many old superstitions and ghost stories about these valleys; I am sure they were quite frightened. We returned to the tribes, and laughed and feasted through the night, and as all tribes do, wove long, scary, exaggerated tales. Myself having no real understanding of what happened, I let the stories swell, and wanting to add to the fun, and of course make sure my blossoming legend would be remembered, thought up the most dramatic exit I could come up with. The next morning, when the tribes awoke, I was gone!

✳ ✳ ✳

Yogis are given stern warnings about using occult powers or even trying to develop them, rather than trying to attain union with God. On the pathway back to civilization, I considered carefully what had happened in the cave. To try and gain conscious control over these powers, and use them at will, like some kind of circus act, is the target of the warnings. There is no need to try and attain them; they are simply there, unhesitant to serve anyone sincerely on a path of loving-kindness toward their fellow human beings. I never gave much consideration to where I might stand in the hierarchy of evolution, but I took this as a 'pat on the back', and was thankful. Assuming I had no control over these things, a quiet acceptance of these phenomena seemed a better way to go. In Hindu lore, they are controlled by the various Goddesses; In Judeo- Christian and Muslim lore, they are controlled by Guardian Angels. Having experienced the angel while in the Northern

California ashram, I was primed and ready to give credence to all of this, and it was integrated into my reality. After purging myself of the neural consequences of Catholicism's excessive use of the images of Jesus' broken body on the cross, which for myself, only served as a warning not to be open and loving because this is what will happen to you, I was now, at least a little more free to choose which images and realities I wanted to fill my aura with. The realization of one's own connection with the Universe and being open to the incomings of unqualified Truth, always acted as sword and shield, even without conscious intention. Whether by divine beings, or the intricacies of synchronicity, one always found themselves in the right place at the right time, and apparently I was; a friend who had heard news that the Yogi had come to the islands and was now on Oahu, met me at the edge of civilization.

✳ ✳ ✳

In the midst of a sea of white clad students, I entered the ashram in my best Hawaiian flowered shirt, and a scraggily pair of shorts that scandalously showed off my tanned, sinewy legs. Under the high eyebrows of the senior students, the Yogi met me with much laughter and warmth. He stuck me by his side for the next three days, as I told him of my adventures. Much to the astonishment of the teachers, he laughed merrily at the stories of the naked yoga classes on the beach; he was genuinely happy to see me, and I him; all the judgments about the organization I had made a year ago, were now pushed aside in the enjoyment of friendship. Except for some friends from the 'den of wild beast' the senior teachers were very formal, and asked many questions about the rumors that had surfaced about me since leaving the ashram in Northern California. I assured them that they were all true. The Yogi enjoyed this immensely, especially because he sensed many of them becoming angry, and even jealous at the attention I was getting after being too cavalier about my running off, as they abashingly put it. The more controversy, the more the Yogi seemed to enjoy himself.

The end result of this strange confluence and astral pyrotechnics was that I was now to be made the head teacher at the international headquarters in Los Angeles, where the Yogi lived. Also I was to become one of his personal bodyguards. This was a lot of responsibility, because I had to teach the 4:00 a.m. classes every morning, work in the center's restaurant during the day, and then be watch guard at the main ashram at night. After a year of *no time* in the Hawaiian valleys, I knew he was setting me the challenge of a new kind of growth: being

firmly in the world of time schedules, and having many others depending on me to do it right. I wanted to spend more time with the Yogi,
and of course, see Leila again, so I took the position. When I asked
about Leila, he suddenly became very serious and took me off to the
side by myself, then told me that Leila was now engaged to someone,
and I must forget that. My heart jumped a beat and he caught it.
Peering deeply into me he spoke, "You have a big destiny that you can't
fight, if you do, you will only become very sad. You can cause trouble,
act crazy, run away, do what you want, but you made an agreement with
God along time ago, and God will hold you to it." Destiny! Agreement
with God! What did that mean to me, I wanted to be with Leila! I had
developed the habit of never seeing outer reality as the final say, so I
quietly accepted what he said, while hiding an inner capricious smile

* * *

Because of all the teaching and meditating, or maybe just lack of
sleep, the fast pace of Los Angeles didn't seem to bother me. One class
floated into another, and I was also staying up most of the night on
guard. We were expected to meet these challenges with the knowledge
of diet and yoga that we had been given. I adjusted my diet to foods that
gave maximum energy without a lot of digestion time, and practiced
the breathing and postures that created heightened alertness. The air-
tight schedule created a kind of security, which once I got used to,
allowed me to go into meditation even more. To others I looked quite
normal going about my routines, my outer life on automatic pilot,
while on the inside I was filled with beautiful sounds and feelings of the
interior worlds. I saw Leila only a few times and met the young man she
was engaged to. He was in his early 20's, and studying to be a minister
in the tradition we practiced, learning to read the scriptures in the old
original Indian language, and officiate at ceremonies. Leila was kept
busy doing various task in the Yogi's household, and they did not see
each other very much, which I of course gratefully accepted in silence.
The year went by without much change in my routine except when I
was asked on many occasions to act as the Yogi's personal bodyguard.
This kind of guarding was different from the typical understanding of
the word. Through the magic inherent in meditation, one was expected to *create* a blanket of security; if you were watching and waiting for
something to happen, you weren't doing your job. So no problems ever
appeared in the peaceful force field I had cultivated, but I did get to sit
with the Yogi for many hours at a time, watching and listening as he

give counsel to many sorts people with their various problems. There
were many things he would say that I didn't agree with, but he always
knew what I was thinking, and after the people left, he would give me
insight into why he would say what he did. He was a very shrewd and
humorous man and I truly loved this time with him, drinking up his
wisdom as he explained to me what he was trying to make these people
understand. He enjoyed that I would try and think of alternative ways
to do the same thing, and when I did disagree, he was always ready for
a good argument. The man loved to talk, and would sometimes spend
many hours with those who came with problems. I felt people should
be made to be more self-reliant and find their own answers in meditation. His answer was that Americans were too crazy, and not humble
enough to really open in meditation. He said I needed more patience
with people, and teased me that I was more of a Saturn teacher than
even he, though in outward demeanor I was more Jupiter. He looked
on with fatherly pride as I challenged him to stop trying to get me off
the point, and came back at him with the factual statement, there was
not supposed to be a Guru in this path. This path had been made democratic in the 1700's, and he was setting himself up as a king. He would
answer,

"I am not doing it." "These crazy people are doing it to me."

With this I had to agree. In the early days of this group, I remembered him saying over and over again, "if you put a middleman between
you and God, you will create hell for yourself." But no matter what he
said, many people just wanted a giant 'daddy' to take care of everything
for them. For many years I watched as the group continued to put the
Yogi in this role, and at some point, it seemed like he just thought,
"what's the use", and started to go along with it. If people were going
to create hell for themselves, they were going to do it with or without
him, so he might as well profit from it instead of someone else, and he
did profit. The Yogi bought up acres of land, expensive Peruvian horses, and like all Indian potentates, he liked lots of jewels.

I did not begrudge him for the wealth he accumulated; after all he
did work for it. He was one of the hardest working men I had ever met,
and he did genuinely care about people; I saw this again and again. But
he was a very smart man and knew how Americans loved to set someone on a pedestal, and then knock them down. So the Yogi took care of
himself, and setup his family quite well, as any person who works hard
is entitled to do.

One night, the head secretary came to me and asked if I would go
to a neighboring city as the Yogi's bodyguard; a large Tantrik Yoga class

was being given over the weekend. While standing outside the teaching center, a man came running out of the crowd screaming curses at the Yogi, and would have physically attacked him, but with the help of the other well trained guards, he was easily stopped before getting close enough to do any harm. He turned out to be a former student who had supposedly fallen in love with one of the secretaries, and had made threatening phone calls on previous occasions. Even though nobody was hurt, the Yogi was visibly upset by the incident, the secretaries also. I had an uneasy feeling about the whole incident, like there was something I didn't understand, but put it aside when asked to guard in front of the Yogi's door through the night. I could not help but hear some of the conversations on the other side of the door. The way the he dealt with trouble was to work. He grabbed his phone and started to call on some of his teachers in other parts of the country, and I could hear him counseling, arguing, giving his wisdom—for hours he talked and talked. Into the late hours I could hear the Yogi speaking, and I began to feel a deep admiration for this man. For seven years I had watched him helping, generously giving of himself, a tireless soldier doing his duty; he had given me a place to live and invaluable training that had changed my life. That night I bowed. Not because I was supposed to, but purely out of love and respect for the man. My bow started as an admiration for him, but then turned to something much more. I was mercifully propelled beyond my admiration for the Yogi, and found myself in awareness of the perfection of *synchronicity* in my life, which I had previously named *coincidence*. I viewed years of chance encounters and meetings, as now having a coherent pattern and map, leading to this very moment. It was not important that I was bowing to him, what was important was that "I" bow. I saw that if I always had complete control in my life, I could have never come up with such an interesting and fascinating story, connections, chance encounters to usher me into a life of gratefulness.

To bow is to trust, and I saw the function of ego was to control everything, make sure everything is running smoothly, and be on top of it all. The intention is mostly altruistic, and one of self-protection in a fast scary world. But once the ego understands that there is already a perfection in Space that happens without "it," then out of this wisdom it dissolves itself; there is no need to control what is perfect. Trying to destroy the ego with punishment or force, or seeing it as the devil or enemy, was an ultimately fruitless activity with very temporary results. The wisdom appearing by experience, and the swoon of thankfulness, was the only way the ego bowed in humility, and while basking in this new feeling, I began to compose a song. The song took on a life of it's own and became an expression of Love for all Life, and the thankfulness to be able to taste it; I became infused in the words and rhythm. But while in this state of ecstasy, a further, ironic synchronicity appeared at the same time.

It is interesting how the mind can become very selective in what it wants to deal with at moments like this. The implication of what I was hearing was such an anathema to the song that was being born, I quickly partitioned the sounds, rationalizing it to be something else. Anything else! But alas, a chosen path of awareness doesn't allow for such trickery; the seed of painful doubt had dropped. On the other side of the door, I heard sounds and words that I knew to be the declaration of seduction between lovers; the Yogi was alone with one of his secretaries.

Two weeks later I was asked to accompany the Yogi again, this time to San Francisco. I was happy to see my old friends from the Northern California ashrams. On the last night of the course, he asked me to stand up and sing in front of the few hundred people in the auditorium. He jokingly said, "Sing the most beautiful love song you have ever written." For the first time in public, I sang the song that had been composed in front of his door. The Yogi and audience were stunned. He peered at me in silence for a few moments, and then declared, in front of everyone, I was now a Master of Laya Yoga. The next morning I was given the title of "Khalsa" to be used as my name. This was one of the highest honors that could be given in this path, and had never been done before.

I had no idea what this all meant, and can't say that it meant all that much to me. In my own mind I was a yogi who sang pretty well, and had some pretty cool experiences. But the way people treated me changed drastically; some smiled and were proud of me, others were cold and jealous. I had become a celebrity overnight, and this brought me no comfort; in fact, it was downright scary to be the object of hundreds of people's expectations and personal definitions of the meaning of Khalsa. It seemed that everyone knew something that I didn't, and I decided to ask for a new assignment in another State.

A few months passed when a tragedy struck. The young minister who was engaged to Leila had been killed in an automobile accident. I didn't know him well, but had much respect for him, and felt the pain of the whole group, and I was asked to accompany the Yogi's wife and two other women to India to bury his ashes. I was honored, and excited to see India for the first time.

* * *

I awoke bleary eyed at New Delhi airport, after a long, smoky flight. The Yogi's wife handed me a box filled with the ashes, then put a picture of the young minister on top of the box so all could see. Her only words were, "Stand straight", and the gate leading us out of Customs was opened. My first impression of India was a swarm of hundreds of emotional Indians running straight towards me. Within seconds, I could barely stand with all the wreaths and flowers hanging all over the box of ashes and myself. A taxi pulled up, and I was told to dump it all in the back seat and get in. The driver was a crazed mad man, using his horn every five seconds, racing through the streets, coming within inches of people, other cars, monkeys running across the road, and giant cows leisurely sunning themselves in the middle of the street. We came to a screeching halt in front of a beautiful temple, and the box, all the flowers, and I were unceremoniously pulled from the back seat and rushed into a side entrance, then seated in a honored place near the book of scriptures. It was then that I knew why I had really come to India. The music began to rise and swirl around the temple, caressing me, opening me in places I didn't even know I had. I couldn't understand the language, but it didn't matter; the songs were an ecstatic worship of God unlike anything I had ever heard. The western music of worship had it's own stately beauty, but these songs were from men who were fools for God, mad with love and unafraid to express it. All tension left me, and tears rolled down my cheeks. It was like being washed with a gentle white fire that passed through you, in and out, pulling apart one's fears, weaving together one's strengths and courage. At the end of two hours, my former self had become a sheet of silk flowing in a soft wind. Forces, fires, and lights took over my body and mind, and I started to feel fever in my head.

We were whisked back to the airport then caught a plane heading north, to the city where the main temple of this religion was located. I was introduced to the Yogi's father, a saintly looking man with a long white beard and a gentle voice. He taught me all the rituals of the temple, and introduced me to the elders. They were gracious and curious, and because they had been told I was a singer, they had already set up many gatherings for me to sing at. I was rushed all over Northern India, and stuffed with more food in one sitting than I would normally eat in a week. I felt the strange fever becoming stronger and taking over my body, and would have fasted to cure myself if I were back in the US, but to these people feeding you was a great honor; I couldn't say no. The lore of the temple said, "if you bath in the water surrounding the temple, then pray inside, all your karma or sins would be washed from you." In a few more days I was flat on my back; the Yogi's wife left me in the care of her father-in-law, and the spirits of the temple.

Chapter 3

Dark Night of the Soul

The little birdman passed his pendulum over my body. I felt as if a wave of cool liquid passed through me, and in the days that followed, the fever began to subside. In the six weeks I laid on my back, I had seen my whole life pass in front of me, right up till this coordinate in time. My body, my thoughts, the way I breathed, had transformed into a new instrument of active awareness, the range of perception pushed to the super-sensual. It was as if I had died and come back in a strange new body, fit to explore a strange new world. On this day I knew the little man would not return. I took his hands and thanked him in the silent communication that passed between us; he bowed and shuffled out of the room. I wanted to bring him some gift of my appreciation, and learn more about the way he used his pendulum, but when I asked the other doctors who he was, they just said he was one of the local villagers, and they weren't exactly sure where he lived; he came and went, as he wanted. Wanting my memory of him to remain as it was, I didn't pursue anymore questioning; it was just one of those things that happen in India.

With the Yogi's wife still in New Delhi, I had no duties, and decided to take off and explore on my own. I found my way to the bus depot, and headed for Dharmasala, the new home of the exiled Dalai Lama; taking my time, I stopped at many small temples along the way. It was these simple village people that I fell in love with. I sang at the temples, channeling back to them their joyous and un-breakable spirit, and I was treated like a young king. Before the fever, I tore into spiritual life as if it were a football game, smashing my way through the gates of heaven, learning all the required attitudes as if in college. But now, by seeing the strength and love of these people, and because they made me feel that I was one of them, the first infant understanding of humility began to arise in me, a richness of feeling and thankfulness beyond what any material riches could give; joy can only be given, never taken.

I arrived in Dharmasala with the idea of staying at the Tibetan library, but the village leader, who had been told of my coming by his friends down the mountain, immediately snatched me off the bus. Again I was breakfasted, lunched, and dinnered, all over the little town. The villagers were in awe that an American who knew some of their sacred songs, would come all this way to sing with them. Though I had to insist upon a break from the feedings, singing with them in their ceremonies was always thick with joy. Eventually, I traveled further up the mountain to visit the Tibetan community. After taking a small room at the library, I wandered all through the town, meeting many friendly Tibetans and western students, and through them, I was shown many things that a casual tourist would never get to see. Soon I was the guest of young Tibetans who worked in the carpet factories, and after a few hours of swapping stories, the subject turned to politics. These young people were very open and friendly, but somewhat frustrated by their circumstances, and I was told a different story about the take over of Tibet, one that was not spoken of in the West. The happy little tale of a people gratefully under the care and protection of the Dalai Lama, was a fantasy, and in fact, many of the common working class had sided with the Chinese when they first came. Tibet was a feudal society with the Dalai Lama owning everything, and the people had to give much of the fruits of their labor to support the thousands of monks who stayed in the lush monasteries. Now in exile, they certainly had no love for the Chinese, but found themselves between a rock and a hard place; they didn't want to live as Communists, but neither did they want a life in a feudal society. These young people worked long hours, with almost no pay, and all wanted to come to the West for the possibility of a better future.

I had seen this all before. In all religions, there was the wisdom intended by their founders, and then there was the political side, a cancerous growth that grew stronger over the hundreds of years, as followers found it easier to acquiesce to middlemen rather than live in the original spark. As the middlemen accumulated property and power over people, impressive dogma and ritual became more elaborate in order to compensate for the loss of original experience. The common people and monks had been indoctrinated to believe that a monk, or someone with a religious practice, was the highest incarnation available to humans, and others of a lower intelligence where there to serve them. The society was broken into caste of servers and those to be served, with no chance of advancement unless one was accepted to study as a monk. Women were thought of as having about as much chance at enlightenment as a dog, an attitude that is not hard to find in all religions of the world, if you look under today's politically correct veneer. Once leaving Tibet and exposed to more of the world, these young people broke from the spell in a very simple and logical way. All the power of the lamas, the magic, incantations and hoopla they had been taught to believe and fear, had been useless against the Chinese; therefore, it didn't work. They knew the Dalai Lama had been smuggled out of Tibet by the CIA, for use in the future as a political tool against the Communists. But what struck me most was they had no bitterness toward anyone, and even though they saw the whole game, they had a compassion and love for the Dalai Lama, understanding that he had been trapped by his past also. From what I saw, these were the most intelligent and enlightened 'class' of people; the compassion of the Buddha had become a part of their being, and was expressed in the most natural un-pretentious way.

The price one pays for leaving behind old emotional baggage is a new larger room and capacity to sense and feel the world around them, for good or ill. I was very saddened by what I had seen here, and overwhelmed by a glimpse of the hierarchical, feudal thinking that most of the world still operated under; even with the creation of democracy, it still carried on as a subconscious force. And it was not just the beings that exploited others that were at fault, but also the ingrained tendency in the masses to allow themselves to be exploited; both groups of people worked in complicity. After finally meeting and studying with the Dalai Lama, I was even more confused. He was truly a wonderful and humble human being; how could someone of this quality be used as an instrument of other's suffering? After traveling and teaching around the world, he openly admitted that what happened in Tibet was created by the Lama's own karma for having been so closed off to the people. The value of having shared the Buddhist teachings with the rest of the world has proven that statement to be right; for in the presence of such humility and intelligence, questions of why and wherefore of the past, are extinguished, and a deeper compassion for the human condition and the forces that keep us from evolving, become a new burning.

I knew I was yet too young to grasp the Tantrik teachings I was given, but received the initiations with a still gratitude, and knew that a seed had been planted, a great tool for my quest to understand the causes of human violence. I left the Himalayas hoping the world would take heed of what had happened to these wonderful people. Change and grow, or perish. The biblical quote came to mind; "There are those now last who will be first, and those now first who will be last."

* * *

India had stretched my frame of reference, my emotions, and my body, to the breaking point; I'd had enough. Maybe I should have been on my knees in humble thankfulness for all that had happened, but truthfully, I wanted to get back to California, catch some waves, sit in with a good rock band, and watch a mindless car wreck movie. But Mother Kundalini had something else in mind, the cherry on my Indian cake! As I slowly made my way out of the mountains toward New Delhi, I kept running in to large groups of Sikhs, all heading the same direction, and as the roadways became wider so did the masses of people. In perfect synchronicity, I had merged with the largest religious pilgrimage India had seen in a hundred years. Every road, every highway was clogged for hundreds of miles, with truckloads of pilgrims; the Sikhs were celebrating the anniversary of their beloved ninth leader, Guru Teg Bahadur. In 1675, the Moghul authorities beheaded Teg Bahadur for openly condemning the Emperor Aurangzeb, for his forced conversions of the Hindus to Islam. He chose to die rather than bow to tyranny, which set the character of the Sikhs as a people that would defend any or all people of any religion, who were suffering from religious repression. After his death, Teg Bahadur's son, Guru Gobind Singh, only nine years old at the time, then became the next and last human Guru for the Sikhs. He grew up to be a great warrior, and in 1699 established the order of the Khalsa, a casteless warrior society that became the earmark of the Sikh religion.

I now became the guest of hundreds of Nihung Sikhs. Nihungs were the last of the old world warriors; most still traveled by horseback, and were armed to the teeth with swords, spears, guns, and various other gruesome instruments. They still practiced the old warrior arts as part of their spiritual discipline, and we sat up raucously through the night, singing songs of worship while sipping on strong tea laced with bhang (hashish). The spirit, kindness and humor of these men were infectious, and swelled to an ocean of blissful devotion, as we moved like locusts over the land. At night, we slept in fields on tarps placed over hay that had been set out for the pilgrims, and in the day, thousands were fed in the free kitchens along the route; we were swept along by a mass of energy that enveloped the whole of North India. On the last night before reaching New Delhi, we stopped at the beautiful temple of Patiala, were we listened to the stories and songs of Guru Teg Bahadur late into the night. I wanted to stay with these men through the night, but I had felt my fever returning for the last few days, and much to the amusement of the Nihungs, I began to fall-over while singing. A kind old Nihung picked me up, dragged me to a tarp in a large darkened courtyard, and left me for sleep.

In the morning I awoke in the middle of a mass of sleeping bodies. I rolled onto my other side, and my mouth dropped open; there right in front of my face was the beautiful smiling eyes of Leila! My heart leaped, but she quietly told me to be still; I immediately understood. She was supposed to be the grieving fiancée of the young minister whose ashes we had carried to India. Everything had to look good; all we could do was silently stare, and smile upon each other; the pull between us unbearable. The hundred Americans had arrived during the night on their way from Amritsar, where they had stayed for the last week. I was surprised and happy and to see many of my former students and classmates, but they were aghast to see me. Not finding me in Amritsar, stories had begun to spin out of control; I had wandered off in feverish delirium and was now lost somewhere in India. After assuring them I was fine, and receiving a scolding from the senior teachers, the whole group was placed into trucks and we were taken to the river where the founder of the Sikhs, Guru Nanak, had received his enlightenment. With many Sikhs singing prayers from the shoreline, Leila, the Yogi's wife, and myself as honor guard, rowed out into the river, and the ashes of the young man were thrown into the water.

Leila had never really known him all that well, but played her role for the benefit of the solemn ceremony. When the ceremony was over, we rejoined the larger group and continued on our pilgrimage, and I could think of nothing but her; she flashed her laughing mischievous eyes at me whenever no one was watching. I was deeply in love and could not keep my eyes off of her, even during the ceremonies in New Delhi. But that quality of spark cannot be hidden for long, and though we were oblivious to it, we were being watched; we were separated and put on different flights back to America. In my heart, I formed a plan to wait for the appropriate amount of mourning time, and then I was going to ask the Yogi to marry us.

* * *

After arriving in Los Angeles, my enthusiasm for marrying Leila was cut short by another bout of sickness. A tropical disease specialist found that I had amebic dysentery, malaria, and hepatitis all at once; I laughed that it took all this to slow me down from my frantic drive for what, I still didn't know. But I did get to go surfing! I was invited to stay with a friend in the beautiful beach town of Leucadia, where the Yogananda hermitage overlooked the ocean. Back in the 30's, out of respect for Yogananda, the surfers had named the surfing spot below, "Swamis", and it now was one of the most famous breaks in California. The fever never returned, but I felt I should make a long, slow recovery, mostly to mentally process and integrate my experiences of India. After a few months, I returned to Los Angeles ready to resume my teaching duties, and look for Leila. I was surprised to find that I had been assigned to the teaching center in New Mexico, to take over the directorship of the experimental drug rehabilitation program. I gladly took the assignment because it was the Yogi's second house and teaching center; I would have the chance to see him more, and the secretaries would also be there, including Leila.

The drug program was in shambles; it didn't take long to realize I had been handed a big smelly albatross. There were ten addicts living in one house, with only one, seriously stressed out supervisor, who walked around with an icky sweet smile trying to hide his fuming anger. As I explored the sprawling center for the next few days, I meet many people in the same passive—aggressive state of mind. This center was shabbily run, but with the old ashram adage of never speaking up when something was wrong, because you might be branded as being *negative*, the stuffed emotions created a dark and stifling ambiance. The larger the hidden darkness, the more sweet the front to hide it; something was wrong here. I decided maybe I could turn it into something better, and began by interviewing the ten clients. They ranged in ages from sixteen to forty; all had been arrested for drugs abuse, using and selling, and now were assigned to this new experimental program. The program was funded by a government grant, and on paper it looked fantastic, using dietary and yoga techniques to detoxify serious drug users. But what I found in the center looked nothing like what I had read in the grant proposal. The clients told me they had been dumped into this house out in the desert, and basically pretty much left on their own; occasionally someone came to teach a yoga class. We were given a weekly ration of food, which was not enough to feed them, let alone detox them, and I was given one helper who spent most of his time scrounging for throw away produce at the markets in town. I traveled to the main office to speak with the head teacher about the program, but was given the run-around and was not allowed to see the bookkeeping. I tried to make do with what I had, mostly because I liked the ten clients, and we had a good time even though there was no real program. Once the directors of the center felt me out to see if I would go along with the deception, I was really expected to act as a baby sitter and chain gang boss, using the clients for many various ashram work projects. Our part of the center was off limits to the rest of the students, and the holier-than-thou attitude towards the clients was beginning to anger me, as well as make us all feel pretty isolated. Some days I walked down the road to speak with the younger women, many who had been students in Los Angeles, and soon the ugly gossip began to flow. This whole place was starting to feel very repressive to me, and I decided to investigate a little deeper. Apparently there had been a rash of unfaithful married couples in this center, and it had caused such a panic, that now single men were not allowed to talk to any women. I had never seen this kind of repression before, in any of the centers, and carefully considered what to do.

Because no one would answer my questions about the drug program, I broke into the main office one night and found the files and bookkeeping for the drug program. The grant was in the six-digit range. There were six teachers on the payroll, including the Yogi; they received the bulk of the money as payroll, the rest was for operating expenses. A few days later I talked with three of the teachers, who told me that they all donated their wages to the organization. Though the clients had been here for a year, they had never seen any of these teachers; the Yogi had come out once on opening day. It wasn't hard to find out what happened to the money; it went to purchase land and expensive Peruvian horses.

I was furious that I was soon to be considered one of the 'good old boys', and expected to go along with it. Having never faced this kind of deception before, let alone what it did to me emotionally because I was part of this organization, my first thoughts were, I didn't want to face the implications of it all, and I should say nothing. Everyone else walked around here like things were just 'peachy', why shouldn't I? But I remembered the simple village Sikhs in India, and the honors they had bestowed; this was supposed to be a path based on truth, living the truth, and speaking the truth. This deception was bad enough, but also, I lived with these addicts, and cared about them, they were human beings who had come to the House of Guru Nanak, reaching out for help. My anger filled the center and I readied myself for the confrontation; the opportunity soon presented itself. At the monthly meeting, in front of the whole group, I was singled out for discipline because

I had been seen talking to the single women. This was against the rules; therefore I was to receive some form of punishment recommended by the governing committee. I turned white hot. I jumped to my feet and raged.

"You are sick! Just because somebody was stupid enough to get it on with some married person, you are trying to keep me from talking with my friends... You are out of your... minds, look at what you are doing here."

I raged on and on.

"You think I've done something wrong...what about the drug program, how come I don't have the money to feed these guys? Where did the money go?"

I was just getting started.

"I'll tell you where it went."

With a look of great alarm on his face, the head teacher stood up and yelled,

"I call this meeting closed?"

The room was dead silence. Suddenly, the biggest guard in the center sprang to his feet, with hate in his eyes. His wife had been one of the women who had committed adultery. From across the room, he started for me. More people sprang to their feet; guards from all directions jumped into separate us. The room turned to pandemonium, men yelling at their wives, women crying, accusations flew back and forth, as if a festering boil had exploded.

I was called into the main office. The head teacher was ready for confrontation, but because of what I knew, I wasn't going to back down. He must have felt it in me, and never said a word; I was glaringly dismissed and sent back to the drug center. Two days later I was called back and informed that I was now to become a member of the governing council; I was insulted that these people thought I couldn't see through their tactics. I walked out of the council, and nothing more was said for another week.

Two things happened in that week to change the nasty mood of the ashram. The government-funding inspector came to check on the program; he didn't like what he saw and promptly closed it down; I was never allowed to speak to him. Seven of the clients found other programs, but the three youngest were sent back to jail. I was heartbroken and outraged. The next day, one of the senior women teachers was sent to inform me that they were writing a new grant proposal, and wanted me to be the head of the program. I threw her out, and prepared to leave for Los Angeles; I set my sights on the Yogi. But the night before, someone had broken into the compound and tried to get into the young single women's quarters. The Yogi called and requested that I be sent to sleep in their house as a guard. I was suspicious, but after seeing that the women were genuinely scared, a sense of duty stopped me from leaving, and I moved into the women's center.

Another month went by. Many people in the center ignored me, and walked the other way when I came around, but I'd always had a nasty habit of shoving it in people's faces when I was mad. There I was, all by myself in the single women's quarters, talking to them anytime I wanted, and although it was amusing to watch the faces of the people who didn't like me, it did nothing to sweep away the images of my boys being taken off to jail.

I arrived in Los Angeles, only to receive the cold evasion from the secretaries; no appointment to see the Yogi was given. In the front section of the ashram, where the Yogi gave his appointments, was a reading room where the Sikh scriptures were kept. All I could think to do was to come everyday and read for two hours. The vibrations of focused prayer cannot be ignored, and after three weeks of reading everyday, I was finally given an appointment.

The Yogi was sitting in his reclining chair, being worked on, and fussed over by one of his doctors. He greeted me with a big smile, as if nothing had happened. When I questioned him about the drug program, his only answer was,

"The money is gone."

He kept repeating himself over and over again.

"What's done is done, why are you going crazy over this."

When I told him about the three young boys having to go back to jail, his only answer was, as he lay on his couch being massaged,

"There is nothing I can do."

After an hour of useless banter, I was thoroughly disgusted, and started to see him with different eyes and heart; this was the turning point in my relationship with him. He was a very shrewd man when it came to business, but this time he was caught in a lie, and knew it. It took time, and some serious stripping away of organizationally induced apathy, to realize he really didn't care. "The money is gone", meant to him that the event had passed, why should he have to justify his actions; it was done, over. He had a way of pressing his reality into you; I had seen him do it many times while watching him counsel people. I could feel the pressure, and knew that I was expected to bow to some unspoken agreement that he wanted me to feel I had made with him. The man's powers were formidable when focused on you, but I could not forget the faces of my boys as they were taken to jail, and my anger and disgust only increased as he lay there being massaged.

One night while in the scripture-room by myself, the curtain opened and Leila walked in. She was dressed in white and had a silken veil over her head, so I could not see her face very clearly. She sat quietly and began to sway gently back and forth to the rhythm of my chanting, as we communed together in the sound of the beautiful poems and songs. It was the custom to not stop the reading once the two-hour session began, so she would show up right after I started my session, and leave right before I finished, never allowing me to speak with her. She came every night, always following the same pattern of leaving just before I finished. I knew something was terribly wrong for her not to talk to me, and grew sad and concerned when I also couldn't find her during the day. After a month of this, I decided now was the time to ask for her hand, and made another appointment with the Yogi.

I walked into the room and was greeted by the Yogi and four of his live-in secretaries. They were overly cordial and the Yogi was all smiles. I became a little shy, but looked at all of them and announced,

"I've come to ask to marry Leila."

The room fell into dead silence. I saw the Yogi put his head down and jump into some deep hole in himself and disappear. The secretaries began stammering and stuttering, and suddenly I felt as if a knife had been plunged into my guts; there was a sense of panic, and I had no idea where it came from. One of the secretaries put on her best sweet smile, and said,

"We'll discuss this, and then speak to you soon."

I stood up and walked out, the sickening feeling in my stomach swirling through my body. I didn't know what had happened, or why I felt so bad, and could think of nothing else to do but go back to reading the scriptures and wait for my answer. After a week had passed, Leila met me at the door of the temple one evening as I finished my reading session. She looked so frail and scared; the knot twisted in my stomach.

"Leila, what's wrong with you?"

She ignored the question; looking down at the ground, she spoke slowly.

"I can't marry you, please don't ever ask that again."

"But why? I protested.

"Please, we can't see each other any more."

She looked up at me for a brief moment, and I saw tears of anguish in her eyes.

"Please, just don't ever ask again."

She lowered her head and walked back through the gate, back into her world.

I drove to the ocean and walked. That's all I could do for months; left foot, right foot, left foot, right foot— the sound of the waves, and a knot in my stomach. I went back to the scriptures and prayed for help, but could not bear to be in the scripture-room any longer. Finally, with sheer will, I forced it all out of my mind and slowly moved out of the influence of the organization.

Two months later I met Cheryl, and three months after that we were married. I heard that Leila had run off and couldn't be found. She had openly accused the Yogi of having sex with her; so many rumors started circulating, that the Yogi finally had to deny it in public, and ridiculed Leila mercilessly. I drove it from my mind, wanting nothing to do with any of it; but the knot turned to steel. All the sheep fell into his trance, the story was buried, until months later more stories surfaced; I no longer cared. The skill of meditation that had taken so many years to learn now became solely a means of suppression of emotions, and I became a very glum yogi.

Six months later I received a phone call from Leila; she desperately wanted to see me. She knew that I was married now, so we both felt safe to meet. She had been traveling up and down California, and was now sleeping on the floor of some friend's apartment in Santa Monica. We sat on the floor as she told me her story.

At first he had forced her into having sex with him, then after some time, she just submitted to it. He was also sleeping with his other women, and trying to get her into lesbian relationships with them, so that orgies could take place. That's when she ran. Since running away, she had slept with many men, had already had an abortion, and thought she might be pregnant again. I felt helpless; I couldn't even touch her; I was so afraid of what might ignite in me. She wept like a child for an hour; I was frozen, my stomach twisted, my hands sweating. After a while her sobbing turned to whimpers; I touched her leg to try and comfort her. The excitement shot through both of us. I pulled back, and we sat staring at each other.

"I knew you wouldn't break your marriage vows, that's why I felt safe to call you."

She was right. No matter how much I wanted her, I wouldn't break a vow. She had come to me because she knew I wouldn't judge her, and in that non-judgment, maybe find some healing. We promised to keep in touch, and told each other "I love you". I walked out of the apartment, and never saw her again. On that day, a very naive young man awoke to the realities of the world, a great gift for someone on a search for Truth, but a costly one. I stuck my guitar in the closet, and didn't play or sing for the next ten years.

✳ ✳ ✳

The years of formal practice had certainly given me discipline, if not a lot of answers, and the momentum of my search now lead me into Zen Buddhism, martial arts, and mountain climbing. The woman I married was a healing angel sent to me by God, that's the only thing she could have been to put up with me. I was constantly depressed, had no sexual energy for married life; I no longer knew who I was, nor could I find that place of internal observation and calm because the pain in my spine and stomach increased as I pushed with shear will power to suppress my dark feelings. The aura of "I can" that used to surround me, collapsed into a shriveled up prune, and all the tension and anxieties of the world now had their way with me. Hard physical yoga practice and martial arts were the best I could do to siphon off the energy that once went into prayer and song. But this loving woman didn't seem to mind. She took it all in stride, and had a natural capacity for finding interesting things to do and staying happy. What we lacked in communication skills, we made up for in the intensity of our martial arts and vipassana meditation practice, which eventually lead to a beautiful but quiet harmony with each other. She also inspired me to go back to the mountains and forest. Cheryl was an outdoor adventurer who had hiked across the Canadian Arctic, and climbed some highest peaks in the Himalayas. She taught me many new outdoor survival skills, to the point where I could spend months by myself in the woods, and with the Buddhist meditation, and yoga practice, I was becoming more and more an ascetic monk. I sat in the freezing cold mountain pools, concentrating on my navel point, learning to generate heat through my body. Other times, I would meditate underneath waterfalls, finding a fall that would hit the top of my head with just the right amount of pressure, massaging the skull bones, gently vibrating the brain, and causing trance.

On the surface I was very happy with this woman, and to my friends and family this seemed to be the case; I was becoming a good actor. But underneath, I was a critically hurt animal: scared, confused, and backed into a corner. Cheryl's positive attitude and joy only made me feel that much more a failure, and the pain in my body continued to increase. I told no one, not because I wanted to be some silent suffering martyr, but because I knew there was no physical cause for the pain, and didn't want to be thought of as a hypochondriac. There was no one who understood Kundalini phenomena that I trusted, and in some moments of honest clarity, I realized I no longer trusted anybody, not even myself.

The strict vipassana meditation practice was very useful for controlling pain, but it really had no spiritual value for me, though I tried hard to make it so. I then met a Tibetan Buddhist Lama and studied with him for a while, but could not accept the same old Guru-disciple relationship after what I had gone through with the Yogi. With newer eyes of discernment, I was able to see right through many of these Tibetan Gurus who were playing the same game as he had. There were others teachers who were sincere, but eventually I came across a disturbing core difference in my make up, from that of a fundamentalist Buddhist. Even though I was suffering terribly, I just couldn't bring myself to believe the first noble truth of Buddhism: Life is suffering. The arguments in my head went on for days at a time:

> *Well at least he didn't accept that and came up with three more noble truths to get out of suffering... But hey!— the dude's ultimate solution was to denounce the world and become a monk... can't blame him for that...doesn't like women, pretty obvious...but... wouldn't you be pissed off at your mother if she kept you in a castle and you never saw anyone suffering till you were in your thirties...Geeesh! That must have freaked him out big time...pretty sensitive guy too... pretty strong dude though...fasting like that...sitting there till ya see holes in everything...it's all shifting ,changing, passing away...But ya know man...then you say life is dissatisfactory because of that... Don't you think that is your own opinion?...I mean, what makes life suffering to you, is what makes it interesting to me...(everything is changing)...but now these monks of yours have turned everything you said into dogma...scripture...come on man, I'm a democrat!... What about trying to change the world to make it work... What's all this running away becoming a monk...Geeesh! I should talk!....I haven't gotten it up in so damned long there is probably a blank space down there!... hey did you ever get together with St. Paul...you guys think an awful lot a like... Nirvana...Heaven... sounds pretty boring to me...Why can't we make this earth into Heaven....Are you sure your not just copping out...you and Paul...maybe your just a couple of wussys...can't tow the line...Ah man...I should talk...who the fuck*

wants to tow a line?...can't we dance through this?...but hey! Your
cool man...I can understand you... It's all a bit much, isn't it?...I
don't know though...you can keep your opinions...don't be trying to
tell me it's THE TRUTH...you keep your opinions...I'll keep
mine...Ha!... Soon as I get some!

There was really no choice left to me. Having lost trust in anyone's spiritual system, I launched into my own path and practice, based
upon all I had learned over the years, and what I myself found to be
real. There were the different forms of earth, air, fire, water, space, and
my relationship to them—no Gods, no Gurus, Saviors, or philosophers. Some Tibetan friends told me that this was really the practice of
Tantra in the Tibetan Buddhist system, and of course I was doing it all
wrong, then I was told that it was the American Indian way, and again
I was doing it all wrong. But it worked for me, and after a few years I
found the same devotion and spirituality in the body and natural things,
as others found in their religious philosophies, gurus, and saviors. This
was all fine except for one thing; I still could not forgive the Yogi. After
seven years, Cheryl started to understand that she couldn't save or
change me, and she became sad. It all ended on one horrible day when
her father died of a heart attack in our arms. I watched in agony as she
tried to revive him. I knew he was gone, but she was a trained nurse and
had to try. The picture of her trying to bring her father back to life
burned through my mind and turned into a plethora of darker images
about myself. I didn't know how to comfort her; I wasn't even emotionally there for myself, what could I do for her. That was just a simple fact, but it did nothing to ward off the cloud of guilt and self-hatred
that was swallowing me. It turned to one of those Catch 22's; the more
I wasn't present to help her, the more I hated myself—the more I hated
myself, the more I wasn't there for her. I was sucked down into the pit.
After a few weeks of silence, Cheryl told me she now needed to be
alone. I wanted to leave, knowing that I was only making her feel worse.
I had already abandoned her and myself emotionally and spiritually; the
only thing left to do was physically leave. Without Cheryl to cover for
me, the anger at the Yogi, my physical pain, the fact that I hadn't played
music in seven years, and my own self hatred because I didn't know how
to help a woman who had given me nothing but love, all surfaced at
once. I sold my belongings, and headed back to Hawaii, but for a much
different reason this time.

* * *

A broken heart can kill as sure as a bullet. But why wait around for a slow unhappy death, why not just finish it? I was going back to Hawaii to commit suicide. Suicide meant to me, something other then the learned psycho-spiritual pundits espoused; to me it was a call for more life, or better life, not an end to life. After years of excursions out of my body while living in the ashram, I had no belief in death. Suicide meant to me that this planet just wasn't a good place for me, and I was going to go somewhere else. Like I had stepped into some smoky, smelly, bar room, and instead of enduring it, why not just walk out. But this was not going to be some messy unskillful suicide, I was a trained yogi and wanted my last actions on earth to be done perfectly, right down to the end; I was going to leave this earth by fasting to death in a cave, high in the mountains. I knew of some large lava tubes near the top of Mauna Kea on the island of Hawaii. This seemed to be the perfect place, because breathing practice in the rarefied air of high elevation made one sort of drunk, and dulled the pain of fasting. Before making the two-day ascent, I prepared my self with a cleansing diet, then fasted for a few days, thinking that if I spent most of my energy on the way up, then I would not have so many days left to fast once I reached a proper cave. Suicide should be orderly! After the first days climb, I reached the half way cabin with a terrible headache and nausea. I knew from previous experience at high altitude that I was coming down with altitude sickness. So far-so good! But to my dismay, the cabin was filled with ten-year-old kids on a camping trip with their expert-outdoor-mountain-counselor. She was a very sweet Jewish girl with the largest breasts I had ever seen; I could not keep my eyes off of them. This young woman oozed of compassion, and being an outdoor expert she wanted to know why I was going to the top with so little equipment. In my sickened condition, I made up all kinds of ridiculous stories that she saw right through. She knew my sadness, and probably would have done something about it if all the kids hadn't been there; and I was greatly amused that I could still find a strong male pride at feeling lust, even after four days of no food. Alas, we both fell asleep and with difficulty, parted ways in the morning. Though I never told her what I was up to, this was a wise lady, and I was forced to silently assert mental pressure for her to weigh her duty to these children as more important than me. But she was not made of the stuff of acquiescence, and in a strange inexplicable way, I felt she wouldn't let go.

That day I made it to the top of Mauna Kea and searched for a cave. The landscape of the volcano was like landing on the moon, nothing but rocks in strange formations; at night the shapes could turn into anything. I found a small cave, but found it to be too cold during the night, so the next day I headed down the backside of the volcano toward the active craters. I found a suitable lava tube, big enough, and warm enough to indicate that it was still an active tube connected to the lava lake far below.

I began my daily breathing practice, and the days went by. I was puzzled why I wasn't thinking about all the problems that had lead me to this place, instead, all I could think of were the giant breasts. All my training told me I should be thinking about God in my last days, but there didn't seem to be much I could do about it. There was nothing to be done except keep meditating, hoping the salacious images would eventually turn to something else. One morning I was awakened by a deep rumbling sound. My first thought was that I was having some kind of Kundalini experience, and this could be the big send off. Then the rocks started falling from loose spots on the ceiling, and steam rolled up from deep in the tube. I ran outside in time to see a huge boulder sink into the earth, and then everything started to move. The volcano was erupting! Fasting to death was one thing, burning to death was not what I had in mind! I ran back into the cave, put my boots on, and ran for my life. To get away from the erupting side of the mountain, I had to scamper up the volcano and down the other side, taking a whole day of running to reach the bottom. I hadn't eaten in many days, and after a few hours of running wildly, I began to hallucinate giant walls of lava chasing after me and meeting me at every turn. Finally reaching an old fire road at the foot of the mountain, covered with black soot and blood from cuts by the sharp lava rock, I began babbling incoherently, and could see the spirits of the dead way down the road coming to take me. They slowed as they moved closer! It was a truck and the spirit got out and slowly approached me! The being stopped and called out to me. I said nothing. What a scary sight I must have been, standing there alone in the middle of nowhere. They came closer! When it was standing right in front of me, I saw giant breasts, and I went for them. She put up her hand and said, "Wait here, I'll be right back," in the most pleasant singsong voice. The outdoor expert knew I was in shock from exposure, and quickly took complete control of the situation, giving me just the right amount of water, calmed me down, and plopped me into the truck full of wide-eyed kids, all trying to help. They drove me to a friend's house at the tip of the island, and stayed for a long time, giving my friend instructions how to feed and water me until I was complete-ly back, then left after I fell asleep. What was the quote from the Bible? "To those who believe in God, all things happen for the good." I guess that can also include lust.

I stayed around for a few days catching waves and eating every-thing in sight. Mauna Kea continued to blow up for two months, wip-ing out a few villages and adding considerable acreage to the island.

Chapter 4

Goddesses and Witches

Coming back to Los Angeles, I took a job managing a vitamin and herb store at the beach, and also started my own yoga studio in Santa Monica. At this popular store, I began meeting many young women and had to start considering the whole dating and sexuality issue all over again. For years I had drained off my sexual energy in self–pity and sadness, and suffered from premature embarrassments when I did have energy, but now with the help of some advanced yoga and herbs, I quickly remedied this and started my adult sexual life with a vengeance. Before too long I was in a relationship with a beautiful young artist, willing to take on my newfound sexual imagination.

Skirting so close to death can be a very sobering experience, and I now found a new joy and curiosity in living; what was left of my depression was quickly written off as the last residue of obsession with the so-called "spiritual path". I was now determined to explore what a normal, healthy, American male was; the only problem being, no one seemed to know what that was at this time in the shifting human culture. The feminist movement began to generate a lot of good questions, and men started their own groups to consider where they now stood in all this. The general consensus of the day, for a man wanting to be considered in-step with the times, was to be overly sensitive and accommodating to women's needs and wants, but again, the problem being, women weren't sure what they wanted. It was a very confusing time to launch a career in dating. I asked the young woman I was dating what she was doing for birth control, like the new male was supposed to; I was met with the cryptic answer that she didn't need any because she could control her fertility with her mind and certain herbs; she had no intention of becoming pregnant, so she just wouldn't conceive. If I had not seen many incredible feats of mind control, I would have never believed her, but I had met yogis in India, who had complete control of their bodies, and this was actually now my goal as well; I believed her. I quickly found out that the cultural, popular male myth of being able to have sex with anybody, anytime, and not care about them, moving on to the next available site when it shows, was a hideous lie; I was not capable of having sex so intensely, and not bonding with my mate. Jana loved my innocent explorations, but as soon as that bond was made, she told me she had become pregnant. When I asked her how this happened after what she had told me, she said that secretly she really wanted to have a child with me. I angrily told her I didn't want a child, and she had no right to make that choice without the both of us deciding it; I was incensed, and pulled away from her. In our angry exchange, she broke into crying and told me why she had allowed this to happen. When she was a young teenager she had experienced an abortion, and it had been so traumatizing to her, that now she needed to go through a similar experience as an adult, so she could heal the shame and helplessness she felt as a young girl. I couldn't believe what I was hearing! This was the strangest logic I had ever heard, but to her it made perfect sense. But the key element was me! She had used spells to draw me into a relationship, because somehow she knew I would not judge or condemn her; apparently (to her) the soul of the child had agreed to do this for her, but she needed me to go through this with her. I was flabbergasted; Jana was a witch. My mind spun out.

She used spells!!!!....Should I be pissed off or flattered?!!!....How did she know I wouldn't condemn or judge her?....Who the hell does she think she is telling me what I'll do or not do?...Man, I'm in trouble here, this girl is whacked ....Why do I feel so sad?...But ya know you ran away from Cheryl...I don't want to run away anymore if this girl is really in trouble...Abortion!!!! — What the hell have I gotten myself into?!!

I was surprised at myself — how badly I felt about this. I had no connection with Christianity, and had never even considered their teachings on abortion, so why did I feel so bad? This was not getting off to a good start in my new life in society, and I decided to go back to the mountains for some serious scrutiny of this whole society sexual thing.

I was having sex with a woman I knew I would never marry, so what was I doing? It was mutual masturbation, a mere release of tension; and the most horrifying realization was seeing that I would always attract partners who were just as selfish as myself, just as afraid of life.

After a long pondering of my feelings about this matter, I gave the emotions words: I felt weak and cowardly that I didn't have my life together enough to feel good about bringing a child into the world. For me it was the making of a statement to myself, in the strongest possible terms, that I no longer trusted life to support me, or that it would bring me joy through a child or any other way. And since Life was God, I no longer trusted God. God was an abstract to me, but still, to state this to myself in such clear terms was startling, and kicked up deep subconscious fears and taboos. My circumcision, and all the many hidden thought forms connected to it, flamed to the surface, and I was faced with the ancient miasmas alive in the race mind, of the prejudice, mistrust, and fear of the feminine. The thought forms flew out of me and circled on display for my conscious mind's eye: clouds of mental fabrications of gorgeous temples and churches, scriptures from around the world, celibate priest and monks, golden sacred ornaments, all the things that so-called spiritual people felt to be more significant and holy than women and children — everyday normal life. No wonder humans allowed the brutal killing of men, women and children to continue, the disrespect and rape of women; in the darks of the minds of those who had placed their philosophies above human life, was the hatred of women for being the doorways into the world of our so-called fall from grace. The propensity for hierarchically placing philosophy above human life was scared into me at my circumcision: humans and the feminine through which they came, were nothing, dirt, compared to the gods and their realms, so who cares what happens to them. My mind turned to Jana.

Oh my God...what she must be going through...Someone tell me what I can do to love her, honor her, and help her now in whatever she needs to do.

The answer came!

Listen!

Seeing my conditioning about women, angered me to no end, and I rushed back to be with Jana. After her abortion, Jana bought a tree and asked me to go with her back to the mountains. She planted the tree, then prayed to Nature, which she called Goddess. She told the Goddess that this tree was her affirmation that she respected and loved life; she thanked Her for the healing this had brought her; she thanked the soul of the child that had come to help her through this, and asked

her to come again when she herself was more ready; then she thanked
the Goddess for bringing me to her. I had to agree; for this abortion set
off in me a series of questions about life, that I would have never
reached, and it was with such a depth of sincerity that I thought I had
completely wasted my time in the years of more formal paths.

On the way home, Jana told me her story. As a young teen, she
had become the sexual prey of a senior minister in her Christian
church. The minister branded her as an abomination of Satan.
Terrified, she ran off on her own to have a brutal abortion, and for
many years, she had cowered in guilt and terror of men. We both wept
and held each other; the demons ran from the Light of our embrace;
and thus began one of the longest, most enlightening, most healing,
and most tender conversations with the feminine that I had ever
encountered.

There were now two issues in my life to consider: what is a man,
and what is my relationship to the feminine? No problem, right! I
began with myself first. I was still uneasy that I had been drawn into
this new chapter in my life by spells and incantations. Jana and I dis-
continued our sexual relationship (well, sort of) but our friendship continued to grow, and I was thankful for that; but what if someone whose
intentions were not benevolent used spells on me? The question
became: how does one stay psychically open and sensitive, and at the
same time, protected from negative influence. Los Angeles was a great
town to explore the issue, for it was filled with powerful wizards who
had more influence on the world than any other group of people — the
entertainment industry; and then there was all the young men and
women willing to sell their souls to be part of it.

My experience in Hawaii was a psychic re-birth into the world,
but now I was wide open with no clear direction and no religious system to hold on to. That felt all-right, but without anybody else's experience to hold as my center, it was clear that I had now to define who I
was from my own experiences; coming back into the psychic influence
of society without any grounded center of ethics, was like taking a stroll
across the freeway. In this new pressure of search, a new ability unfolded, one that I had seen a glimpse of when first being upset about the
abortion. I now began to sense thought forms as if they were clouds;
(tendencies, fueling mechanical behavior in the world) with their ten-
drils running all through history, I could now see them as a whole picture. I was alarmed at how easily humans would interface with the mental environment, taking on society's ways and morals, seldom questioning who was the initiator of their actions. It was like putting on a coat

made from mental material, then walking through the world seeing everything through the particular filter that one tried on. It was a huge task to stay conscious of all this prompting material; in myself I saw how easy it was to be influenced by these clouds when wanting to fit-in became more desirable than self-knowledge, in fact the clouds were designed to be desirable. I sometimes caught myself acting unconsciously without any volition that I remembered putting into motion, speaking words without any sense of myself behind them; it seemed almost like possession. Yet this kind of behavior was a cherished social survival skill in the entertainment industry, and since I was still learning and defining myself, I felt I should put no judgment on it, which only made it more fascinating to observe.

It was the sifting and questioning of all this that attracted grace into my life, for it was only the questions that gave me a sense of my Self, beyond the thought forms of the society in which I lived. Without this constant questioning, I am sure total possession would have taken place, and I would have ended up as wallpaper in a house of decadence. The questioning had been with me for many years, but this was the first time I recognized it as an action of grace, the only vehicle to carve out a Self in a sea of chaos. Without a clearly defined purpose of one's own, the world was filled with people who were more than happy to define it for you, and use you for their purposes. Blinded by the desire to be ego-less, (the proverbial goal of spiritual life), I drowned in my own furious momentum, and it never occurred to me that I was already ego-less from the years of intense chanting and meditation, and was easily swept up by any strong influence that came along. Even the desire for enlightenment was just part of one of the clouds, an ancient knee-jerk tendency trying to counter the trauma one found in the world. To become ego-less was easy: a little sleep deprivation, a little fasting, a few postures and deep breathing sustained over six weeks or so, and you were an empty container. To create a functional ego in the world was much harder work. These two conditions seemed to be the established polarities of this world, but in the months of driving back and forth from the mountains to the city, to consider all this, I discovered a further articulation of mental evolution; I learned to dissolve or create an ego at will. There were times to dissolve into the life-force, and other times that an ego was needed to participate in society. From this ability, effortlessly arose the next logical question: who was it that decided when to do what? The answer, in the realm of words could be endlessly articulated, so I just named it Will. The terror of religions to honor the freedom of Will, came from the belief that left on one's own without governing rules, we will do harm, it is our nature to do so — we are sinners. I found no such currents in the stance of Will; on the contrary, with Will, one could create what ever they wanted without hurting anyone, or taking away from anyone, so why would we want to harm. From the stance of Will, it was easy to see that all the worry was just one of those floating clouds, a lie; harm was created by people who put on that cloud, and felt they had no power or Will. And this became my best definition of a man: Will—constant and steady.

That meditation and commitment was easy enough — No problem! But the second part of the question, how a man stood in relationship to the feminine—

Oh my God save me! Take this cup from me!

Jana was a remarkable young woman. She practiced a form of primal magic in her artwork, taking natural objects and weaving them into patterns that had a most soothing effect. She was humorously dramatic in her work and expressions, and our conversations took on titanic dimensions, with candles, incense and all the pomp and reverence of a high mass in the church. We became the Universal archetypes of all men and women, asking questions for all humanity, interspaced with beautiful exotic rituals to seal the answers or disperse the malevolent clouds opposed to our conclusions. The ticket for entrance into the world of the Goddess was: no judgment, tender respect, and listen. Jana taught me the rituals and meaning of the Hindu god Ganesha, which was the proper beginning for anything having to do with the Goddess. In Hindu mythology, the Goddess created Ganesha as her personal guard, that even her husband could not get through without the proper attitude; he was a fearless warrior in the Goddess' defense. Ganesha had the body of a plump little boy and the head of an elephant, rode standing on the back of a little mouse, and was quite jolly. The symbology for men was: when you approach the Goddess, leave your logical mind behind, be ready for the impossible to become normal, and come with lightness and humor. The idea that spirituality was heavy, somber and dark was not the Goddess' way. Her protection came from the fact that people, who live their lives with lightness and humor, do not hurt or dishonor other beings; and if you thought you could force the Goddess in any way, Ganesha was the magic that would thump you.

Because the abortion had such a powerful effect on both of us, this is where we began our dialogs. Jana fell into meditation than began to speak:

"Long ago, when humans were still in hunter gatherer tribes, the women often had to abort for the good of the tribe. In times of famine when food could not be found, too many new children would jeopardize the harmony of the whole tribe. The hunters of the tribe understood this, and honored women for their wisdom and power over life and death. No man knows what goes on in the heart of a woman who has to abort her own child. This was part of women's ways and mysteries, and was to be respected."

I answered her back:

" But today we don't have those problems; there is food, and no one need starve. Abortion creates a vibration — a morphological field around the earth, of the casualness by which we accept death and violence — a lack of sacredness for life; it adds to the acceptance of war and other institutional violence — a passive acceptance of violence in our movies, music, and literature, which only serves to numb us."

She answered:

" You are seeing this backwards — remember that women abort for the good of the tribe; there is no woman who wants to abort. Stop dis-honoring us by thinking that. You are not asking the right questions — How and what are men doing to create a world where women no longer feel safe, and no longer want to bring children into it?"

I shot back:

"And what are women also doing to create that same world?"

Jana sat in silence for a long time, then answered:

"Yes! How many women have jumped up and down like cheerleaders, goading men on to war? What man would fight if women had the courage to look in their eyes and call them murderers? Woman is the first teacher! What this world could be if women had the courage to say NO from their guts, and teach their children to!

In a cloud of frankincense, we held each other and rocked back and forth in release. Together, we had created this uncaring world where we no longer felt good about bringing children into it. The lack of food in prehistoric days had turned into atomic bombs and pollution, and now, all felt small and helpless — men and women. But abortion brought no peace of mind to anyone, it only added to the feeling of helplessness to change the overwhelming forces that ran the world.

Our dialogue ran on for weeks at a time, as next we considered religion and abortion. The religions that were openly against abortion, looked weak and impotent under any serious scrutiny; they had lost true moral authority, or power to make changes, because they themselves had been responsible for killing billions of people in their fanatical wars and witch hunts. How can any institution that looks the other way at the killing of millions when it serves their needs, expect to be listened to by any thinking human being. The problems of birth control, contraception and young people trying to control their hormones, could be taken care of easily in five to ten minutes a day of simple yogic techniques, and if taught to children in the 6th or 7th year of education, they could learn easy control of their sexuality before it could be exploited by commercialism. These techniques have been around for thousands of years, and were certainly known and documented by the Catholics, who had gathered libraries of information from the eastern cultures. But these techniques also increased one's capacity for pleasure and intelligence, which led to the experience of one's own Will, exactly what the religions didn't want you to have — Will must be controlled, separated from ourselves by a philosophical dogma called "God's Will," and controlled by "God's chosen authorities." But as I had seen earlier, people who felt they had no personal power were the ones who created violence, so who was really responsible for violence in the world? Any institution or individual operating in this paranoia, loses the support of the natural forces of Life, which are spontaneous and instinctively moral. Once this happens, the religion has lost the ability to give people the experience of God, and falls upon a feckless enthusiasm created by alignment with the current social issues. But that kind of enthusiasm is not the 'Peace that defies understanding,' and only creates the antithesis: emptiness, which turns to anger, which turns to violence. A real follower of Wicca had no such ponderous philosophies to separate them from the forces of Nature. Innately knowing there is no separation of spirit from matter, (indeed these were just two words describing different octaves of the same substance), God and Goddess was felt a part of everything and everybody and needed no outside control, because IT always acted with Universal Intelligence and wisdom. To a true wiccan, there is no society, and you can have no relationship with Catholics, Jews, Muslims, whites, blacks, Russians, Americans, etc. You can only have a relationship with an individual, and if you are to change society, the only way is to change yourself, because society is made of individuals; whatever we want the world to be, we must first be ourselves. Society was a mess because hierarchy was backwards; without our awakened intelligence to enter in and psychically and physically run them, religions and governments could do nothing but reflect the natural condition of chaos.

As a male living in a Judeo-Christian culture, I had been duped into thinking that men were somehow higher incarnations, or more blessed, or more powerful, than women, though I could have found that in the east too; even in the Tantick systems, woman was used as an instrument for man's growth. But under the surface is where the real root of the violence was committed; women didn't really exist, they were merely extensions of my male ego, and expected to be what I, conditioned by society, fantasized them to be. But what I found in Jana was a whole separate universe of knowledge and wisdom that had nothing to do with me, and in her gentleness, I saw a power that surpassed and would out live patriarchy's brutal power. We did not solve all the problems of the world, but one thing I learned for sure— a patriarchy, working with only one half of it's intelligence, (half a brain), would never solve anything.

After a year of our wonderful talks, Jana's old boy friend came back to town with the intention of marriage; I saw that he loved her very much and gladly moved out of the picture. Jana was the gentle side of the Goddess, and that gentleness was a power that I had never understood before. Because of it I changed the way I practiced martial arts, yoga, meditation, just about everything, and the greatest gift, I re-strung my guitar and began another journey in music. But there was also a dark side to the Goddess, and without knowing it, one's education is incomplete.

* * *

After Jana's wedding, I returned to my beloved mountains, feeling blessed with a deeper respect for the feminine, and understood that as a man in society, it was necessary to set a clear direction and intention. I no longer battled with the question of desire as opposed to desire-lessness; they became the notes and the rest in my own symphony, each appearing at the proper time, the rhythm organically created by the intention of the piece; intention was the key to the result. By allowing myself to be open to the gentle feminine, I had found my own masculine, and saw it was not enough to merely find out the reasons for violence in the world, I had to actually create something; understanding the past was useless without also pioneering ahead with the knowledge gained. In meditating on my next move, an old Tantrik aphorism began appearing in my awareness: "Love is selflessness within oneself." There is a further state beyond having an ego — or not having one: the experiencing of both at once. There must be the joy of giving all of oneself, but yet there must still be a self to experience that joy. How could this be, it was not logical in our worldview created by black and white dualistic thinking. But that really was the point. Love is not logical; it takes one beyond all systems and philosophies. This could only be experienced in relationship; giving all yourself to your beloved, yet finding yourself in them at the same time, and if they were doing the same thing at the same moment, this was Love. So this is what I decided was next for me, to consciously fall in Love. I, whoever that was, was going to make myself fall in Love, whatever that was; I had it all figured out! Then I reasoned I must have some money in order to do this responsibly, because it might lead to marriage and children.

All my old recording industry connections in Hollywood had moved on, so I began anew, positioning myself to meet different entertainment executives and other recording artist and writers. I watched carefully how this business worked, and with an un-judging childlike innocence, learned the skills to fit in: I became skillful at telling big lies about myself at parties, (exaggeration —one of the big tools of Hollywood), learned to speak critically, but with style, about anybody that was currently out of favor with the people I hung out with, (cliques — another big tool), and spent large amounts of time scheming and plotting how to make huge sums of money — who we'd have to meet — how to get leverage in the deal, (strategy). From a meditative center, I saw nothing wrong with the Hollywood behavior, it was simply the standard operating procedure that I had to learn to fit into.

One evening, at one of the many networking parties, an actor friend introduced me to CiCi. She was a beautiful tall actress-singer with coal black hair and eyes, and we were immediately attracted to each other, and within a week we were swept away in a steamy, delicious affair. CiCi was the ultimate sexual fantasy! She was as beautiful as any cosmopolitan model, with a voracious sexual appetite, and absolutely no inhibitions. In the past, she had many colorful lovers, and had such an interest in sex, that she had watched hundreds of porno movies, and could become any actress she had ever seen. She also had the ability to have as many orgasms as she wanted, —fifteen, —twenty in an hour, all of them loud, screaming flights into what for her was a religious ecstasy; she fed the energy back to me through magical circuits of pleasure, fueling a lovemaking that was inexhaustible. CiCi was a seriously practicing sorceress! One could meet many of these in Hollywood, actors and actresses using sorcery, spells and incantations, and various forms of ego-enhancement props, to hopefully reach stardom. I felt she should be very successful at this, but could also sense something about her that was self-sabotaging, and would not let her excel into the fulfillment of her desires for success. She made a better living teaching classes on the occult, hypnosis, and practicing a form of exorcism on her Hollywood clients, all sent to her by word of mouth. We soon began working together, writing and singing, and I started to come to her classes, learning the more formal side of magic and her powerful style of exorcism. Behind CiCi's purposeful eroticism and sometimes-complex behavior, she had a very giving and soft heart, and once the sexual intensity turned to a deeper knowing of each other, I found a greater treasure; CiCi had impeccable integrity. In the middle of insane, backstabbing, lying, Hollywood, CiCi was refreshingly honest, clear and witty — even in her fiery temper, she still spoke coherently and truthfully. With her I was able to lose my fear of strong emotions, and saw even more lies about women that I had unconsciously absorbed: emotions are the antithesis of reason. Before long I was having loud, screaming, and sometimes fun fights with her, and completely lost my fear of this kind of passion. She was not afraid of the intensity of my anger, because she knew I would never hit a woman, and I began to see that truth and clarity could be expressed no matter how emotional one became. It was like adding many different shades of colors to my black and white world of trying to speak the truth. This led to such a freedom of expression, it propelled us through the many fears surrounding the human heart, and soon we noticed there were no boundaries between us; we were in love.

On many occasions I was invited to assist her in exorcisms. Sometimes powerful hypnotic herbs and drugs were used, depending on the receptivity and desires of her varied Hollywood clientele. CiCi was a prodigy at reaching into the subconscious and pulling to the surface, hidden fears and pent up energies that no one ever suspected were there. By watching someone's mannerisms, and listening for key words they spoke during the forced heavy breathing, she could see the hidden life as easily as reading a book. Nothing slipped by CiCi; she was a natural physic and intuitive with the sharpest ability in observation. Most of the time, what surfaced were repressed emotions, but on many occasions I felt the presence of other entities, some horrifying, causing people to go into strange contortions, and make sounds that brought up visions of the bowels of Hell — unearthly demonic screams and babbling. But CiCi being very skilled, and sometimes taking up to five hours, always led the person out again, and into a peaceful calm. Over the three years we spent together, I slowly learned her craft, and we trusted in each other enough to begin using the techniques on one another.

One evening I allowed CiCi to put me into a hypnotic preparation for exorcism. My conscious mind's eye began to sink into the deeper layers of memory, contrary to the popular belief that the conscious mind dissolves, or is given over to the hypnotist; there is always self-control, as you the observer allow yourself to be taken into parts of yourself you would never, or could never go alone. It is rather like tickling; one can't tickle oneself, but someone else can. She told me to focus on the pain that I still carried in my stomach and spine, and I sank deeper and deeper into the feelings. Suddenly I was in rage, the most intense hatred imaginable. I could see that I was in a dungeon of an old medieval castle. I was tied to a wooden table, and was screaming in pain; robed Catholic monks were breaking my arms. Then they poured water down my throat, repeatedly punching me in the stomach until I passed out. I was actually there! I could not feel the physical pain, but felt all the emotions and saw the thoughts going through my mind. I had been caught and put on trial by the Inquisition for being almost exactly the kind of person I was today, a wandering poet-musician, and because women were attracted to me, I was accused of sorcery. My hands were tied behind my back, then I was lifted high into the air by a rope tied to my wrist, then dropped. The weight of my body pulled my arms from their sockets. This was done to me ten times, then I was put back on the table, filled with water and beaten again; the torture continued for many hours. In CiCi's time frame the recording tape was up to three hours; I screamed, pleaded, and cried for two of those hours. I felt a connection with CiCi that somehow allowed me to feel the emotions and terror, but also still be an observer free of the physical pain; I was fascinated and horrified at the same time. I hated the monks, and the whole corrupt church, yet still had a love for God. But in my pleadings for God to save me, no help came. This was the true horror of the torture; when God didn't come to my rescue, I began to curse God in my screaming, which only made the monks feel justified in torturing me more. In my own mind I was losing faith that God even existed, and this became the real terror, that all my life had come to this — being killed by sadistic monks, my belief in any afterlife shattered, nothing left but total black extinction — the ultimate terror. I took a long look, deep into its face, but I hated these monks so much that I would rather face extinction, than ask forgiveness from the church, for doing nothing but being myself. From my perspective in CiCi's room, I saw that this would have been a far worse extinction. I died in black hatred. CiCi slowly, and carefully pulled me out of the pit, and closed the door.

Listening to the audiotape was a chilling experience. My screams, and the dialogue with the monks put me into a catharsis that lasted for three days. But I had left the Catholic Church long ago, and as far as I was concerned, it no longer existed; the great historic event of the Vatican II Council was coming to its close, and I never even heard about it. So the exorcism was a great curiosity to me, but I could not see what it had to do with me now. But CiCi taught that the images that came up in these sessions were not as important as the emotional and chemical release that happened in the many hours of breathing. The chemistry of anger in the body had to be released no matter where it came from, and after the purge, all I noticed was that my body felt much more at ease. The lack of concern for the images is the sure sign that it was successful, for when it is exorcised, it is truly gone. There is not even enough left to ponder on how powerful this technique is, it's almost as if it never happened!

The Christian world of today condemns belief in past lives, but from my own experienced, I saw that both sides of the issue were right. Past life memories do exist in the cells of our bodies, the whole history of the human race is there to be seen; and also there is another way of living in the Now that has no connection with the past or future at all. But exploring like this did not hold my interest for long, and I began to see that many of CiCi's clients were addicted to the drama of it all, but never moved ahead with any change of life style. To empty oneself of past garbage was one thing, but to fill the empty container with positive habits was quite another. If one took seven days or seven years to explore their past hurts, healing still only took place by an act of Will to move out of the pattern one was stuck in. In the various occult groups around Hollywood that I was introduced to, the same pattern that I had found in the major religions seemed to prevail: a self-satisfying excursion into outer ritual, which skirted the issue of the real work of change, the real manual labor to be done in ones own cells.

I did not wish to fall into a state of judgment about a tendency so wide spread in our world, and tried to assume the attitude that people were right where they were supposed to be in evolution, and were doing the best they could. But then, being introduced to a different sort of Wiccan groups of a more militant, feminist nature, I quickly learned that though I did not judge, discernment was still required. I define a feminist as someone who demands respect, rather than inspires it; and many of these women downright hated men, using all kinds of trickery to exact revenge. I was allured in many different ways, and when declined, I was accused of "being afraid of the feminine", "being a closet passive-aggressive-woman-hater", "being an alien of the Grey Race

— here to prey on women", and many other colorful descriptions of my stupidity. Many of these women felt that worshipping the Goddess, and grasping the philosophy that we are all one, was a license to have sex with as many partners as they could, because they were on a crusade to crush any kind of moral rules created by the patriarchical religions. I would have supported them in their quest, except for the observance that out of the hundreds of these women I met, never did I meet anyone who radiated any kind of true joy that was consistent through even a few days. It was easy to see that their behavior was not so divinely inspired and was merely a reaction against past patriarchal dominance. To break away from anyone's dominance was certainly a worthwhile quest, but if one became worse than who they were trying to get away from, something in their reasoning was obviously amiss. Blinded by their anger at men, it was almost impossible to tell one of these women what a turn off it was to be propositioned by someone who came at you with the attitude there was something wrong with you because you made discriminative choices. I was truly amazed to meet creatures that didn't seem to have any self-reflective ability; if you didn't want them, it was because *you* had a problem — it couldn't be because they had put all their eggs in the basket of seduction, rather than attraction, which ironically made them energetically repulsive. Instead of finding the attractive feminine in themselves, they had been trapped in a knee-jerk flip-flop, and now treated men as objects, as they had been treated. But in the years of association with these groups I made a deeper, sad discovery; most of the women I met in these groups, came from a background of some kind of sexual abuse from men. This truly saddened me, and after awhile I felt honored that I was even allowed to be around them at all. Being so damaged by the male, there was nothing I could say or do in the way of action that would help. Sometimes it is best to be silent and do nothing but respectfully listen with no judgment, and though I was not perfect at this while under a barrage of abusive language, I saw it as a worthwhile effort to learn, hoping it might possibly be healing to them. Anyone in anger is acting out because they are hurt; the last thing they need is retaliation and condemnation.

I was beginning to love Ganesha, for in learning a deeper compassion and honoring of the Goddess in all women, again I was thrown back upon my own manhood, considering what I had done as a man to help 'create a world where we no longer wanted to bring children into it', and this kind of inquiry could only deepen and expand the potential of the human heart, whether man or woman.

CiCi was remarkably without jealousy at her sisters who came on to me, and was amused by the ones who dis-liked me. Our love was growing, and that allows for this kind of security, but in talking with her about sexual abuse, I noticed she got a far away look in her eyes and felt uneasy with the subject, though she would ramble on about anything and everything else; my suspicions were raised. When spring came, I told CiCi I wanted to go back into the mountains for a month, for my yearly Spring-cleaning fast and renewal; she had never showed any interest in the outdoors and I thought nothing of it. She flew into a rage that I couldn't bring her out of: I was leaving her, I was cheating, running away, on and on she cried and raged. I just needed to leave Hollywood and be in nature for a while, she didn't like the mountains, and so what's the problem? She wouldn't hear of it; CiCi was sure I was abandoning her, and that something bad was being directed against her. Those two words, *abandoning* and *bad* had lots of energy on them for her, and we both knew that this was not about me going to the mountains. I invited her to come, but she declined and instead decided to go see the women who had taught her, and work on her own hidden issues. When I came back, CiCi wanted to break up with me, and within a week had another love. A few weeks later she called me up and wanted to get back together; she went back and forth for almost a year. This kind of questioning would have been acceptable as long as truthful communication was maintained, but what started to disturb us both was that she would make love with me with all her dynamic passion, then turn around and do the same with someone else a week later. Many of her sisters applauded such behavior, but even CiCi started not to respect her own lack of control. Through her therapy sessions with her teacher, she began to realize that sex was all she really felt she had to offer a man, and behind her expertise was the fear of being abandoned; she felt she had no choice but to control with her sheer sexual power— if that's all men wanted, then she would learn to get the upper hand. With a core belief that all men really wanted was sex, and then they would abandon you, when she could stand the pressure of her inner fears no longer, she herself would abandon before the other person had a chance to abandon her, thus creating her own self-fulfilling prophecy.

One day CiCi came home from therapy white as a sheet. She had seen in a hypnotic regression, that when she was just a child, her mother had sexually molested her. She knew that not all stories in regression were necessarily true, so she flew back to her then separated parents in Chicago, and confronted them. The mother denied it. But after a week, her father couldn't bear the pressure any longer and told CiCi that it

was true. The mother had 'problems' with other children in the neigh-
borhood too, and had once been institutionalized because of the problem. CiCi came back to Los Angeles in pieces. Not only did she no
longer trust women and hate herself, now she also hated men because
her father didn't protect her. When she made a decision about something, it became the gospel truth of her life, and her venom knew no
end. She grew more abusive to me, and on two different occasions,
insulted me in public, but at the same time she had decided the healing
answer was for us to get married, and possibly have children. I had no
understanding at all about child molestation, and what that might do to
somebody, but I knew enough to know that marriage was definitely not
the solution. Again I started to withdraw into myself, and again took
the blame unto myself because I didn't have the understanding to help
her, or the courage to marry her. We stayed together for another year,
trying to hide from the problems by using our sexual life, which became
addiction beyond bounds — a trap of pleasure and pain with all the
comforts of a spider web. I made more and more ridiculous excuses why
I could not marry her, until again I fell into the hole of self-hatred and
desire for suicide, and with both of us feeling the same way, we sadly
split apart. My experiment of "Love" had landed me in hell —again.

The next two years were spent in an intensive research of my family psychology. The tools I used at this time were the "Twelve Steps for
Adult Children of Alcoholics" programs. I found the information about
the behavior of people coming from any kind of obsessive home life to
be very helpful. I worked the program sincerely, and got good results,
especially in not blaming myself for not knowing things about life that
no one had ever taught me. For awhile I went into PLOM (Poor Little
Old Me) mode, but slowly took the information and applied it to my
life experiences, and curiously, I began to pray "The Lords Prayer." It
felt good to be in prayer with these people, many who jokingly called
themselves "recovering Catholics." There was true magic and healing
grace in these programs, that seemed to be created by the up-against-
the-wall intensity of the members. No matter what you stood up and
said about your life, there were always the old timers who had been-
there-done-that, so there was little judgment in the room. But there
was a lot of compassion and understanding from people who had surrendered to their own understanding of divine power, and had now
come back to help others. In lieu of the great healing to so many 'recovering Catholics' that I witnessed in these programs, I wondered how
Christianity had gotten so far off the path and had become a religion of
judgment, condemnation and Thou shalt nots.

＊ ＊ ＊

After a year of inner work, and beginning to pray again, I felt more confident that I would attract a good relationship, and soon met another beautiful young woman to try the game of love with; it turned out to be one of the most important relationships of all, but in a totally unexpected way. Alexis was another dark haired beauty — half Jewish-half Italian — an accomplished pianist and composer who came from a wealthy, New York family. Our first interest in each other was the shared world of music, and soon we were writing very interesting compositions. I wanted to go very slowly this time, but Alexis was a woman in a hurry about everything, and my resistance only turned her on more. She loved to smoke pot and sit around in the sexiest cloths, taunting me, while draped over her piano like a honky-tonk crooner. She was a very funny and enjoyable person, and with the help of her marijuana-fudge-cookies, my lofty intentions wilted and we succumbed to hilarious sexual breaks in the middle of our composing schedule; soon, our break time was longer than our composing time. Sexually, she was not as adept as CiCi, but Alexis captivated me with her humorous flights of talking dirty, and her bizarre sexual fantasies. In her everyday life she was cultured and serene; in bed she had the foulest and funniest mouth I had ever heard. One fantasy she had fulfilled in her colorful past, was having sex with dogs. This fascinated me, and I spent endless hours fantasizing about it. When trying to analyze why this bewitched me so much, I came to the conclusion that it was because it was a snub in the face of the thousands of years of biblical conditioning, and the warnings from the tales of Sodom and Gomorra. She had a certain power by the fact that she was free of all cultural taboos, and had been that way since she was thirteen. For a Catholic boy, it was a titillating turn on, and source of great humor, considering she came from a proper Jewish family. If you can get a Catholic to talk honestly about sex, they all say it is more fun when you are not supposed to do it, and I often suspected this was a hidden Catholic secret, a way of getting all those Catholics to have big families. Tell someone they shouldn't have a lot of sex, or particularly enjoy it, like the early church did, and it only makes it more irresistible. Though I personally never saw her do it with a dog, I had great fun pretending to be a ferocious wild beast ravaging her in her bedroom. The yogi's powers of concentrated visualization, I don't think were designed for this, but none the less, it worked pretty well, and was a barrel of laughs, which I sorely needed.

Alexis was certainly full of humor, passion and creativity, however, she had one problem — she was a liar. Many times in the two years we were together I had a gnawing feeling that she was cheating in our relationship, and lying to me. I had never cheated on a woman, and had no secret fears of any kind of karmic retribution; this kind of game was unknown territory for me. When I talked to her about it, she looked me straight in the eyes and continued to assure me she was being true. But I began to have many strong feelings and dreams, which increasingly became an alert that something was wrong.

During this time I went to visit my mother, and in our conversation, casually mentioned what I was feeling about my relationship. She became very serious then began to talk about my father, for the first time, telling me the truth about their marriage. After becoming successful in the film industry, my father turned to womanizing, and she had caught him in many lies before he finally left with a younger woman. Flashes went off in my brain, as if large hidden pieces of a puzzle all of a sudden appeared and fell into their proper place. For the first time I could feel my father's tendencies and energies, as separate from my own. Taken as a matter of self-pride, I never cheated on my mates, but did often have the desire and urging. I knew I would not break my word or vow, that being one of the only feelings of self worth that I did have; so why even have the desire, why even fool with that uncomfortable feeling — always wanting more — never being satisfied? It always seemed to me to be a stupid and useless waste of energy, already knowing I wouldn't act it out. Now I understood that it was not I, but my father's tendencies in me. I saw that while growing up, my mother and father always hid what was going on, the fights and trauma they were having. The parents want to protect the child from 'adult things', but that turned out to be one of the most destructive deceptions in my life. I was taught to look only at the surface of things and ignore my gut feelings; but the family is a unit connected on many different levels, how could one not feel the trauma. The result of this, is growing up not trusting one's own gut feelings and intuition; one is then powerless to sense when people are good, bad, or lying to you, and you are easy prey for the promptings of others —religions, governments, advertising. One literally becomes split in oneself, and loses the natural compass that directs you through life — ones own intuition. Seeing all this, crashed the spell of my slowly-creeping-sexual-addiction, and I was inspired to re-dedicate myself to finding the answers that I had started out to find so many years earlier. Being manipulated by any one, angered me to no end, and I turned this new fire in on myself, launch-

ing a fierce effort of interior questions, and after years of spiritual discipline and experience, I now felt ready to tackle the whole problem.
Not a simplistic, who am I? — but rather — what, and whose thoughts
and ideas am I living? — what are MY own thoughts and ideas, and
what are fantasies, and half-truths created by my culture, religions,
mythology and even science? I felt tangled up and resentful that I lived
in a world that was more concerned with teaching 'what to think' more
than 'how to think.' But now I had tools given to me by more enlightened cultures, and I rediscovered the precise Tantrik Buddhist methods
of mental analysis. Much of Buddhist teaching is about the structure of
separation — how it forms and why; what is the structure and nature of
the layers of information we put together to form a belief that we are a
separate entity, all by itself, afloat in an unfriendly universe; it proved
to be a whole scientific laboratory in itself, and an invaluable tool.

My questions were becoming more precise, and answers were
almost immediate, and with this, my self-esteem grew too strong to
allow me to be in relationships with someone who was lying to me.
Alexis called after a month, and confirmed my suspicions, but instead
of anger, I met her with a kindness that surprised me; a deeper understanding and compassion for the human condition seemed to have
imperceptibly found it's way into my demeanor, no doubt a by-product
of the Tantrik chants and practice, and of course my new friend
Ganesha. I understood intuitively why she lied, and learned to look
through it, seeing that one way or other, men and women shared the
same pain and fear, even though their outer appearance and expression
were different. We were all in the same boat.

* * *

The mountains were only five hours away, and as I raced back and
forth like an obsessed madman, my family and friends becoming more
concerned about my sanity. I never considered how I looked from the
outside, but in their faces I could see I was right on the edge. In order
to head off any problems with health authorities (the very thought of
that set me off into mad laughter), I spent more time alone; and if I did-
n't know how to survive alone in the mountains, I'm sure I would have
ended up institutionalized. I had two problems : I was by myself with
no support from a teacher to guide me through the rough spots; I could
not get over my suspicion of gurus, and was too scared and stubborn to
ask anyone for help. I looked at this as giving away of my power. It was
my power I was trying to find so I couldn't give it away just because I

was scared. And secondly, I could see my answers coming clearly into focus and understanding, but wasn't sure that I wanted to face the consequences of awakening. Loneliness was taking it's toll and I didn't want to be isolated further; it is one thing to see Truth, and quite another to live it in a world that ran from it, and many times persecuted it. But being stuck in this ditch only increased the adrenaline, and feeling I had no more options, I followed my thinking process to it's alarming end, slipped past society's comfort zone, walked deep into the mountains and broke:

Junk in—junk out—junk in—junk? … Endless cycle…broken wheel…broken arrow

I'm defective…born a sinner…How can you possibly trust yourself?…

Look at the suffering in the world…You did that man!… Your part of the human race…greedy killers…Junk in…Junk out…I want OUT…Let me OUT…I'll kill myself… NO…better do what they taught me…or I'll burn in eternal fire…forever…This is my hell you motherfuckers…Stay away from me or I'll kill you…See!…I am a killer!…Can't be trusted ….

My nervous system twitched and burned, from the tip of my penis — up my spine to the tip of my tongue. My brain felt like it was on fire—then—violent bloody images in front of my mind's eye:

You sliced me up…drove my power up into my head…away from pleasure…up into your thoughts and philosophies…systems…no feeling…numb…I can be a killer…but only the ones you tell me it is ok to kill…them…out there!… If I kill myself…I am condemned…but it's ok to commit suicide in one of your fanatical wars …See how nuts I am…I can't trust myself…Yeah…better do as I'm told…better to kill THEM before they kill us…That's the way it has always been man…who the fuck am I to change it…..

I don't believe you man…I think Attila the Hun was a good guy…trying to protect his people…he wanted trade…you lied to make us afraid… so we'd buy into your rules and give away our lives to you. No…don't think that man…they will torture you Remember?!!!

They can do anything they want to you… Remember?… Anything can happen…anytime… anywhere… that's why you have to kill first…No…I want to Love…

Images of Jesus, stretched out and bloody on the cross, poured through my head:

See! See what will happen if you try and love...see what will happen to you...They will get you and you will end up like this...Only Jesus can love...you're nothing...bow down and worship...or burn .....

Images of priests came and whispered in my ear:

Never listen to yourself...that is Satan tricking you...listen to us brother...and have eternal life, you'll rape and kill if you don't listen to us...it is your human nature...

Satan's face appeared — the same one I had seen in Greece — he sneered and cursed at me — images of atomic bomb explosions — mutilated, burned bodies and limbs. Then a huge caged beast, representing all of society of all time, appeared in front of me. It was sad beyond description. Bearded priests yelled and slashed at the beast, "You are evil." The beast was choking on its own self-mistrust; scared into anger, it shook itself in fear and slashed out in all directions. I looked deeply into it, and saw my own eyes in its sad face.

Over a period of three days of fasting, the images slowly broke into tiny patterns and dissolved. Then one last image appeared: all of mankind as a huge lake full of joy, creativity, goodness, at one with the harmony and intelligence of all the creative power of the Universe. Then I saw that the rivers and tributaries coming out of the lake were all dammed up, the water was not allowed to flow out on its own natural course; it backed up and slowly became stagnant and stale. Mosquitoes and other bloodsuckers began to spawn in the clear water, and soon it was filled with strange ugly creatures of violence. The images were horrible, and waves of sadness past through me. Only the reflexes of hard training kept me from going insane or leaping off a cliff. If someone had watched me during all this, they would have been very bored; all they would have seen was a silent man, sitting in perfect posture!

Chapter 5

Grace: The Vision

After a few weeks in the mountains, I jumped in my van and hit the road, driving across the states playing music where ever I could. It had been many years since performing publicly, but the music came out with a new ease and depth, in spite of the years of neglect. One day I came back to Los Angeles to stay with my mother and visit with some old friends. She had a wonderful house that I loved to stay in and take care of when she was off traveling. I enjoyed my life more now, but like a slowly creeping vine, I was becoming concerned with not having a mate or family, that having very much to do with being in the proximity of my mother, and the universal trait of mothers to worry about their children's future. My mother certainly had her own spiritual ordeals to bare in dealing with me, and I had compassion for her plight; both my brother and sister were married with children, and to all of them I was an enigma. But some of the concern was also my own; though I loved traveling and living in my van, still when winter came, I slept alone, and at times, finding the right mate took on the dimensions of an obsession.

One morning I awoke at 4:00 a.m., like any other normal day that I would get up to begin meditation. There had been no visions or flights out of my body for many years, and still operating from the unconscious believe that fulfillment was somewhere else, I felt no fulfillment in my daily practices. The pain in my spine was still present, but now more than two decades had gone by and I merely accepted it as part of my life and never spoke of it to anyone. Without knowing when or how it happened, the journey to God—Nirvana— Enlightenment— Whatever, had turned to a sluggish ritual with a life of it's own. Still pushed and pulled by the undercurrents of a society that judged anyone as suspect and useless if they didn't fit into the norm, I began to suspect that the intensity of my practice was merely a last stronghold of self-esteem against the onslaught. And worst of all, I myself immaturely judged this, as not a good reason for continuing; I was bored. I watched my thoughts of dissatisfaction begin to surge:

Here I am at 4:00 a.m. in the morning... tired and grumpy... no wife... no family... no home of my own... a bent up car.

I started to rage at God:

I've been getting up and doing this for all these years and this is all I get? Well screw you buddy!

I began to swear, letting the years of frustration and anger surface. I really let God have it, using all the choice words that were sure to land me in Hell—wouldn't have been real otherwise:

I quit! It's all over! I am going to stop these silly practices, no more yoga teaching or writing songs... I quit, I am going to go to work in a bank or something...this is all a bunch of bullshit...look where it's gotten me...I'm a nobody...hell!...if there was a murder down the street, I'd be the first person they'd look at...I fit the psycho- wacko profiles...

I laughed hideously, threw my meditation pillow at the door, and dove back into bed with a new sense of righteous liberation. I laid my head down on the pillow, and swoosh—suddenly I was in another world. I knew I hadn't fallen asleep, but somehow I found myself in what I thought was a waking dream. I had studied the dreaming practices in Tantrik Buddhism, and had trained myself to become conscious in the dream state, but this was something unfamiliar, even from my out-of-body experiences. In the dreaming practices I had been taught to identify certain symbols, and ask a set of questions, which lead to being fully conscious and functional while still in the dream. Even though it did not feel like a dream to me, I employed the training I had been given in a logical sequence of questions about my new environment. To become more fully functional in an unfamiliar world, the first step is to ask yourself, what is the over all "feeling" of the place, thus, engaging one's emotional intelligence into the situation. The feeling felt very light and humorous to me, almost comical. I found myself squatting down, hiding behind the bushes of a long hedge that wound up a hill to the left of me. From a deeper place than my normal mental banter, I heard the words:

THE MAN WHO SAW THE FACE OF GOD

It is time to be found!

This thought moved through my mind, as I looked up to my left and noticed a small winding road on the other side of the hedge. A man dressed like some kind of guard, came strolling down the hill. He was very comical looking, all filled with self-importance, and as he came closer I purposely shook the bushes.

"Ah Ha! You, I see you, come out and come with me," he declared.

I jumped over the hedge and allowed him the feelings of his big capture, and then we turned together and walked up the road. As we reached the top of the hill, I notice that we were coming upon a school yard, and continued walking towards a small school house further up the hill. The yard was decorated with banners and balloons, as if they were going to be a festival. Then, twelve young girls, looking around thirteen to sixteen years of age, appeared near the school house. They see me coming and start to run towards me; I can see that they are all sexually aroused, but their sexual energy does not seem to interest me— I am in a state of childlike curiosity. Then a school master came running out the door, and stood in front of the girls with his arms out to protect them, keeping them away from me. They young girls stood behind his arms, but were trying to push him so they could get closer. I innocently and excitedly spoke to him,

"You are going to have a festival, I'll come and play some music."

He tries to act politely, but I can see he is seriously worried,

"No it's OK we don't need any, I think you should leave."

In my normal waking consciousness, if someone doesn't want me around, I leave, but now I don't seem to be affected by his impoliteness. I answer back.

"No it's OK you'll see, it'll be fun."

Again he refuses me, and asks me to leave, as the young girls are still peaking around him, trying to figure out who I am. Before I can reply, five older women in their forties and fifties walk into the scene. One taps the school master on the shoulder and speaks,

"We want you to let him play."

I don't know who this women is, but she has obvious authority, because he changes his attitude quickly,

"OK, but come back later."

He then takes all the young girls and goes back into the school-house, leaving me alone with the older women. The woman who spoke to him now looks at me and asks,

"Are you going to sing Anand Sahib?"

Anand Sahib is a famous Sikh prayer written in the late fourteenth century by the third Sikh leader, Guru Amar Das. The Guru wrote this song when he became God realized, spontaneously speaking the words while in a God intoxicated state; it means "Song of Bliss." I had heard the song many times, but had never memorized it in the original Gurmuki language, but instinctively I knew and understood what she was asking me— am I going to sing my own Anand Sahib, my Song of Bliss in my own state of union. I also understood it to mean, will my music be for the glorifying of God and uplifting of humanity? I happily answered yes. Again I am noticing the feeling of light joyous humor—nothing solemn about this at all. The woman then took me by the arm and gently spoke,

"Now you can come with me."

We walked down a pathway, away from the school, and I notice mountains in the background; we seemed to be in some older third world country. We came upon a house, where she seated me upon an adobe wall, and then silently walked away, leaving me alone with my own thoughts and feelings. I was still using the techniques of observation for dreamscapes, taking in the colors, hues and emotional feelings; again I was struck and surprised out how light and humorous it all felt. Looking down, I notice that I was sitting on the side wall of somebody's backyard—there is hay all over the ground, and a grass like roof covering over the yard. I noted to myself that I had seen many houses like this in the rural areas of India and Pakistan. Then, sitting in the middle of the yard, in a cross legged position, is a Yogi—long hair and beard, wearing only shorts, he looks like he is in good physical condition, but I can not guess his age. I immediately like this man, as if all the light humor is radiating from him. I am not surprised or overly impressed, because I had met many Yogis', but this man had a warm attraction to him. I then noticed that the humor and lightness begins to dissolve my own self-caused seriousness, created by my own effort to read the cues and look for signs, as taught in the dreaming practices. Sometimes in waking dreams, the action becomes a little overwhelming, and causes one to feel out of control; the crux of the training is to try and take control the events in a dream, giving one more control in the areas of the deep subconscious, but I felt very at ease, and so far, my observing ego was left intact. I could register my own feelings and conclusions while observing, just like in normal daily consciousness. My thoughts were my own as I watched the yogi:

I wish I could go back to being a student again...I miss those days...

I was tired of the burden of my spiritual experiences, and all the trauma that came with them; I wanted the innocent days of being a beginner, with a teacher that I respected and trusted.

The man did not notice me. Suddenly, he began to move in spontaneous *kryia*, (the body begins to move by itself so it can loosen, as the inner energy builds in the beginning stages of meditation. It can be very slow and snake like, or intense, shaking with strange sounds made to loosen the jaws). In his kryia, he began to flop around and cluck like a chicken, and I began to smile, watching this funny Yogi, when suddenly— beautiful rays of light came out of his hands—long rays of about ten to twelve feet. These were lights I had never experienced before in all my inner or outer encounters!!!!!!!!! Intensely shimmering, electric and alive! About every three feet down the rays of light, was a spinning chakra of thousands of tiny colored explosions. I was in a state of awe, and knew that I had crossed into another dimension of mind, deeper than the experience I was already in. Then, I heard a voice in the center of my own head,

"You must be like a child to enter the Kingdom."

Watching the lights, I was a little child again, in a state of awe, but still with an adult questioning observer left intact; I was not overwhelmed in anyway, and still allowed my own separate thoughts and feelings. A quick scan of my life, and I was sure I had never seen or experienced anything like this. It surpassed any psychedelic experience I had ever had twenty years earlier, so I eliminated the thought that it might be some psychedelic flash back. The humor prevailed! My next thought was:

Wow this is some very high magical yogi... I want to learn that trick with the lights...

I jumped off the wall into the yard. The electric lights withdrew back into his hands, and he immediately stood up and turned his back to me, acting as if I was totally unexpected and he needed to prepare himself in some way. He seemed to settle himself, then he turned to me and together we sat down cross legged, facing each other. I knew I was in the presence of some great spiritual master, greater than I had ever met before, and I had no idea what to say. Sensing my discomfort, he graciously put me at ease, by saying,

"You have some questions for me?"

It was so gentle an invitation! The first thought that came into my head was:

Who is my mate going to be?

Then, I began to lightly and humorously poke fun at myself.
   Hear you are with some great master, and you are still thinking of chicks.....

He sat passively watching. What finally came out of my mouth, was the most deeply honest and sincere question,
   "When are things going to get better?"
   Immediately, the skin of his bare chest began to roll open like the petals of a flower. As the petals rolled open, a mirror appeared in his chest. As I gazed into the mirror, I began to see a picture of myself, probably in my late 50's—I was old, fat, balding, and modestly success-ful in the world, lecherous, still lusting after young girls—then instan-taneously—outside of time—I understood what he was silently saying:

   By following this line of energy or life path—always feeling like— "when are things going to get better"—this is where I was heading—this is how you end up...

I looked at myself in the future and was appalled. Also, instanta-neously and simultaneously, I had the choice to change right then and there. This all happened outside of time.

   Are you going to spend your life complaining, or be thankful?
   OK, I get it...

It was not easy to look at, but at the same time, I humorously and lightly made the choice to change, all this in one instant—time was not involved.

   Whoever this guy is, man-o-man, he certainly has no time to mess around....

The skin on his chest rolled back together. Again, I noticed how I was allowed my own separate reactions, as the humorous and light feel-ing continued:

this is as real as having a conversation in everyday life, there is nothing dreamy or trance-like about this at all...what a trip!

I was allowed all my doubts and mental mechanisms to try and figure out what was going on. Suddenly I felt humbled, and knew that I was in the most powerful, spiritual initiation of my soul. I sat dumbfounded on the precipice of the fulfillment of all the many years of search. I looked at him, and simply asked,

"Who are you?"

He smiled whimsically, and spoke,

"You can call me Jesus."

My reaction was complete astonishment, and immense humor. In the annuls of spiritual literature, perhaps one would want to be remembered for saying something different than I did at a moment like this, but I must be honest; I answered back,

"No fucking way,"

and laughingly shook my head in disbelief. Thoughts flashed through my head:

No! No! No! How could this be? No way! I left Christianity decades ago...go through all the eastern religions... I meet the heaviest guy I have ever met in my life, and he is Jesus...??? !!!!!

This was terribly funny to me, and he enjoyed the moment with me, smiling and gently shaking his head—Yes it is so. My thinking exploded. I noted that he did not say, "I am Jesus," he had said "you can call me Jesus." As soon as I thought this, I was silently asked to watch. His face began to open as his chest had done. An indescribable multicolored flower opened in front of me, then his face began to change in slow continuous movement, into every religious icon I had ever seen in the world. Hindu, Tibetan, African, Mexican Gods and Goddesses, appearing then dissolving into something else. I was completely transfixed, and in each moment that I recognized a face and tried to name it, before I could finish the thought of the name, the face changed to something else; I was left tumbling in a state of awe as it moved and changed. The beauty of what was unfolding before me, was on the edge of insanity and ecstasy, but the humor and gentleness still prevailed, which gently and graciously allowed me a feeling of a separate self, in control, with no fear; at no time did I feel overwhelmed. As the face continued to change, so did the realizations evolve in my mind. The Christ existed in all forms, in billions of different ways, had infinite names and faces, yet could never be defined, so magnificent a mystery it is. The Logos appeared in whatever form was needed for the time and place. But I was given the gentlest invitation— if I liked, I could call him Jesus. A movement of healing fluid began to surge in me as I realized the meaning of this, for me personally. I had studied all the eastern religions, and respected them all, but had thrown out my own family religion, indeed, my whole western culture. I thought that Christianity, it's root of Judaism, and the shadow of both, Islam, was total insanity, and had shut the door on it long ago. But this being, in the only way it could possibly have been done, with subtle, gentle humor, and not by ordering me, but rather invitation, had slipped pass all my hurt and armor, and invited me to heal with my own genetic and cultural roots, showing me that God was also present in all I had left behind.

The impact moved through me in waves of joy. The feelings and images I held of Christianity were a serious, somber heaviness—blood and torture, but this Jesus was everything but that, and as the two feelings clashed in my body, my astonishment increased at what was happening to me. The feelings led me into neural memories of all cultures, showing me that God existed in all of them, but I was re-introduced to my own immediate place in time and space, and the honoring of my own culture and family, in other words, myself!

Again, I was allowed my own private thoughts and doubts. There was absolute acceptance and honoring of the integrity of my separate self by the being in front of me. My inner thoughts became much calmer and respectful, every doubt was explored in order to milk from this experience all that was revealed:

I have seen all these different faces in books and temples around the world. Maybe this is really some super dream, and I am just seeing the contents of my own subconscious?.

As soon as I thought this, the face began to change into shapes and forms that I had never seen before. Strange plant and insect life, changing shape and color—almost as if I were underwater looking at the great Barrier Reef changing into living things—then it changed even beyond anything that could be described in human language, very alien looking forms. In my self, more realizations exploded. The Christ exists in all worlds and dimensions, in whatever form is necessary to the dimensions and various ways of expression in the vast expression of the Universe. Within my own body I felt movement and change, as if my own genetic structure followed the shapes, colors and patterns of what I was seeing. I began to understand that Humanity was one family that existed throughout the Universe, and saw that my own earthly human biology was capable of change far beyond our current scientific understanding. The face continued to change into more alien forms, as if I were being shown the religious icons of other worlds. Then for one moment, it all became too much; I was downloading too much at once and fear surfaced.. At this time in the United States there were many movies and books going around about alien abduction. The thought forms of my culture raised their head:

O My God!!!…I'm being abducted!!!

I was immediately washed with a gentle wave of humor and kindness. It seemed that every doubt and fear was being gently stripped from me, I was allowed to surrender at my own pace— what felt safe to me—a total respect for who I was. The pace of surrender was almost imperceptibly gentle. The Christ face was now beyond any description of gender or description of any one species, when it slowly ceased changing, and settled into an amorphous triangular face of slowly moving opaque color. There were three enormous eye-like slits or openings of shiny, pitch-black darkness. I was left floating in this humorous, gentle love, and now knew that I was ready to surrender. I projected into the black eye at the top of the triangle, and suddenly I was no more. I was not in the void, I had become the void—the All Infinite.
No boundaries,
No time,
No up,
No down,
No inside or outside.
A naked pool of infinite cosmic nothingness
Prior to all manifest creation
No gust of Will or Desire
An equal cause of all things
Perfect warm peace…
Then after billions of year—a micro movement of current—a thin tinsel of luminous! And I was back in my bedroom!

❋ ❋ ❋

For three days I sat in shock, though a very humorous shock. I tried to push it out of my head, but it wasn't in my head. I tried to convince myself that it was really a dream, after all, I was still here now in my same reality. It couldn't convince myself; the very nature of spiritual vision is certainty, with no need to try and convince anyone. I had spent my whole life in questions and doubt. Should I do this or that, is this the right job, the right mate, the right timing, am I good enough, which way should I go, what path? Endless questions continue through our lives. But now I just knew; it was the first time in my life that I just simply knew without any doubts. Because I had so much experience of doubt, and thoroughly knew what that felt like, I now had those feelings to compare with the feelings of *knowing*, and that is how one *knows*. When I looked at my hand, how did I know it was a hand? One just knows— it is that simple! But for many months following, I watched my mind still try to deny what had happened, by splitting itself into three parts and playing a cat and mouse game within itself. It reminded me of a song:

> *...my good self got into a fight with my bad self...it was a terrible brawl...I would have jumped in and broken it up...but I didn't want to get involved...*

The vision seemed to me to be like a cloud over my head, and then there was me down here on earth. Between the two, there was dark cloud that separated us; this was how I experienced it. I had experienced the ideal, but how was I going to bring it into my everyday life. The part of me that 'didn't want to get involved' knew there was going to be more years of work ahead, probably the hardest years, and I played every game with myself not to have to look at that; even though it was the crowning experience of my spiritual search, the vision did not bring me much joy. I would like to say I was a glowing, positive person, cheerfully marching on the path to God, and sometimes that was true. But now I was going to have to confront all those other times when it wasn't true. My mind shifted into grumble gear:

Shit! When am I going to get a break?"

I felt I had every right to feel that way:

"Be Ye therefore perfect"...man you got to be kidding ...you mean to tell me I can spoil the whole thing with just one negative thought... like one drop of sour milk turns the whole carton to yogurt...you mean the path really does become more narrow...man no one told me it was going to be like this...why can't I be a gigolo or something....

Things about ourselves, that years earlier we would not bother with, one day become a blaring road block. I now knew that one tidbit of —'When are things going to get better?'— would change my whole life. But after what I saw in the vision, I was too scared not to go further. Again, discipline is what saved me. In one strong meditation, I turned what I felt was a well deserved 'When are things going to get better?'—into— 'Quit your whining, and get to work.'

It felt as if I was starting all over again; that was what I had asked for, but had I seen that big bag of 'stuff' over my head, I might not have asked .

The months passed and I began to come to terms with an intimate relationship with Jesus. This was not so easy because the vision had left me with the ability to ask a question and have it immediately answered, like in the vision. It is very hard to fool yourself under such circumstances, and I began to seriously ponder some of Jesus' words, as written in traditional sources. The passage that caught my attention for many months was " Call no man on earth your father" and "I came to separate mother from daughter, brother from sister." In my own being, I felt the battle with my own family, and through them, the cultural conditioning against the realities of Christ. But I saw that I was now embarking on a journey that was to clearly define the difference between the Sacred, and the backlash of darkness created by those who tried to manipulate the sacred for their own ends. Anger and suspicion of religions was justified, but now I had seen the spark behind it all, and in myself, had to separate the two streams. From my readings of the gospels, it seemed that this was the same problem Jesus had in his day, and the story was clearly pointing out what we all must face while living in this world; the lesson of discernment. When Jesus spoke of the father with a small "f" he was speaking in imagery to a Jewish audience. The whole tradition of authority, which kept the tribe together, was based upon the authority of the father, the Old Testament even said the father had the right to kill his son if he didn't obey. There are no records of any Jewish father ever having done this, so obviously, scare tactics to keep authority was a big thing with this tribe; they must have invented plea-bargaining early on. But then Jesus comes along and says don't accept the father's authority (outside authority), the Law. The kingdom, more Life, healing, all that you need comes from within from the Father with a capital "F." But physically and psychically we are entangled with our families ways and traditions. Jesus says when this becomes more important than the individual, we have the right to go past that conditioning; if our family religion or culture is narrow mind-ed or prejudiced, we have the right and ability, with the help of Holy Spirit, to break off from that conditioning; Jesus was the ultimate rebel. It didn't mean to stop loving my family, it meant I had a right to my on unique experience of God, a separate reality from theirs, ever separate from the whole culture. This was the first gift the vision gave to me— the authority or blessing to not rely on outside authority— to take what was unique to me, and fully and lovingly accept it, as Jesus had shown, while in the vision, he accepted, loved and trusted everything about me. I had tried to do this anyway, but now I felt a blessing and connection to an ancient lineage stretching far back into time. I had seen the thoughts about being conditioned by society and authority before, but now there was a definite power to let go of them, a feeling in my whole body, not just intellectual platitudes. Acknowledging this blessing, now I could begin to work with the vision, which remained as fresh in my memory as the morning on which it had happened.

✱ ✱ ✱

First, I am hiding in the bushes, I decide it is time to be found. God is always there to reveal to us, it is we who must decide we want it. The young girls who were sexually excited as I came into the school yard, represented the raw sexual energies that I worked with in Tantrik yoga— I wasn't interested anymore. These practices, or at least the way in which I used them, were not fulfilling me. The school teacher asks me to leave, but I wasn't bothered by his rudeness, my only concern being playing the wonderful music. This meant to me "resist not evil." Don't bother fighting against established authorities who don't under-stand, just go around them and do what you must. The older woman with the authority to make the teacher bow, appears, and then asks me if I will sing "Anand Sahib." Help always comes if we don't give up, and circumvents the illusionary oppositions—also, it would be a very bene-ficial thing for the whole world to think of God Power as feminine as well as masculine. I had a Catholic friend whose father used to beat and sexually abuse him. He told me that God as Father was not a good image for him. Jesus himself suggest in Thomas' gospel, found in the Dead Sea Scrolls, it is ok to give up the image of God as Father, and even to give up the image of a Son. These were just Jesus' favorite ways of trying to explain the loving relationship between God and man. But then He says we must always revere the Holy Spirit, more than the images and the stories, because it is the Holy Spirit that gives the revelation of the images evolving through time and cultures. (The love is the same, our concepts of God are changeable). The women asked if I would sing "Anand Sahib," my own Song of Bliss— will I use the powers and gifts given to me for the uplifting of all, the giving of the attributes and healing of God, through my music and my own union with God? Also the tie-in with the Sikh path; to the Sikh, the singing of the sacred songs is the worship; music is raised to the spiritual level of Holy Sacrament. It is only when I say "yes" to all this, that she takes me to the further revelation of Christ. The schoolteacher said "come back later,"— only after surrender to Christ can I truly sing and create the festival. After seeing the lights and 'becoming as a child' , the first primal question of the flesh comes to the surface. "Who is my mate going to be?" But then I myself decide to drop that question, and ask something else. As I had said earlier, finding a mate had become an obsession with me, and I knew I needed to stop this behavior. It wasn't that there was no mate for me, it was the fact I had turned this normal instinct into a self-inflicted painful Miss Universe contest. Who was it going to be? Who was the winner? To know Christ, I had to drop this tension out of my biology. It was not hard to do, but rather light and humorous, because there was a feeling that this was already taken care of on some level, why was I so worried about it? Finding a mate should not be my concern, it is already done. So I humorously decided to drop it. In my early Catholic days, I had been immersed in a morose vibration; it was shocking to feel the lightness and humor of this being, then discovering it was Jesus. Never at any time in the vision did I get the feeling of Christ as "King," or "Lord," or even my teacher. These are our own images that we put on Christ, but it is ok because it is from an expression of devotion; we have a true need for expression of devotion, but must also remember that the images are not necessarily true. Instead of hierarchy, the feeling that was being projected on me was one of an absolute trust in me—he had no need to teach me what he knew I already understood. This being was there to love and reveal me to myself, and that is all. It was a silent acknowledgement of, "You have the answers in yourself"— "I trust you to know what is right"— "You know what to do." Christ is met in the realm of Truth, it was impossible to not know what was right and wrong for us. We all know when we are doing something we shouldn't, but we have many elaborate games to pretend to ourselves that we don't know, then when it comes back on us we feign victim-hood. Christ won't play this game with us, indeed, has no *time* for it because Christ does not exist in that orbit of deceit; he has total confidence in us and never wavers from this. I ask, "When will things get better?" In the mirror of his heart I see where I am heading following this quality of energy, (a self pitying hope for the future). The seeing of myself as I am, the choices I've been given, and the making of the choice, are all revealed in one moment, telepathic and instantaneous. This means the kingdom of God is always Now; the choice cannot be made in the past nor in the future, it must be Now and immediate. The Christ does not indulge us in our self-destructive choices, they don't even happen in Christ' peaceful kingdom of Nowness; the trauma is absolutely of our own making. The image of Jesus hanging on the cross forever, taking on everyone's suffering is really our own self pitying image, this was not Christ as he exist Now and therefore, Always. Sitting across from me was the reality of what I could be, what we all could be—or by my own choices, I could be an unhappy, unhealthy, lecherous, self-important boob. I had to make the choice Now. (The Indian teacher Krishnamurti used to say, "Freedom is now or never"). Then I ask, "Who are you?" Still today I marvel at the subtle answer and, the gentleness of healing.

"You can call me Jesus"

I had no trust in teachers or religions, I was barricaded behind memories of the Yogi, that still hurt even after the many years that had past. I had seen obnoxious 'born again Christians' down at the beach, accosting people to turn to Christ. Burn in hell if you don't become a born again Christian, we feel sorry for you, you sinner— Big judgment; big self-importance there. But Christ said to me, you can call me what you like, because I am all those Gods and Goddesses and much more. I *invite* you to look at the big hurt that is stuck in your subconscious concerning Christianity and Jesus. On my mother's side, I had come from an old Irish-Polish Catholic family, Christianity was in my genes, and so why fight against the currents of my own spiritual river, if God was there too; it was an invitation to heal with my past, to become fully myself. I wasn't born into a Jewish, Buddhist, Sikh, Moslem or Hindu family, I was born into a Roman Catholic family. This was a big chunk of myself that I didn't accept; somehow God had made a big mistake, I thought. To walk through life thinking that God, or Life, or Fate, whatever we call it, makes big mistakes, is a hell in itself; we either trust life or not trust it. Then his face changed to reveal some of the possibilities of what Christ is, yet I could not name any of the faces because they kept changing before I could *name* it, put a label on it—any description of Christ or God was a limitation. That was the real blasphemy, to try and limit what Christ is; because it is so magnificent, it is beyond description and uniquely revealed to each individual being.

The only thing that stayed the same throughout the whole experience, was the feeling of basking in humor, and loving kindness. And this became the signature, the flavor of Christ for me, the way in which I was able to recognize It in the exterior or interior worlds, no matter what the outer appearances. "You can call me Jesus," became even more significant to me because he used his proper name; He didn't say Christ or Lord, he said Jesus. Lineage is very important in spiritual training; the old lineages are kept fresh and alive by the revelation of the Source and Spirit of the lineage to the current heirs of the day. If he had said "Christ," I still wouldn't have known what lineage I was entrusted with. I had seen that the Christ was founder of many lineages, but Jesus the man, was the founder of this particular lineage of the revelation of Christ. Even though I knew His name would have been Jeshua in his time, it only further revealed to me that the name and form can change as long as the Spirit is the Same. I also felt relieved in a very comical way; because I had become so self-reliant in my spiritual path and untrusting of any earthly teacher, I often thought I was totally alone. I had met most of the famous holy men of the east, and though some were very loving, I never found any that I felt knew more than I did. Even some of the so called miracle workers I met, had no idea how they did what they did. It sounds arrogant, but this was my feeling at the time. To know that I did have an "elder brother" as St. Paul said, was a great relief and joy to me, but at the same time, there was a warm mystery. I experienced Jesus as a separate being, indeed, one of the most striking understandings of the experience was how every part of me was allowed to stand un-touched—every thought, every doubt, and every decision made during and after, were my own, yet at the same time, I knew I was seeing the unfolding of myself, and not just myself, but what we all are at the core of our being, behind all the discursive layers of false images we wear. Jesus revealed me to myself, layer by layer, then became a doorway for me to pass through into the experience of the All of myself—and no Self at the same time. It was as if Jesus was so at one with the All, the only thing left of him was a sliver of color or filter. We are cleansed white, then dyed in this color as we pass through to our own experience of unity with God. The color, the filter, is Love; nothing else can pass through into Universal Life. Jesus was the guardian at the gate, and also the gateway itself, standing between our bickering world and the world of peace, through which we are born into our own Universal Self, able to travel the Universe at will—" Life of abundance!" Another realization that was very much different from my Catholic upbringing, was that the whole experience was erotic. (Sexual, meaning all your energy is stuck in the loins, and erotic meaning, it flows throughout the entire body). It was the most pleasurable, physical, erotic feeling, as my body changed while watching the face of Christ unfold. It was only by pleasure and the feeling of being safe that the body relaxed into its further potential. And finally, I realized that all this happened by grace! My spiritual path was a macho 'smash your way through the gates of heaven' kind of strife. It had its moments, but the payoffs were minimal compared to the effort I put into it. I had to learn that it was the "Father's pleasure to *give* one the kingdom." There was nothing I could have ever done to force this opening, and what being enjoys giving a gift when you are always trying to *take it* instead of happily *receiving it*.

✳ ✳ ✳

In the beginning was the Word, and the Word was with God, and the Word was God (John 1: 1-2). This Word is found in all religions and spiritual paths, and from the unifying view of God, religions do not clash or oppose each other, but rather compliment each other, bring a different and unique piece to the puzzle, give a different flavor or color. If we take an apple, the English name (*apple*) changes in the different cultural languages, but the nature of the apple stays the same. In just this way does Christ exist in all religions. The Word is the first creation out of the Void, called God in the language of our times, and this Word is the only doorway into Universal Life beyond our earthly concepts. In Islam it is sometimes called Saut-i-Sarmadi, (the Divine Song), or Kalam-i-qadim, (the Ancient Sound), and the Kalma or Word, Nid-e-Asmani (the Sound coming down from Heaven). In the Old Testament of the Jews, the "Word" is spoken of many times in Psalms, Isaiah, Proverbs and Genesis. In Hinduism and Buddhism the "Word" or "Holy Sound" is described in many fascinating ways. The Sikh religion, the newest of the world religions calls it the "Nam", or "Shabad". They also believe that a human can become so in union with the "Word" that they become one in the same, "God and Guru are One". In Christianity we say the "Word became flesh" and is called Jesus, and because Jesus was Human, he shows the way for all Humans. The path or method of

Jesus was to treat each other with the same respect and love that we feel towards God. St. Paul says that all who are touched by spirit are "Sons of God". But the message of Jesus is lost when we think that our particular path is the best or highest path. There are many ways to experience the "Word", they are endless, and no true lover of God would ever allow themselves to be limited. So in this way there is only one door, one Christ (the word I choose to use) that exist in all paths and in all forms of Humanity, (unique to all) including those of which we have no understanding. I also choose to name it Love.

I had been shown the personal mystery of my connection with Christ, and through that doorway, the whole Universe—seen and unseen. I had seen that I was a separate being, and yet somehow the same as what I had experienced, but the revelation that excited me the most was seeing the unity of all paths and religions. As I was distinct, yet one with Christ, so I had seen that all paths were distinct yet one at their roots with the Word. Personal fulfillment is a wonderful gift, but I had started out my quest with the question of violence in the world, and unexpectedly received an answer to both questions at once. God is Great! What can I say?

Completion Stage

Chapter 6

The Test

Imperceptibly, over the following years, I changed. One day I simply noticed that I no longer chanted to God like some whining beggar, but rather, the chanting became an expression of God, a giving out to my environment; there was now not only a faith in God, but more so, the faith of God. My questions about life were no longer "What is the right way?", as in wanting to know the future, but rather, "What do I want to create?" Not the daily wants and needs of struggling humans, but rather what had I come to this earth to do. My spiritual practice became a daily task of keeping my mind clear, like bathing every day, instead of trying to reach some kind of enlightenment. In this position of clarity, I merely had to make a decision and it would be given. But to make a decision about the direction of one's life takes a total commitment to self-honesty, and the giving up of the victim mentality. I had thought for many years that I wanted to be a recording artist, but after careful truthful analysis of my situation, I knew that I myself had stopped it from happening all along. I really did not want to be an 'entertainer', someone who takes people out of their thoughts and troubles for awhile; I wanted to stir up trouble, not let people or myself hide from their problems, because if one faces it and lets it hurt, then the effort to change is born from that; I wanted change. I had seen too many friends with contracts on major labels, whose lives' were almost completely controlled by the record company. They changed the lyrics to the songs, tried to change their image, even their names. I also had friends with two or three released albums out on the radio, but they had never played live in front of an audience— they had no connection with the people and were very sad about it. I had too much fun playing for whomever and whenever I pleased, even if it was not to large audiences, to let that happen. Also, I had said I wanted to marry again and have children, but again truthfully, I loved my freedom and lifestyle. It allowed me the time to evolve in a very particular way, that I wouldn't have been able to do had I the responsibilities of a family. Some of my friends with large homes and all the symbols of success, wondered how I could live the way I did with so little, but when I asked further about their accumulations, it always turned out that the bank really owned everything. These people were hundreds of thousands of dollars in debt, and felt trapped on a wheel, trying to keep up the payments on everything. I on the other hand, didn't owe a cent to anyone; I could earn money when I needed it, then take off and travel the world when I wanted. I never needed doctors or medicine, and never worried about what would happen when I got old; through yoga, a good diet and fasting, I just didn't get old. There is only one way to truthfully look at what one really wants— look at what you have. But I had been stuck in a cultural thought form or habit, to always want more, always look for tomorrow for my fulfillment, instead of sinking deeply into the experience of Now, and being thankful for what I had. So what had I come to accomplish? I knew I had much more to go through before that answer became clear. But for now, I was amused and amazed that all the reasons I cursed God for on the fateful morning of the vision, now, having gone through an imperceptible passage, I was grateful for.

* * *

I went back to the mountains and stayed for a year, and during this time I became totally absorbed in writing a screenplay. The vision was ever present with me, and I began to sense that their was much more work to do with it, but I didn't know exactly what. In Tibetan Tantrik work, the first part of the path to spiritual development is called the Generation stage; the second half is called Completion stage. In working with a specific deity or angel, the practitioner first has to visualize and find their devotion and unique connection with the deity; this can take many years. The deity's are really symbolic codes, representing real archetypal energies existing in the universe that the practitioner tries to tap into. Then much later in the completion stage, the practitioner actually takes the deity into themselves and becomes the embodiment of the actual energy, like very fine actors who totally become the person they are playing. There is no clear or definite path of how this happens. The path of Tantra has developed many different ways to try and suit different personalities, but the actual becoming of the deity is a mystery, and seems to be controlled by that old bugaboo— grace. I began to see my own predicament in terms of this Generation-

Completion model. I had seen the potential, the primal archetypal being, that we truly are. Then there was me, now on earth, in the mountains. Between the two realities was a sea of conditioned doubts and habitual tendencies, created in my genetic make up long before I was even born. All that had to be overcome before the two realities on either side of this seething soup could become one. The paradox for me was, "How could I be in this perfect state where all 'desires' dissolve in an ocean of peace, when I 'desired' it so much?" It didn't matter what one wanted, God or material things, it was still being tangled up in the energies of 'wanting.' How could I dissolve from my being, the dynamic energies of 'wanting', that I had amplified so furiously over many years of incorrect Kundalini practice. It was going to have to be something powerful to knock me out of my rut, and I prayed for it to come. What's that old saying? "Be careful what you ask for."

* * *

After finishing writing, I came back to Los Angeles and was offered a job with a successful young rock and roll singer. He was in his teens when he had made his first million, and had bought into the whole rock and roll scene; fast cars and fast women. Now he found himself almost thirty and full of disillusion about his life. Because he was successful he was surrounded by people who wanted something from him, usually an "in" with the industry. He was very generous and a genuinely good soul, but seemed to lack ability to put up some boundaries and say No to people, feeling he needed their approval. He had heard about me from his cook, whose husband had lived in one of the ashrams I had taught in, and I was hired as a kind of physic bodyguard; I moved into his house and we started meditating together. Within ten days the house was cleared. No one came around, the phone didn't even ring. Even I was impressed. Most of my practice of sending out vibratory waves to clear a *free space* had been done in the mountains. I had forgotten how powerful these practices could be until seeing the results down in the city. We went to business meetings at Warner Brothers Records and even the executives starting acting more respectfully. After a few months of calm had passed, we decided a celebration was called for and planned a party for some close friends. A friend called me and said he was bringing his girlfriend and her sister, whom he thought I had some kind of 'connection' with; this was the way people talked in Hollywood and I didn't pay much attention. That evening, Carissa and Veena walked into the house, and my life changed.

They were not the American standard model type of beauty, which was how men rated the women here, rather, they glowed with intelligence, wit and humor. They were French, very feminine and mysterious in a most unpretentious way. My friend told me that Veena, the younger one, had just found out that her boyfriend had cheated on her and this was why he was bringing her to see me. Maybe there was something I could do to cheer her up. Veena was introduced to me in the middle of the loud party and surprisingly I did feel this 'connection' my friend had spoken of. Behind the gloom and sadness, was a tiny, beautiful young woman, with curly brown hair and blue green eyes, that opened into a realm of power and intelligence. She looked into my soul for one second and we 'met.' She sized me up instantly, then politely sat in the corner, never bothering to remove her bulky long coat. It seemed as though she wrapped it around her as if it were her only security left in the world.

Music started up in another part of the house, and I went over to play drums with some of the musicians and a few of the children who were present. After awhile I saw her come into the room, sit down and begin to watch me, turning her head the other way every time I would look up at her. I began to feel very uncomfortable, knowing it was the kind of discomfort that comes when you are about to take one of those big leaps into the unknown. Later, I found her in another room looking at a picture book, so I sat down next to her and began telling her a story to try and cheer her up. It was just a simple story about how things that look bad, sometimes turn out to be not so bad after all; with her head down, she listened intently. When I finished my story, she remained sitting in stillness for a long time, then slowly lifted her head and smiled. For the second time our eyes met—and I was in love.

Within a week we were talking long hours on the phone, happily discussing how we were going to spend more time together. After another week, she started backing off. The following week, we were on again, then off, then on again; this went on for a few weeks until I took the warning sign, and backed off too. The old boyfriend now wanted her back, and in her confusion, she wavered back and forth about what to do. I had set a strict policy on myself to stay away from women who were in this kind of situation, because it always spelled trouble, but the more I pulled back the more she would call and try to patch things up. She was so sincere, and tried so hard to make things go smoothly, at times it was even comical. Through listening to her bizarre explanations, I learned that the French had a real flair for romantic complications, and slowly learned to see it with a little more humor. What had happened to us on the first night of our meeting, was a very powerful and compelling experience, I couldn't deny it, but I began to sense that this young women had some hidden problems and complications that would interfere in our relationship, and I became afraid for my own heart.

There is a humbling nature to love: when it isn't there, there is nothing you can do to make it happen; when it is there, there is nothing you can do to make it go away. If it could be controlled by ego, it wouldn't be Love. My only choice was to honor what had happened to me and make up my mind to not have any sexual relations for a long time, in other words, a more traditional courtship. This dance went on for almost a year, and though complicated, it was one of the smartest and nicest things I had ever done for myself, and for her. I slowly came to know and respect her as a person *(not an object of my desire)* in that year, something I had never learned to do in the fast past dating track of Hollywood. She tried so hard not to hurt me or her boyfriend in her long break-up process, and although I was impatient, I became more impressed with her compassion for everyone concerned; I felt genuine soul growth here, something I hadn't felt in a long time. I had seen so many friends, both men and women, jump into sex too fast, bonding with their partner, only to find that we are really not compatible with the person; then there's the painful separation and broken heart. After a few broken hearts under their belts, they bravely set out looking for new mates, only now, with a huge shopping list of do's and don'ts, likes and dislikes. All the spontaneity and innocence had died in the rush. I didn't notice when I stopped being that kind of person, all I knew was that for the first time in my life I was taking my time, and finding out about this person before leaping, and it felt warm and nourishing.

Eight months flew by before I ever kissed Veena, yet we grew closer and closer as we worked our way through the ups and downs of it all. To my spoiled, 'want everything, when I want it' American male ego, this was all a whole lot of trouble, but the orgasms were daily in my heart, before I ever thought of a sexual relationship with her, and that was something no one should ever miss in earthly experience. But then there were those days when I was in terror:

> *She's playing you for a chump...All this bullshit about not wanting to hurt her boyfriend...She's been with him so many years...So what...What about me?...What about my needs?....All this soul growth stuff...your just making that up...look where all this spiritual shit got you before...Just sleep with her...she's French...they're*

used to that!

The thinking mind knows no shame!!!!

> *You are going to get hurt here…you are falling too deep…she is better at all these games than you…Man you don't know what you are doing…You are not listening to your intuition again…after all it took to learn to listen to yourself…There is trouble here…your turning into a wussy…*

Yes, there was trouble, but sometimes so-what! I'd never had an orgasm in my heart before!

One night I drove to Veena's house and we sat around talking with Carissa and a few other friends. There was a young man from England there, who had been around the scene for about a year, whom nobody seemed to like. He was often gloomy and depressed and when he drank too much, he launched off a canticle of insulting remarks about everyone and every race of people except the English. After he left, everyone started to talk about how unpleasant it was to be around him, all except Veena. Even though she was young, she had an innate, deep insight into people, and a very generous compassion in dealing with them. She was the only one who stuck up for the Brit, saying that he was just in a lot of pain because he was feeling kind of lost in America, and that was why he acted so badly. Other people in the room were not anywhere near this level of understanding and compassion for the young man, and I watched Veena hold her own in a one sided discussion about this matter. I looked on with joy, and that night I asked the Universe for this women, that she be mine and I be hers, and that I was willing to give it all for this. With Veena, all concepts of what that was supposed to look like, melted away; we knew each other so well and thought so much alike, that we were often intimidated by each other. Because I was older I was expected to have a lot of answers, but now I felt I was flowing down a path I had never been before, and was as alarmed as she was. There was nothing to do but fasten my seatbelt, and go for the ride.

One evening Veena came to visit me when she had become very upset over a dream she had the night before. She suspected that something had happened in her childhood that scared and angered her, but didn't know what it was. She knew of my exorcism work and asked if I would help her find out what had happened to her, if anything. I had known her long enough to know she really was extremely upset by something, and innocently wanting to be her hero, I immediately took on the case. She was frightened by the word Exorcism, and I explained to her that it was really an extreme word in most cases for this kind of work. I had performed eight of them and assisted in many more, and only twice had I seen outside entities attached to people rise to the surface; the rest of the time, it could really be called emotional release work. Over the years of studying with the Tibetans, I learned to see things that went far outside my own culturally agreed upon reality—what to us was emotional release, was to them a release of demons, and they actually saw them because in their agreed upon reality, this was normal. I never slipped into the argument of which was the right way to see it; the universe was a big and strange place, big enough for all kinds of realities; whatever worked was my motto. But there was one rule no matter how one did the work—never work on someone that you are emotionally involved with. I foolishly ignored that, and thought just maybe this would help our relationship move forward a little, convincing myself it would be ok if I took some precautions. For normal release work, it would be ok; the warning was a precaution for real exorcism. I spent a few days in fasting and meditation as a preparation, thinking I would not become entangled in anything that I heard or saw. With people I didn't know very well, I became so concentrated in the moment that I rarely remembered anything that surfaced. My job was to act like a filter, or vortex, so the intense emotional energies could dissolve, by passing through me because of no judgment on my part; having no judgment is the essential key to the success of the ritual.

A few days later Veena came to my house and we began. First I gave her the powerful hypnotic herbs that I was careful to mix myself. I put her into a breathing pattern and focused in on her body movements, watching for the openings into her hidden mental doorways. Within minutes she was crying and I could see from the movements of her body that she was in extreme turmoil. After an hour into the session I knew I had made a mistake. To see someone you love going through so much pain, there was no way I could stay neutral, and soon, I was also filled with her feelings. Two hours into the session, and the core of her feelings began to surface. At five years of age, she had been put on a jet plane with her sister, to come to California. A man sat beside her and molested her for many hours, putting his coat over her lap as he stuck his hand under her dress and fondled her, telling her that if she made a sound he would hurt her sister. I raged inside, listening to all the images come to the surface. Experiencing almost as much trauma as she was in, I felt lost, but my training took over and I was able to safely lead her through it. The session was taped and after a few days of listening to the tape and processing her feelings, Veena felt much better. The person on the table goes through the worst of it in one swoop. They have faced their worst nightmares, see the decisions and choices they made while it was happening, breath and sweat out the stress from the body; in most cases, it is finished, almost as if it never happened. But I was a wreck. Without the breathing and heat, and because it was Veena, I was stuck with horrible feelings. I immediately cut off from her and spent many agonizing days sifting through the feelings, and finally came to the conclusion, that the reason I felt so bad was because there was something more that hadn't surfaced in the session; I could feel some brooding darkness, but could not see it, and I knew there was trouble ahead. This was a horrible position to be in with someone I was in love with. While I consulted with the Tibetans, Veena wisely decided to make some moves of her own. She told me she was going to go back to France for a while so she could break off the relationship with her old boyfriend once and for all. She wanted to feel what it was like to be alone for awhile. I was going to miss her but was happy she was doing what she needed to do for herself, and complete her healing. I knew her healing depended on her learning to trust her own decisions and stand on her own two feet. But I was left with these dark feelings and had to deal with the consequences of my mistake. I had used a sacred ritual to try and influence an outcome for myself. Even if it was because of my loving her, still there were consequences to pay if I wanted to keep my craft pure. The next two months were spent in fasting and breathing practice, in order to break up and let go of the feelings I had accumulated. It finally felt ok to call her, but when I did, she complained to me that her old boyfriend had been calling her almost everyday, trying to talk her into coming back. I wanted to ring his neck. The demons of anger and jealousy thumped me good. Maybe I had to become more French to be with her, I didn't know, but this was foul territory for my yogi self image, and I began to spend more time wondering if this was all worth it. I tightened the seat belt!

You're such a damned wussy!

Another month went by, when Carissa called me and told me that Veena had come back to Los Angeles, and had embroiled herself in a terrible fight with their mother, and was now living with her old boyfriend. I was crushed. I knew she felt too ashamed to call me, but I could still feel her calling out to me, now, more than ever, even if she was with her boyfriend. For the next three months I could not talk to her, but felt constant deep depression, and though I felt the pain of missing her, I knew that most of this pain was not mine. If she was happy and wanted to be with this person I would have been fine with that, but I knew something was terribly wrong.

During this time, I stayed in San Diego with an old friend who had recently left the Yogi's organization and was in need of some emotional help. Two big earthquakes hit Southern California, and it seemed like the whole state was scared and agitated. I could reach no peaceful place in meditation, as if the very space in which all phenomena happens was in turbulence. The year of daily talks had forged a telepathic link between Veena and myself, and I knew she wanted to talk, but I also knew she had to make the first move. Mentally, I had to tell her to leave me alone and use the telephone if she wanted to connect. For a few weeks I felt her go away, until the Christmas season came; her feelings and images began to haunt me. Knowing that she felt she had hurt me so much she shouldn't call me, I had to give her a hint that it was ok. I took a Christmas present for her and her sister, delivering it to Carissa who was now living in her parent's house while they were in France. The next day Veena called! It was as if nothing had ever happened. We were both so happy to speak to each other after so long a time, that we chatted away for hours just like we used to. With her French dramatics and she told me the whole complicated story. Veena had fought with her volatile Sicilian mother and was thrown out of the house with no support. She came from a well to do family and had always been given a generous allowance, she wanted to move out on her own anyway, but was not prepared to be cut off overnight like this. At this time, the old boyfriend was so insistent that they try again, she decided to give it a try, convincing herself that she still loved him. Deep inside she knew she was doing this because she had no place to go, and was depressed and ashamed of herself. The boyfriend practically kept her a prisoner, giving her marijuana, which she had been smoking almost everyday for months. She hated herself and finally told him she wanted to leave, but wasn't sure where to go. She rambled on. All this was just soap-opera to me, I was just happy to talk to her. We chatted and laughed for hours, but even though I felt happy, I could tell she was a little off, so I decided to move cautiously; this women could turn my heart to pulp, and I was scared. Since the parents were now in Europe, I suggested she go live with her sister, but I didn't push it. I wanted to make sure she was really reaching out for help before doing anything. Two days later, she called again and sounded as if she was falling apart. She had told the boyfriend she wanted to leave and he had kicked her in the stomach. She was in shock and I could tell she was slowly losing touch with reality. Suddenly, Veena became very serious and told me she had something to tell me, but was scared. I knew that my guard had to come down now, and I would open to her again; her trust in me had always been able to melt away any barriers that I put up. We found that old loving space with each other, and she told me her incredible vision.

After being kicked, Veena walked downstairs by herself, and sat in the dark. Suddenly a little being appeared to her and identified himself as the Devil. He came in the shape of a demon about two feet high, with pale skin and pinkish eyes. He was sad and scared. He knew that his time on earth was coming to an end, and he was afraid of the death and transformation that he would have to go through. Veena told him "yes it was true, people now want to be happy on earth, but there is no need to worry because you will transform into something else, something happier." I could just see her talking to this scared little fellow. If the devil did come to someone for some understanding and kindness, it surely would have been Veena; she was the only person I knew with that sort of fearless kindness towards all beings. And I was the only person she knew she could tell this too, and not think she had gone crazy or judge her, or worse, think that she was being tricked by the devil, as some fundamentalist types would have done.

In western psychological values these things are handled very differently, but I had seen enough strange happenings in healing and spiritual work, to not be disturbed by what she said. What she had told me was consistent with my own realizations, and that of many other mystics and seers that I knew, including some old Catholic monks that I had met in a monastery on the east coast. One Catholic monk saw a vision of Satan being forgiven, and invited back to heaven with great celebration. Many Muslim Sufis' had also seen the same vision. Others saw similar visions, but interpreted them according to their own religious backgrounds. Whatever the imagery was, everyone felt that the earth was going to be a happier place in a few more years. Even the fundamentalist believed this, the difference being that Satan would be crushed rather than forgiven and saved, and in the process much of the world and its people would be destroyed. I had never discussed my own views of evil with Veena, so I knew she was not just rearranging my ideas in her head; she was a very conservative young woman, who did not read occult books, or even meditate. Veena was very confused by the vision, and having come from a Catholic family she was on the edge of fright, but held on to me for some kind of center. The only thing I could think to do at that moment was to tell her the Sufi story of God and Lucifer:

God, being by Himself, wanted someone else to share love with. His first creation was Lucifer, made out of pure light. Lucifer loved and worshipped God because this was the purpose of his being. Later God created mankind and told Lucifer that he was now to serve mankind and also God. Lucifer refused saying "You created me only to love You and serve You so I will not serve this mankind." God became angry and created Hell and told Lucifer to leave Heaven. Before leaving he turned to God and said, "Just remember that this mankind will forget you, but I love you so much, that when they do forget you, I will make their life so miserable for them, they will have to turn back to you." God wept because of Lucifer's devotion, and the tears formed the rings of Saturn.

Veena laughed with glee!

"They are in cahoots...they are in cahoots."

She musically sang out between spurts of laughter.

"Well that's a really hard job for Lucifer...poor angel." She laughed hysterically. She laughed so hard she started to speak in French to me, forgetting that I knew very little of the language. Then she stopped abruptly and said,

"Ok, I have to go now, see you soon."

This is one bizarre girl...man, you better get out of this...she is whacked ...this one's over your head ...run...don't walk!!!

When Veena told me her story, I had two separate reactions; an inner one of joy, a feeling of "of course", and a more clinical one of alarm. Veena was a powerful expression of the all-compassionate female, and even if this little being was a demon, there must always be someone in existence to love him and offer healing. My alarm came from knowing that she was still in a very stressful environment, and without any training in how to integrate different realities in her own ego, I knew she could be in some danger. She called back a few minutes later, and still laughing, she told me she was moving in with her sister and would contact me. I felt some relief.

Two days passed when she called from her parents' house, but this time she was talking nonsense on the phone. She switched back and forth from English to French to gibberish, and then talked about blue celestial realms, and beings that told her we should give up all electrical appliances. I slowed her down and got her to focus, then asked her what had happened, how did she get to her parents house with her sister? She said she just left, but the boyfriend had followed her to her parents house and beat her up. I was ready to run out the door and teach this worm a lesson, but Veena started screaming at me on the phone. She had let him hit her because it was the only way she could make the break from him. She had been trying for a long time to break up, but he wouldn't leave her alone. Now he was so ashamed at what he did, he knew it was over. Her logic made sense, even though I didn't like it; I let it go; it was just one of those French things.

Veena had not asked me to come visit her yet, and I really considered if I wanted to get more involved in this anyway. The thoughts of running away ran havoc through my mind. I decided to slowly back out, but two days later, Carissa called; she was hysterical. She and her boyfriend had taken Veena to a nightclub, and Veena had started dancing wildly, ending up on the floor babbling incoherently. They picked her up and brought her back home, but Carissa was crying and scared that Veena had gone crazy, and would I please come at once. I had a good relationship with Carissa and knew she would not ask me to come unless it was very serious. They both met me at the door. I saw the look on Veena's face and melted; she had a black eye and a bruised cheek, but her eyes grew large with joy at seeing me, yet afraid that I would be judgmental. We held each other for a long time. She kept whispering, "please don't judge me, don't judge me." What had happened to her since I saw her last, I couldn't imagine, but I was holding a destroyed human being, someone who had lost all self-esteem and she was terrified. She held me like I was her last hope—if I rejected her she would be lost in some dark, self-imposed torture chamber. I had been in that place before, and held on to her with all my strength. In spite of herself she invited me into her house with her best French manners and charm. I felt joy and foreboding at once when I walked through the door; I fastened the seatbelt tighter.

Carissa told me that Veena had been awake for two days, constantly talking about things she was seeing in the future. Veena chatted on and on, and I could tell from her descriptions that she was seeing the inner spiritual worlds. Many eastern seers had described these worlds in their literature and I had seen some myself, so we all listened with great interest. Veena was normally a quiet person, so to see her so animated was a treat for everyone. Even though in western psychology she would have been diagnosed as having a psychotic break, I had seen this before in India and some of the ashrams I had lived in. She flew off on fantastic descriptions that took hours, but was also able to focus in her environment when we spoke to her, so her condition was not beyond my ability to facilitate. The eastern mindset did not consider this as an illness, but rather an opening to a higher intelligence, providing the person had the right kind of support to go through the strain; the stories of yogis and saints, acting crazy as they opened into their higher brain functions were common knowledge in these cultures. There were many schools and monasteries where people could go when they reached this crisis in their lives, and at the invitation of Carissa, I decided to stay and try and create this kind of environment while Veena went on her inner journey Though I was concerned she hadn't slept for three days, I had spent weeks like this myself, so I understood it from the inside out and was able to track her by listening carefully to her descriptions. After two more days of this, I knew she wasn't going any further, because in her dialogue she started to repeat herself. I suggested to Carissa that I would call a doctor friend of mine to prescribe some strong drug to put her to sleep. Carissa panicked! The whole family had a terrible fear of doctors and medicine. Carissa told me that once her mother had been institutionalized for a few days of observation and I could see that this meant a huge shame and fear in her family. She was scared that Veena would be taken away. I kept having the feeling of being pulled deeper and deeper into some place I had no business being, but I agreed to stay with them at the house and ride it out. I had been in the middle of a recording project when all this started, so now I had to cancel the rest of the sessions, and already felt great pressure to get all this business over with. But as soon as I would begin to think I didn't want to be there, Veena would become scared. I realized that she was using me as her center of stability and love while she passed through whatever she needed to do, and because I loved her, I put my concerns aside and surrendered to whatever I needed to go through for her. This time I was going to be there for someone I loved no matter what happened. That night she seemed much better and told me that she knew I was her soul mate, and that we would be together to inherit a happier kingdom than the world had been so far. Any parts of me that were holding back, I now let go and moved deeper in love with her. We both knew the meaning of soul mates and this was what I had longed to hear from her. This was the woman I wanted to be with forever and she had just said, "Yes". I knew that she was not all there to make that kind of decision, but I also knew that in this moment, I had to surrender to her completely, and that was the only way through this. She would not let me doubt. Veena became panicked when any doubts crossed my mind, and when I saw that, there was really no other choice; I surrendered my heart and soul to her. So brief; so brief; but for a few days I experienced the greatest joy with another human that I had ever known. But that night as I sat at the foot of her bed, I felt a wave of pain pass through me that I thought would shatter me. I didn't know why or how, but I knew I would lose her. I was being asked to give all myself in Love, even though I knew I would have to give her up.

Veena tossed and turned as I sat in my sad meditation. About 2 a.m. she let out the most blood curdling of screams. Even in exorcisms I had never heard such horror. She screamed and screamed. Carissa came running in and we tried to calm her, she finally broke into tears and continued to sob the rest of the night. Veena was gone from us. She couldn't hear us or even know we were there. At four a.m. she started to scream again. All I could do was hold her as she cried uncontrollably. I smelled urine and saw she had wet herself. Her earliest infant motor functions of holding on were gone, and her eyes went blank. I knew what had happened to her. She had a spiritual awakening and had gone to the heaven worlds, and now while coming back, because of the lack of proper training and preparation, she had slipped into the hell worlds, or some horrible past in her own life. Whatever model one used, she was in danger of not coming back to us if the trauma was too much. I told Carissa that it was time to call the doctor and get her to sleep, and Carissa trusted me in this. I went back upstairs and sat quietly at Veena's bed. Then I felt it! I was shocked! The same cold calculating, purposeful intelligence, that I knew from Greece, entered the room. This time it was even more powerful, playing chess with my soul, the most terrifying of stakes; the life of the women I loved. The thought of Veena being involved in this enraged me, but again, as soon as I felt anger, Veena would begin to scream in fright. This was a great relief to me, because I knew she was still connected to me, that my thoughts and actions affected her, and then, in one brief moment she came back and talked to me coherently. Veena grabbed me,

"You have to believe it will be OK or I won't get though this."

Then she was gone again. In that moment, knowing that she was still with me, I knew we had won. Even before the real battle began, I knew it would be ok; there is no doubt in that depth of Love, it is all powerful. A peaceful calm came over me, and Veena responded, resting quietly in her bed, but with her eyes wide open. After five days of no sleep I was a little slow in understanding what I had to do, but I felt the attack coming and pulled myself together.

Carissa walked in the room with her boyfriend and also her former boyfriend, and I saw she had changed. Instead of calling the doctor she had called her former boyfriend because he knew something about healers in this town. The two men couldn't stand each other and the previous boyfriend didn't like me much either. What I saw was Carissa become partially possessed. She knew Veena was in danger and had to get to sleep, but she hadn't slept for days too and was losing her boundaries. The former boyfriend, who was involved in all kinds of occult things, in a matter of an hour had convinced Carissa that I should leave and he would take care of everything from here on. He tapped into her fears and told her that by the very fact I wanted to take Veena to a doctor, showed that I had lost control and didn't know what I was doing. Carissa had become some kind of obedient pawn, and suggested that I should leave. Then her new boyfriend announced that he had a gun and I should stay and the old boyfriend leave. The hostility in the room increased to the flashing point. I could have easily overpowered both of them and thrown them all out, but as my anger swelled Veena began to scream again. I couldn't even get angry. My insides were being carved out with the heat of the pressure and were starting to boil over, but Veena was right there with me, and I felt realizations of cosmic dimensions exploding inside me, about the choice between Love and Faith as opposed to anger and violence. I cooked on that edge for days. Anger transmuted to diamond clarity. I knew that Carissa was the key. So attuned to her sister, she was now becoming seriously close to the edge herself and was easily influenced. I could see that any wrong move here could be very dangerous, even a shooting from her jealous boyfriend might get thrown into the pot. I focused all my attention on her and told her that her friend could take over if he wanted, but I was not leaving. Carissa relaxed and thought that was a good idea, and I threw my auric field around her, the same as I was doing for Veena.

The next two days, this jealous boyfriend tried to win back Carissa by showing how competent he was, dragging us around town, first to some Mexican healing lady who only scared Veena more, then to an herbalist, who tried to settle her down with teas; she became worse. I was begging in my prayers, that whatever she was seeing, she wouldn't decide to leave us, but I could do nothing but be with her and watch this play itself out. I watched as these 'healers' tried all their tricks in vain, knowing that if she didn't get some sleep soon, she could be permanently damaged. I could see that the boyfriend and the herbalist would become possessed as soon as they walked into the house. Their weaknesses were their investments in being right, rather than putting Veena first; and that was the entrance point for possession, dark places and holes in ourselves that we refuse to look at. And I began to look at myself to see if I might be becoming infected. This was very dangerous

after seven days of no sleep. There is a time for this kind of introspec-
tion, but now wasn't the time. I knew I would be attacked when I was
at my lowest point. Again Veena came back for a moment,

"Don't leave," she whispered.

She held on to me like I was all there was between her and total
darkness. Then I made a decision from my soul, a place deeper than the
karma I still had to work out, a decision that I had always been afraid
of, knowing I could never turn back from it, I would never be the same.
But this was the woman I truly loved and if she died, I would want to
die also. For myself I never would have gone so far. It took the life of
my beloved to be threatened, for me to unleash all the powers I had
trained for, but held back from my whole life. I went downstairs and
pulled together all my long years of training. I used my yoga to relax
and re-nourish myself. Centering in my own body, I consciously
invoked, for the first time, the deathless, fearless, revengeless, timeless,
unconquerable personality, with all the powers available to a mature
yogi. I bypassed the 'cloud of separation', and fully incarnated my
whole presence into this world.

✳ ✳ ✳

The sun was just sinking beneath the horizon as I came out of
meditation. I walked upstairs and talked directly to Carissa, telling her
that the three ringed circus was over, and Veena was going to the doctor, her two boyfriends and the herbalist had to leave. Carissa came
back to herself and I was able to *think* the rest of them out of the house.
Not able to release my anger because of the way it affected Veena, I was
learning some new skills. Veena had been gone completely for four days
now, never sleeping, in constant movement, and urinating on herself.
Even though Carissa was stretched to the breaking point, her great love
for her sister took over, and I was amazed at how quickly she came back
to life and took care of her Veena. She cleaned her bed every few hours,
put her in the bath and bathed her, brushed her hair, made sure she was
dressed nicely, cooked and fed her. Carissa was a very strong young
women, with a wonderful giving heart, but still, she was young and
started to fracture under the strain. That night it was only Veena,
Carissa and myself in the house. I was sitting in my normal spot at the
foot of Veena's bed when around 1 a.m. Carissa came into the room terrified. She was starting to see demons and was seeing and experiencing
what her sister was going through. I was alone, and now both of them

were lost! But I felt danger and didn't dare take my attention off Veena. Carissa put her hands on my shoulder and I took one of them and stroked her palm. I mentally told her that she was OK, and that she was a very strong and wonderful person. Carissa and I were becoming closer friends through all this, and in her trust of me, she immediately rallied and found her bright calm center that she normally was. The next thing I did was to create a ball of golden white light around the whole house. I sat in posture as Veena tossed on the bed and Carissa laid quietly by my side. About 2 a.m. I felt the ball of energy being probed, then suddenly it was being pressed in upon us. I sat still in a state of *knowing* nothing could enter. That was my only weapon, the willingness to give my life, and with that, the *knowing* that I could not be defeated, and the stopping of any thoughts contrary to that. But they came anyway, I felt the anger, the horror, the demons of all ages of history, enraged and smashing against the ball of light. The walls of the house creaked, pictures moved, the curtains started shivering, it felt like the house would explode under the pressure. I sat still as they came in droves of thousands throughout the night, the rage of ages. I saw a world where evil and misery where the natural state; grief, pain and joylessness, a universal decree from beings whose joy was terror and calamity. Monstrous swarms pressed a noxious hum into the ball. I read epics of horror in the agonized nerves of twisted vile creatures, driven in agonizing passion for blood and death. They chanted sounds that made the mind begin to love what the spirit hated, arrogant princes of torture who despised the sun, darting tongues of deafening acid mantras lusting to annihilate all beings. Through the night they came to do battle, but were met with silence, until finally, the force that drove them all, appeared. A brooding nameless nothing! A presence, yet not a presence. A swarm of fear because it knew it's existence depended solely upon the attention that Humans gave to It; no existence of it's own, without that attention, It would not be. It stayed a long time, sitting on the ball, watching for an opening, and in the heat of the pressure, anything I knew as myself dissolved into energy. I became a doorway in time, the point of Now in which they all tried to pass through into the future. The frequencies of energies, the colors which I had now become, automatically changed to meet whatever tried to pass through, neutralizing any sliver foul odor into my own Delight. Those that held at the threshold became more enraged. I did not hate them or condemn or fear them, I simply sat still, breathing. At sunrise their feeling and color changed, they now came just to touch the ball of light rather than try to crash through it. Then it stopped, so suddenly that I almost collapsed. Veena was awake, but perfectly still. Carissa was sound asleep.

That day the boy friends and herbalist called, and again tried to stop Carissa and I from taking Veena to the doctor. But Carissa was strong as steel, and to my never ending astonishment of theses two sisters, she was humorously polite to them as she clearly took control. We made it to the doctor only because Carissa was now awake and taking responsibility too, and with her gentle humor, keeping me together. The doctor prescribed strong knock out pills and by the afternoon Veena was sleeping. Nine days had past since I first walked into their house, and I had only about six hours of sleep in that whole period, but still felt I could not let the shield down. When Veena awoke the next day, I somehow knew she needed to see her mother, and asked if she wanted me to call her in France before I left. She wept and said, yes. When Carissa's old boyfriend found out that I was trying to call the mother, again, he and the doctor tried to interfere. Veena had many bad fights with her mother, and they all thought I was mad for wanting to call her. But Carissa, though tired and scared, was so happy to see her sister back, she supported the decision. I had met the mother only once for about two minutes many months earlier, but I remembered making good eye contact with her and saw a very wonderful being, in spite of all the stories I had heard about her. Veena knew what she wanted, and that was that.

Veena slept for the next two days and nights. Carissa and I both talked to her parents in France and they asked me to stay in the house with her and said they would come as soon as possible. The mother showed up late the next evening. I met her at the door and tried to assure her that the worst was over. She wanted to wake Veena but I wouldn't let her until I told her the story, at least the parts I felt she could handle. I was very firm that whatever problems she had with her daughter, they had to end now. Part of the pressure that had set Veena off had to do with their fights, and being cut off from the family before she was ready to leave. I would not wake her until I was sure there would be no fights. It was a very awkward situation, telling the mother what she could or couldn't do in her own home, but Veena's well being came first, and I was not willing to take a chance till the mother understood the severity of what had happened. But her mother was wonderful in this awkward situation, gracious and centered, and because of her I started to let go of my grip. Another day went by and I felt Veena awaken. She was groggy and exhausted, but back with us, at least most of her. Her mother and Carissa bounded into the room and sat on the bed, all three holding each other. I stood in the doorway and now with all three of the women from this family together, I saw the most beautiful soft blue light came from the center of them. The light spread out, moving like chiffon in a slight breeze, and filled the entire house, replacing, or rather filling the ball I had put in place. I backed out of the room, knowing that this was some women's mystery that I was not a part of, and walked down the stairs knowing it was over. I sat on the couch and broke into tears. Carissa came down the stairs and put her arms around me, and with my head on her shoulder, I broke down and let go of all the fears that I could not allow myself to feel for the past nine days, and I slept.

✳ ✳ ✳

Veena very slowly and gently pulled herself back into this world. I took her outside everyday and had her walk barefoot on the grass, getting her to ground herself and find her physical balance. She still acted very strange and on a couple of occasions I had to show her mother how to relate to her so Veena wouldn't get upset. Her mother, an exceptional woman, was always gracious, and I saw a great healing take place for her also, as she nursed her daughter back to health. Because she and her husband traveled so much when Veena was young, it looked like they were bonding for the first time. When the father came, it was a much easier situation, because now the mother knew the ropes, and she could show him what needed to be done. After fifteen days, I finally left the house and went home to finish my recordings.

I came to visit Veena every day, and we were in love. Veena asked me to help the rest of her family heal too, from what I didn't know. I did not feel comfortable with this, but she was still not completely stable and I didn't want to upset her by saying no. I began to deeply admire Veena's parents as we had many nights of deep discussions, interspersed with the most wonderful classical music created by Carissa and her father playing together. They shared with me many of their family hurts and pains, and I learned much about the depth of human love as I watched the parents interact with each other. They had a remarkable relationship, and I often laughed as they openly argued with each other as if they were high-school sweethearts who had just met. Everyone seemed to accept that Veena and I were going to be together, and she was happy that she now had a man that could sit and be with her parents. But I still remembered the feeling that I would have to give her up, and over the next few weeks, I began to understand why. As she slowly came back, she finally told the horrible truth of what had happened to her. She described wonderful heaven worlds, then as I had suspected, coming back into her normal consciousness, she fell through a door to some dark hidden memories. For the first time, she saw that when they were very young, she and Carissa had been dropped off at the house next door for baby-sitting. Unknown to their parents, the neighbors were into some kind of Satanism. They had terrified and sexually molested Veena, while showing her cut up animals, sticking them in her face and telling her that if she ever told, they would kill her sister and parents just like these animals. Carissa only had memories of lying in bed with the man, but not much else, and Veena psychically wouldn't let her go to that place. Somehow Veena had taken all the memory into herself, and in some way saved her sister. In the world of mystics, this is not uncommon. Very advanced souls can actually take on another's suffering. The parents were shocked, and I came back to the house to be with them for many following days. Was it true? Was she just making it up in her mind? The torture of doubt is one of the weapons of the Satanic craft. I told them that at this point we had to support Veena's story. The doubt could rip them all apart, and one thing was for sure, after what Carissa and I had seen, nothing seemed beyond possibility. Veena worked her magic, and convinced her parents that she was OK now, and that was all that mattered. But now I understood why I would lose her. As Veena had done for her sister, now I would have to do for her whole family. With me around they could not close the wound. I would be a constant reminder. All of this was part of the first exorcism I had started with her, and I had to take responsibility for transmuting the energies and memories I had opened the door to; I had to complete the healing. I had only read in the Tantrik text that you could actually pull the memories from someone and seal the door for them, leaving them in a Now state. It is not unlike western hypnotism, making a subject forget or remember something. I remember my teacher saying, "It is not hard to do, because people don't really want to remember unpleasant things anyway." Now I had to follow it through to the end, because these wonderful people had trusted me. Also, I knew that Veena had not really made a choice to be with me. When she came back to her normal self, I was just there and we were together. I knew she had not put together a new ego that was capable of making such a serious decision as choosing a life mate. Knowing I would have to give her up, I had merged my soul with her to pull her through the black hole, now I had to go further in love than I had ever known. Now I had to let her go so she could close the door on what had happened to her. She had to find her own self confidence, and define her new self, by herself.

Another month went by, and I saw that Veena was stable enough to go out more into the world. I suggested to her parents to send her to a good workshop on communication skills that I had once attended. In the workshop she now also saw that she needed to be alone. That was the last time I saw her for many years. We created some arguments over the phone and I even fought with her mother, but I knew it was just so we could make a break from each other. I felt that if I got angry enough, it wouldn't hurt as much. It was a stupid tactic and only made everyone feel worse. We sadly said goodbye and she moved back to France. It was strange how I could feel a great joy in my soul that she would heal, but still my ego tried to hold on, and without her, it died a slow painful death over the next few years.

I later found out that during those nine days there had been world wide spiritual celebrations taking place. There are many calendars other then our Roman calendar, and one of the most looked to by our generation is the Mayan calendar. It seems that on this week, a galactic cycle had ended, and a new one began. In the lore of their calendar it was the ending of thousands of years of the dark cycle and the beginning of the cycle of light. At the same time there was a celebration called '11-11' signifying an opening for souls to communicate through the dark influences and connect with light. I haven't much knowledge of these calendars, but it was ironic to me that this celebration happened on the very night that Veena, Carissa and myself were alone in the house. Thousands of people all around the globe were participating in joyous chanting and circular dances, while we three held the line.

Chapter 7

The Return

During the first year after Veena left for France, I took to the road again. Sometimes I felt like the saddest creature on earth, but forced myself to continue the Tantrik breathing practices to keep some kind of positive force field around me. Many times out on the open highways, driving alone, I felt the pressure from those same negative entities I had seen in Veena's house, and had many strange happenings and images of crashing my van on some lonely highway. But after that night at Veena's, I knew I had won, it was just a matter of 'keep moving on', and while driving the wide open spaces of Arizona and Texas at night under the stars, I had plenty of time and space to think about my life. Because of Veena, I had completely opened, and for a few days, become my future self. But I also understood that there were no short cuts, there was still a path that had to be walked, and much more to understand about the 'cloud of separation.' In the spacious desert I let my mind expand till it encompassed the whole winding string of my life, and I knew what Life was asking me was to learn to love all beings with the same selflessness and passion I had loved Veena. After unleashing the fullness of my Self to protect Veena, I knew there could be no turning back.

Damn! Tricked again!

I felt sad at losing Veena, but also confident, and could appreciate the humor in how I stumbled through my life, leading to what I didn't know, but I was always amazed. And to walk around in a state of amazement, well, that's not too bad. 'Keep moving soldier', that was the only answer that came in my nightly meditations under the stars. Learning something new was not hard— giving up the past was, and I knew it was going to take a long discipline to release all the energies, thoughts and feelings that had opened up in Veena's exorcism. In considering how to remain responsible for the success of the exorcism, I perceived that I must continue to pray daily for Veena and her family, and I would become celibate, and continue this until I knew she was completely healed. So much of the devastating cloud of pain on this planet, is caused by sexual perversion, and the only way something as damaging as rape can be healed, is to go back to that state of being before puberty, before we even thought of sex. From this place one can relax and re-birth into healing of their sexual traumas. I knew that Veena could not set such rules for herself. She was young and wanted to go out to explore, she was just awakening to her sexuality. So I decided to create this healing space in myself, so that when she did turn her mind and spirit towards me, she would at least be able to touch that place of healing and take from it whatever she needed. I knew that I still had a great influence on her, and we were very telepathically linked. I also knew that if I told anybody what I was doing, they would think me absolutely crazy, but none-the-less, this was the course I saw laid out before me. What I never suspected, was how healing it would become for me also.

I drove the back roads for a long time, then ended up heading toward New York City when I heard that an executive at Sony Records had listened to my music and liked it. I met this young women and her boyfriend and was invited to stay at her house while she looked into trying to get me a contract; as long as I had control of the music, I'd go for it. It ended in disaster. What a crazy world these record people lived in! The boyfriend had been cheating on her, and decided he was going to leave her for his new girlfriend. One day he took his things and left me there alone while she was on a business trip, not even telling her he was leaving. When she came home, she went crazy, and in her bizarre alcoholic thinking, somehow I ended up as the cause of her loss. At this point it just seemed like another common experience in my life; I laughed it off and acknowledged that I had no clue how to relate to these people. I considered going back to a monastery I had lived in many years before, it was only 100 miles away, and I headed in that direction. I took off from New York and camped in my van in the beautiful New England Fall. By myself, in my own space, I felt freedom and confidence, but out in the world with people, I felt a sadness that I just could not release, and many people seemed to be afraid of me. One of my favorite activities was walking; cities, in the forest, beaches, it didn't matter, I walked many miles every day. I am large in stature and found that people would be frightened as I walked towards them, it didn't take a genius to know why. The newspaper headlines in America were constantly filled with stories of murder and rape; everyone seemed to know that America was the murder capital of the world, and fear pervaded the streets. Civilizations are built on war and killing, lies being sadly accepted as our way of existence. The unrelenting media pumps out these stories that increase peoples feeling of powerlessness to affect change, and according to statistics, one can become a victim at any time. I remembered that it wasn't like this when I was younger, people weren't afraid like this, at least in western civilization. No one was afraid to walk in the streets, even just thirty years ago. But while we weren't paying attention, the world had become a darker and sadder place, and now with the many breakthroughs in communications in the last decades, our sinking situation had become common knowledge. Violence is constantly spoon fed to us through movies and TV, then reflects back at us in the news. People expect governments to lie, and even the religions are now suspected of corruption. Pedophile priests; the Catholic church support of the killing in Vietnam; Moslems and Jews who think they have the rightful duty to kill each other. Everyone is right, no one is humble enough to say they are wrong. So much hopelessness in people, so many trying to find where they could turn for the Truth in these days, but instead, they became subjected to mindless entertainment to numb the feeling of hopelessness. I felt all this cloud pass through me, and even though I had never hurt anybody since football days, still I felt the guilt of being human. Any feeling Human Being feels a vague sense of guilt for what we have allowed to happen in this world. Yet with no clear solution or understanding of how, or when it happened, or what to do about it, the guilt sits on us like a dark cloud and peers at us through the gaps of our 'pursuit of happiness.' I walked down the streets of many cities, and when I saw someone coming I would try and send them vibrations not to be afraid, "I am a decent person, it is OK," I tried to project out. But it rarely worked, and I could see the fear all around them.

The monastery didn't feel like the place to deal with this at this time in my life, and instead I chose to jump right into the fire and returned to New York City; I fell deep into sadness while walking the streets, not knowing anyone and feeling this collective fear in humanity. I began to walk in constant silent prayer:

Oh Creator, what have we done? Why does it have to be this way? I can't even find the thread to grasp, to un-tie this knot... Help us...

On that particular morning I turned a corner and ran into the beautiful St. Patrick's Cathedral in central Manhattan, and entered just in time for the noon mass. I sat down and became transfixed at what paraded in front of my mind's eye. It had been more than twenty-five years since entering a Catholic church, but now with as many years of intensive meditation and yoga training under my belt, I entered a totally different world than the churches of my childhood. The whole building was alive with activity, I could sense and sometimes see angelic presences all over the building. Some were bright, some rather dark, some in quiet repose, others watched everything with great interest. They mixed together, it was as if everyone, every creature was welcome in this house of Christ.

Seeing in this way was becoming natural to me. As a good musician can hear the higher and lower harmonics of a chord, I had imperceptibly, through time, learned to see the higher and lower harmonics of sight. In a vast electromagnetic spectrum, we train ourselves to register only a tiny band of what is all around us, in order to feel coherent with society. But because I had spent much more time outside of society's constraints than in them, I did not feel the need to narrow my senses. It seemed the Church had tried to remind people of these other possibilities, with all their statues and pictures of angelic beings, but they settled for a limp belief rather than solid experience of other dimensions. I'm sure I must have looked like some crazed fool as I sat there staring at the ceiling with my eyes wide in awe. I registered different waves of tension running through the Cathedral, that I was able to identify as the different currents of thought of the many different levels of awareness and spiritual realization of the people there. I felt at ease but not completely at home, as there didn't seem to be anybody else seeing what I was seeing, and I could find no place to completely commune with the people around me. I sat calmly and observed the mass.

The Vatican II council had made some changes since I had left the Church so many years ago, and they had added to the mass something I had never seen. Before the communion, the people turned to each other, acting as Christ, to wish each other the "Peace of Christ." Not the peace the world gives, the temporary peace of having a fat bank account and other such matters, but rather the peace that comes from knowing that whatever condition you are in, whatever station in life, you are loved and accepted right now as you are. I turned to an old Mexican woman behind me. She looked at me straight in the eyes and from the depth of her being she wished me the Peace of Christ. I was aghast! Two human beings, unafraid, not even knowing each other, expressing and accepting love! I turned to a young man, and the same feelings were there, then turned to a little girl who looked at me unafraid, shook my hand and wished me peace!

I have seen and done many strange things in this world, some people would call them miracles, but I am unashamed to say that this was
the most miraculous thing that I had ever experienced. Perfect
strangers unafraid, expressing something from their souls to each other.
In the dark world in which I walked, this one act in the church became
a fountain of warmth and light to me. It quite literally gave me new
Life! I changed right there on the spot! I felt connected to a huge body
of brothers and sisters, many who would give their life for me and I for
them. What had inspired such courageous love? I looked up to the
image of Jesus on the cross, but now it had a whole different meaning
to me than I had ever been taught. There he was in His silent defiance
saying to the world: "You can beat me, insult me, whip me, hang me on
a cross, you can throw all the dirt of the world at me. But there is one
thing you can not do. You can not stop me from loving."

That was God's message to us. Not "Look at what depraved sinners you are", but rather "look at how magnificent you are." This is the
power, beauty and potential of what a human is. God showed us
through Jesus, a Human Being, what magnificent creatures we are.
What wondrous Love and ingenious creativity and healing lies in the
depths of all of us, hiding behind our negative self images. People came
to the mass for many different reasons, and what I saw in this Cathedral
was a Church in the midst of great change and upheaval; some still
came out of habit, some seeking salvation, but many others were there
for no other reason than to celebrate. They had gathered to celebrate
and honor Love— that love did exist in this world, between God and
mankind, and each other. That is where these people wanted to put
their attention, because whatever one puts their attention on increases.

There had been nothing in my vision telling me to go back to the
Catholic Church; I found the presence of Christ in many different
ways, and saw the face of Christ before being involved in any Christian
system. But to be with other people who honored love before all things,
and who sincerely prayed for "peace on earth, good will towards all
beings", touched me in places I had never felt before. I could not
remember the last time I had felt sacred joy with a group of humans,
and I came back again and again. I had trouble listening to the old
authoritarian liturgy, it was not consistent with may own experience of
Christ, and I felt some of my old anger at the Church begin to swell.
But I realized that my anger was at the *political church* and not at the *real
Church*, which was starting to unfold as a great mystery before me. In
meditation I held my vision of Jesus, but as before, it floated above me.
But now, all of a sudden, the cloud of turmoil, separating the vision

from my everyday experience, became more visible and easier to get a handle on. No matter how I had tried to escape, my destiny was intertwined with the Church's, as was everyone on the planet, because the Church had influenced science, politics, and even controlled time; they had created their own calendar, a huge feat of hypnotism to bring the world in line with their influence, for good or bad. The cloud contained much turbulent history to be unraveled, but more for me personally, it contained my anger and distrust for the Church, and any authority that tried to scare or control me. Rightly so, but the cloud also contained the whole history of feelings emotions, courageousness and excesses, generated by the struggle of an unfolding Self through all of history, not just mine, but all of humanity's. Now that's a big sack to carry around! I clearly saw that I could no longer, and didn't want to walk in this world with that kind anger and discursive feelings towards anyone or anything. So this was before me: I had to go back into the Church to learn to forgive. Only this would dissolve the cloud that stood between me and the full vision of Jesus. I was coming back because I hated the Church. An interesting conversion to say the least, but none-the-less, humorously consistent with my life.

I started my journey back across America, stopping at many Catholic Churches along the way. I was fascinated by the variety and flux of feelings I found in these churches. Older priests, who were bored to tears, came out and preached about the reality of Hell, only to be followed in the next Mass by a younger priest filled with love, contradicting everything the previous priest had said. This was mostly in the larger churches in major cities. It didn't seem to be a matter of age either. I saw many younger priests with dark tortured auras, and older ones with the smiles of newborn children. I also stopped at many smaller Christian churches. Some were friendly, others down right sinister. The preachers talked way too much for my taste, and many times I heard them condemn people for some reason or other, using the Bible as their executioner's ax; I even heard them put down the Catholic Church. Not that I cared about defending the Catholic Church at this point, but it seemed to me that many of these preachers worshipped conflict more than Love. I have never heard any Catholic service where anyone was talked ill of, even though I knew the same kinds of feelings were just below the surface. But at least in the Catholic Church I could get moments of silence, and I didn't really care about what someone else might be thinking; I wanted communion with Christ, not ill feelings and conflict. There are two ways of being a better person. One is to really work at it, and the cowards way is to compare yourself to someone else and judge yourself to be better. Too many times I saw the Bible as an instrument of bludgeoning, mixing up verses to add credibility to the preacher's own personal point of view. At first I wanted to say something, but then I remembered my time with the Yogi. People are not victims, they want to be where they are or they would leave. Discernment is a great and valuable lesson, so why should I deprive anyone of the opportunity to learn it. I took it all in— thinking, sifting and praying as I made my way west.

※　※　※

Through many years of being exposed to different religions, I had tried to find the truth in all of them, but in none did I ever feel what I felt when the old men and women who had been faithfully praying for decades, turned to me and offered peace. This is what really kept me returning to the Church. Without this feeling of connection, the taking of the Host would have meant very little to me. It was the people who were the Church to me, not the buildings, or the clergy as an entity in itself, but the people who lived Christ, each in their own unique way. If not for this, it would have been a tangled maze of thoughts and impressions to work through. If I merely listened to the words, everyone had something different to say. I read articles in the major Catholic papers and magazines that seemed like a lot of slick lawyer talk, long pompous articles by overly educated priests, arguing about if they should move the tabernacle from the alter or should they have female alter servers. All these publications were created by religious educators who tried to explain it all by appealing to the intellect. I even saw that many of the publications had lowered themselves into using slick neuro-linguistic programming in their use of words and phrasing, the same techniques used by advertisers and political campaigners to sway peoples opinions without them suspecting how it was done. This angered me, but many of the parishioners had some kind of magic, and it seemed like infinite patience. I went to board meetings for two different churches, and heard many times, "I only come for the people" " if it wasn't for the people, I wouldn't be part of the church." People were displeased with the structure and hierarchy, but I saw they had a very Christ-like attitude in their dissatisfaction—love and respect people and they will finally come around. I also met other more radical groups who were not content to wait for the hierarchy to come around. But whatever the flavors of the many different temperaments were, still everyone wanted change. Whatever the Church was or did in the past, was just that, the past. Now it had been handed down to our generation, what were we going to do with it? This seemed to be the attitude of almost all the many churches I visited.

The modern educated person of today is not willing to be told "shut up and do as you are told", they want to take responsibility and jump in. The hierarchy on the other hand, is concerned that the purity of the teachings be kept intact. This was my point of entrance into the controversy, and where I knew I needed to work. The words and doctrines of religions had changed and clashed with other religious doctrines all through time, religion had killed more people than anything in history. How did the Church move from the wonderful, gentle St. Frances, to Franciscan and Dominican monks horribly torturing people to death in the Inquisition? What did all this have to do with Jesus? I saw It was the *political church's* doctrine of obedience to authority—the very thing that Jesus had warned against— "Call no man on earth your father". He taught that everything you needed was already within you, and must come pouring out. He said, the things He did, we could do even greater. It seemed obvious to me that the first thing that we have to include, is the realization of our oneness with the Father, but the dogmas of Christianity never emphasized this at all. The *political church* never really taught the self-liberating message of Christ, that we were all one with the Father, and now, modern educated people were more informed of all the excesses of cruelty in Church's history. Millions of men, women and children, murdered in the name of Christ. And yet the *political church* still refused to acknowledge it or ask forgiveness. If a criminal commits a crime against you and does not feel sorry for it, and even feels they have the authority to do it again if they want to, how can you trust them? I heard this talk time and time again and felt myself seduced into the fight. To think that religions can't be possessed by evil just because everyone talks about God and goodness is the opiate of the masses that Karl Marx once spoke of. Possession is a very subtle process; priests of good intention, religious scholars and the many lay people who blindly listened, had unknowingly become the Pharisees of our day. They could not see that their intellect had overridden their common sense any better than the Pharisees of Jesus' time. They had become possessed with the dark spirit of "pride of intellect" and "argument", and I certainly knew something about that kind of possession. When Jesus said, "Cast not pearls before swine," he was talking about the intellect. It was not in his nature to call someone a swine in the derogatory sense that we mean it today. A swine was considered a very intelligent animal, and it also referred to the way they put their heads down and ate what was right in front of them, never looking right or left. Very intellectual people are easy to control and possess, because the intellect can never find any permanent solution from controversy. Many Christians were so obsessed with their particular causes and viewpoints; they had absolutely lost the very peace that was supposed to be the gift of Christ. Because of my own tendency to love argument, I became very sensitive to this issue, and watched these dynamics in myself, as I exposed myself to more opinions. I saw that many Christians had a belief that Christ was the opposite of evil, which assumes there must be a battle between the two. But if Christ was involved in battle, then where would we go to experience Peace, and even though Jesus taught, "Resist not evil", it seemed to be running against our very genetic promptings to do so.

I watched all these thoughts and feelings move through me like storm clouds. Often I wanted to run from all this churning; it seemed I had become conditioned by New Age thinking (it all has to feel good), more than I had been aware of. But after a few months of toughing it out, I began to see the Church as a giant teaching laboratory, and I jumped into my work with enthusiasm. It was an ingenious teaching mechanism for being in the world, in fact it was really a microcosm of the world. There were good influences and bad influences. There were people who loved, and others who only cared about control. There was so much contradiction in the attitudes from one church to the other, that I was constantly thrown back upon my own inner resources to find the answers. I became aware of every word that was said in the ceremonies and sermons, every feeling. Because the Church had been a part of my childhood it was too easy to do everything half asleep, like a trained robot, to just say the words and not pay attention, as children do when they are placed into something that bores them. But now after meditation training, I tried to bring an overview of awareness into the whole process of the rituals, and my thoughts and feelings while participating. I wanted to see what words and tricks were being used by the darker elements of the Church to control and program me into unconscious obedience, and also I wanted to see and feel the real Christ that I knew from my vision. Nothing slipped by, not one word, not a glance, not one thought. It was all there in the Church, the dark and the light, and it all finally came down to my own personal decision of which side was I going to choose to relate to; if I didn't learn discernment here, I wouldn't stand a chance out in the world.

The whole Church now became my Guru and teacher. For one

year I came to Mass everyday, taking communion, listening, pondering. I frequented two very different churches so I would learn more. One was a richer parish of highly educated people, run by Paulist priests. They were an order indigenous to America, and saw themselves as Vatican II reformers, and many also worked in movies and various communications. They seemed much more modern and ahead of their time. They had taken down the altar rail, signifying that there was no more separation between priests and people in celebration of the Mass; we were now all responsible for creating the celebration. They freely said "Be Christ to each other." Though their outer form seemed more progressive, still, very few people came to the council meetings, and those I talked with said they craved for more "true deeper religious experience." Not faith, but experience. This was the predominant feeling of this parish. Being more educated and wealthier, simple doctrine and liturgy was no longer enough for these people; they wanted something more. The other parish was poorer, mostly Mexican and Filipino, and these priest were very Papist orientated. There was a lot of talk about authority, and this parish had more of the Old Catholic vibration. There was even an old Monsignor in this parish who would scowl at me when I saw him. So this is where I ended up doing most of my inner work. I decided not to run from my argumentative nature, and instead, elected to take this guy on, and he me; if I was going to get anywhere I had to jump right into the middle of the cloud and work from there.

The Monsignor was close to retirement, a very formidable personality and didn't seem to care what people thought of him. Other priests I could intimidate or 'nice guy' my way through the conversation, but this old bull was fearless, and I knew he could read my every thought, as I could him. For months I sat in the back of his church and boiled through my changes; this guy could really push my buttons. To those around me I looked like a nice, quiet, devoted Catholic, but in my mind I was in conflict with just about everything he said, and in the chambers of my mind, I blasted him in long fiery dialogues. He always seemed to know when I was silently lambasting him, and he would pen me with his icy stare. To me, he represented everything that was wrong with the religion in this world, but after many months I was finally able to have a few days peace by successfully ignoring him, and continued on with my daily routine.

One day in the midst of one of my internal dialogues, I suddenly stopped and put a simple question to myself, "What have I come here for? Did I come to fight or worship?" I could never have imagined how such a simple question could become such a huge epiphany, for I knew that this simple question encompassed the whole of my internal and outer life in this world. I had very little control of what the outside world was thinking and doing, but I could control what I was thinking and doing and how I reacted to the outside world. Even though I knew this, still, I constantly found myself lost in the *seduction of conflict*, as if the whole history of this earth was about fighting and turmoil. It pushed me, goaded me and dared me to act upon my feelings; it was the most uncomfortable pressure, like a hot wind passing through my very genes. Again, I found myself standing as a doorway in the midst of time, as I had experienced on that long horrible night at Veena's house. That encounter showed me the way to meet this challenge, by staying still, not judging, condemning or reacting, but this time my resolve was thoroughly tested, as this uncomfortable tempering went on for a year. My whole spiritual task became to stand in the doorway, the whole history of conflict pushing at my back, trying to seduce me into it's reasoning, and all I had to do was stand there and not let it pass through me into my future. "What had I come here for, to fight or to commune and worship?" My whole destiny hung on that question for a year. If I had not earned an understanding of how that psychic pressure burned through the channels in my mind and body, where those promptings from history could take hold, I surely would have gone mad; without the world's conditioned receptor sights, the tendencies have nothing to latch on to, and dissolve from lack of attention.

One morning I sat in the church, lost in thought, as the Mass went on around me:

> *If I convince myself that it is OK to be angry...(righteous anger)...I'm doing the same thing as everybody else...Now how many jerks have you seen that tell themselves that their anger is righteous?...And they all say it is because they are trying to help the world...man I can get really angry about those yahoo's...I'd like to tell them where to get off the train...But if do that then I am angry and in conflict...So that means I am angry and conflicted in order to help the world?... Man, what the hell are you going to give the world if you are all twisted up inside?...*

I let out a couple of laughs at how ridiculous this was. The Monsignor was in the middle of his sermon. He stopped and glared viciously at me; everyone felt the tension. I glared back, out of habit, but the question had taken control of me:

*No, this conflict isn't what I want, this isn't why I have
come...God, is this all there is to life...show me more or take my life
...*

The Monsignor finished his sermon, then walked to the alter to
continue the mass. Suddenly I was absorbed into the ceremony. I felt a
connection with thousands of beings, in many different dimensions; we
were all connected together, celebrating this Mass. I felt a tremendous
strength and force come into me, as I became one with a huge body of
living faith; amazing minds and selfless courage, all this was there for
anyone to tap into. The Christ was no longer just Jesus; it was a mas-
sive presence that had come to celebrate a loving union with each other,
a celebration that stretched through all history. The Monsignor lifted
the Host, and for me, time stopped. I saw, with a tunnel vision, straight
to the Host. All around this tunnel I saw the history of the world: the
wars and killings, the hate and terror of religions, armies clashing, the
witch burnings, the whole bloody mess intertwined, the turbulence of
all our human history. But in the middle, down at the end of this tunnel was the Host—Gold and White—It was Now, and never had been
touched by all the drama that swirled around it. The pure intention of
God, to love all, had never been touched by all the bloody history. Even
when there were corrupt Popes and a possessed hierarchy, still the
Christ had been kept pure and connected to Earth by some pure saint
in some hidden monastery, by many wonderful people and beings who
kept It alive in their very beings. Whatever had happened, the purity of
Christ (the Word) was in tact through all ages, and I dissolved in communion with the millions who had given lifetimes to make sure it had
been passed down purely; I whispered their thoughts and prayers.
When I finally came out of my reverie, the church was empty.

A month later the old Monsignor retired. I prepared myself in the
same way I had done many times before for the Sikh ceremonies while
in India: cleansing, devotion, and attention. From the same spot I had
sat in while seeing the vision, I watched this man say his Mass, and
thought of all the many years he had given to the service of Church and
to the people. I knew the difficulties of the spiritual path, and respected anyone who sincerely tried to know more of God, even if I didn't
agree with them. In the Monsignor's face, I saw that he had given his
best in a way that he believed to be right. I did not have to agree with
him; if he thought he had some authority over me, it was his problem,
but that had nothing to do with my personal experience of Christ. The
world would be a very boring place if everyone was the way we thought

they should be, and instead of focusing on my differences with him, today I saw only his devotion. This was the marvel of Jesus' teachings— Forgiveness and Compassion; the bottom line was to truly love each other. The ever fresh, living "Word" is the doorway, and none can go around, no matter how long it takes, we all must pass through and be bathed in that love. I received communion from the Monsignor, and for the first time in a year, we smiled at each other. Neither of us could deny the love for Jesus that we saw in each other. We expressed it in our own unique ways, but still, at this doorway, we were joined. For the first time, I walked up and sat in the front rows, feeling the devotion of the people all around me. In spite of our dark human history, we celebrated and gave thanks that Love was real and existed in our world. Now that's where I want to keep my attention! This was a day of rebirth and return!

✳   ✳   ✳

We mature in life as we learn discernment, by seeing the good and the dark side of the world, then taking responsibility for our choices. This is a tremendous spiritual exercise, and to see how both sides, light and dark, work together for the unfolding of the individual, is the perfection of discernment. Many leaders of the major faiths have not had a real experience of God, the kind that leaves no doubt, and in their pain and dissatisfaction, they cannot believe that anybody else can have a true experience of God either, except the officially declared saintly souls, long since dead. This element in all the religions, still feels it needs to control through guilt and manipulation, and this has paralyzed manly people with doubt. For instance a Catholic takes the Host into their own bodies. Christ becomes our own blood, bone and flesh. Communion means to become one with. We are the body of Christ, yet everyday we start the mass by saying we are sinners, and even the children are still taught they are sinners. If people did not think they were sinners, then what would keep them coming back to the church for salvation? With all the expenses and vast amount of property holdings to support, this is a big worry and the point of compromise in presenting the true teachings of Christ. Many church leaders know this, feeling the dichotomy and guilt because of it. This feeling in turn pervades the 'flock.' The pain of doubt is amplified because it is pushed down to subconscious realms in favor of the outer appearance of spirituality. The result is the daily horrific headlines, that will not let society believe in their own self worth, and that keeps them flocking to the churches. And around and around it goes. But in truth, the inconsistencies are there to make us 'work' our faith, to strive for understanding, to put time and effort into it. The pressure of doubt, if taken in the right way, activates us into higher dimensions of understanding of how life works, and the Church's job is to try and provide the opportunity for that, sometimes in ways that they don't even understand.

The old Monsignor represented to me, the 'old church', the old way of thinking. What I learned by my interaction with him was that I really did love and respect him, even though I didn't always agree with him. Respect is always more important than agreement; agreement can come later. I could argue forever about the historical Christ, what He said or didn't say, what his real intentions were for the Church, but if the argument is kept on the level of intellect, how could we possibly find a true answer that would satisfy everyone? What it finally comes down to is, do we have the actual visceral experience of Christ right Now. The Monsignor and I had met in a loving appreciation of each other, and that was real. I was becoming a consistently happy person, that was real. And the greatest miracle of all, when I walked down the street, people were no longer afraid of me. Whatever I had carried in my aura, that collective guilt of humanity, now was gone, and that was real. I was slowly and imperceptibly becoming the humor, lightness and joy of my vision of Jesus. Whoever the Monsignor was, whatever he had done or not done, that my limited viewpoint did not like, and I say again, he represented the whole past history of the church to me, still he had done his job. He had passed down the essence of the teachings in his own way, according to what he needed to do in his time. For me, it had worked, even the parts I had formerly judged as something bad or wrong, had all somehow worked to heal me. I had traveled many formal religious paths of the world, and ended a broken saddened human being. Now, in a silent communion of beings, that each in their own way, strived to be better human beings, I was experiencing "grace"— a consistent joy that had taped me on the shoulder, imperceptibly, somewhere beyond, or in between my formidable ego's effort to "attain" God. Who was I to say how it was supposed to happen.

All religions were eventually going to have to become democratic if they wanted to survive; the evolution of human intelligence was just evolving that way; all beings want to be free and self-governing, and anything that tries to go against evolution eventually falls. The form of things will change and change again, but without love, which gives trust in one's worthiness at the core, it will all end in failure. If the religions could not give this, if they could not adapt, then so be it, for truly, a belief in the Fall/Redemption scenario was not necessary to live a sacred life.

My cup was becoming full. In my present way of life, I could go no further. There was only one thing left to do. Let it flow over.

✳ ✳ ✳

Well that is a wonderful story, isn't it? Such a nice ending I almost hate to tell what happened next. I had become so involved in my own healing process that I had failed to take notice of the darker side of my fellow Catholics. Forgiveness is a tricky business it seems, not nearly as simplistic as I had supposed. I felt it easier to forgive when I could project an idealistic picture upon my antagonist, sugar coated with phrases like "we are all children of God", "we are all brother's and sister's." But as they say in the East "you can put white robes on a donkey, but it's still a donkey." What a dangerous and stupid thing to do—to idealistically think someone else's heart has had a change just because of one's own sincerity. As my mother had been shunned, so was I to have to learn this painful lesson. But what lesson was I learning?

One of my friends at church had heard of my healing work, and asked me to participate in a Mass for a young woman who was dying of cancer. This young schoolteacher, in her early 40's, was very popular and the church was packed. From the moment the priest stepped out on the altar, I felt a wave of sadness and resignation. This Mass was one of the worst displays of spineless lack of faith I had ever seen. Not one person in that church, not even the priest, had ever seemed to hear the words "Pray, believing it is done, and it will be done." I felt no joy, not even the possibility, that in Christ, all things were possible. The modern churchgoers had become brave soldiers ready to suffer, with a stiff upper lip, rather than the joy that opens a space allowing the possibility for anything to happen; rationality had won over faith. As I walked up to the altar for Communion, I looked at the young woman and we smiled at each other, and I knew this women did not have to die. Four days later, I was asked to go visit her in the hospital. I had seen people with cancer many times while studying at the Hippocrates Institute. I was sure this woman could cure herself, as I had seen many people do. She was vibrant and fun with a lean healthy body, but seemed to have no will of her own. She was a Catholic convert and fresh full of doctrine and dogma, the kind of personality who while desperately seeking approval, especially from the priest, still put on an air of strength and absolute faith. The room was filled with smiling faces including the priest who had said the Mass. The young woman stared at me, smiling in silence. She wanted to leave the hospital and go home but was talked into staying because her back hurt and she was told that she would get worse, so it was better that she stay. I normally would not attempt healing work with the room filled with people, but the women who had brought me insisted that I stay and try. The young women seemed very receptive to me, so I helped her through a series of movements for her lower spine. She immediately felt better, and I told her that she should stop taking the pain medication and she would probably be able to walk the next day, and she should go home if she wanted to. She looked at me as if I was her long lost savior, while the other people in the room started to feel uncomfortable. The fact that she could just leave without asking anyone's permission had never occurred to her. The priest and other guests in the room could not hide their anger at such impudence, but no word came out of them. I felt uncomfortable and wanted to leave but the young woman took me by my hand and quietly and innocently asked me, "Why am I dying?" While holding her hand, the impressions from her past started to fill me. It was nothing mysterious; I'd seen it all so many times before. The woman had been sexually abused while very young, had gone through a series of bad relationships, and though she was a fine looking and vibrant woman, she lived alone and was deeply saddened by this. Her faith was supposed to make it all better, but it didn't, so all she heard form her priest and friends was "this is all God's will, we must accept it." She held on to my hand and searched my eyes. I tried to speak quietly but the room was dead silent and she would not let me go. I spoke as quietly as I could.

"You are alone, and you have been alone for a long time" She nodded.

"It makes you feel like there is something wrong with you." She nodded again.

"You have been taught to believe that because Christ suffered, somehow suffering is holy"—"You have been taught to believe that your reward and joy will come after you die, so because you can find no happiness here, you are willing yourself to die."

She looked at me and nodded yes. I said,

"If this is what you want, then go home and die, God always loves you and supports you, but don't play games with yourself and pretend you don't know what you are doing."

She looked at me with relief and thankfulness that someone had talked so openly and truthful to her. The rest of the people in the room were silent with astonishment; the priest was fuming. No hoopla, no miracles, just simple truth and she was ready to go home. She asked if I would visit her at her home and I agreed to help her if she followed my instructions. Everyone became more alarmed, but the next morning she walked out of the hospital.

I had told her that she needed more time to herself right now, time to really examine her own thoughts and decide what she wanted to do, not what the doctor or priest or friends wanted her to do. When I arrived at her house it was a zoo. Friends gave her books to read, bottles of blessed holy water, various 'religious' paraphernalia, everyone was giving her advice, and the priest had told her friends to tell her, concerning me, "don't go the voodoo route", as if a priest with no faith wasn't the "voodoo route." One of the women had told me that people were going out to a place in the desert where an aberration of the 'Blessed Virgin' had appeared in the window of an office building; they were going to attain 'special blessings' for the 'dying' women. The women told me she had spoken to a doctor who said she needed to exercise and oxygenate her blood, and would I teach her the yogic breathing exercises that she had read about. I told her I would, but she had to clear her house of so many people, she needed her own psychic space and clearing to examine what was true for her and what was not, and I was beginning to feel that it was time to listen to my own advice. There was one young woman who brought her the Host everyday, who vehemently disliked me; she made long angry speeches how Christ was the only healer. When I taught the sick woman the breathing practices, using long drawn out sounds to focus the breath in different parts of the body, I was accused of showing her something that was Satanic. That was it for me. I sadly saw that the sick woman did not have the strength to say no to these people. She had no idea how being in their energy fields of doubt was tearing her down, and rather than have their lack of belief exposed, these people could not see that they would rather have the woman die, though on the surface everyone was icky sweet. Rather than experience the miracle of their own living flesh, the life force in their own breath, and the healing power of any loving human who was willing to suspend thinking and dogma long enough to connect with "Life in abundance", instead they put their focus on books, bibles, pictures of saints and any phenomena they hoped to be a real sign from God, as if that was the proof of the divine. Instead of experiencing God in the Sun, the air, the breath, and in the simple relationships with other humans, they searched for something outside themselves to fill their lack of faith, the more "spectacular" the better. They could not see how this cheapened life, as they openly or subconsciously judged humans to be less important than their 'sacred' icons; and I was Satan because I did not comply. All this noise and commotion went on, while no one wanted to see the simple truth that none of them had faith that she could be healed, or heaven forbid, she was never sick in the first place, just lonely and scared. They were too scared themselves to really fast and pray, Knowing the she was healed, because if it did not work, it would be another blow against their already teetering faith; it was safer to not try at all. But as long as they followed the rituals, it created a veneer of spirituality that did not require true self-examination. To admit that their religion did not help her plug her hole was too much to look at. It was better that she dies because it was "God's will", and many of them hoped I would too.

So this was how my return to the 'faith' ended. But I was not saddened, for it was a truer return; a return to myself, and a clear lesson of how I would end up if I didn't learn it— sad, lonely and dead. The young woman died just three weeks later. I forgave my past, but one cannot forgive a church or government or any other sort of group. A living relationship can only be with another individual. People, who give away a part of their spirit to a doctrine or a system or an outside authority over their souls, were not individuals, so there could be no relationship to lose. I decided to focus on rejoicing in the many individual friends I did have, rather than be sad about losing relationships that were never real in the first place. It left me with no opinion about the Catholic faith at all, nor any other group. I had friends who were Catholic who truly lived the faith, and friends of many other faiths who did too, but it did not matter to me what they called themselves, they lived in integrity and loving friendship towards all, and that was the crux of the matter. But it was the last time I was ever lulled into a hypnosis of open trust just because someone belonged to a 'group' that was supposedly spiritual. From this moment on I wanted to talk only to the soul, and not the conditioning of my fellow humans and myself. I still talked to the conditioning, but only to sooth it into knowing that perfect faith was it's true home.

Late that evening I fell asleep and dreamed of the Pope in all his pomp; his Cardinals and Bishops surrounded him. His voice boomed in the great hall,

"You will be excommunicated."

The words reverberated throughout the building. I stood my ground and answered back,

"I do not accept your excommunication from me. I forgive you. I love you, and I will never excommunicate myself from you."

Chapter 8

Service

I sat alone in the big house just outside of Austin, Texas and watched a beautiful thunderstorm slowly move across the sky. I had just finished a month on the road and was resting up for the big folk festival at Kerrville. Night was falling and the old mother cat that I was babysitting walked through her door with one of her kittens in her mouth. She plopped the little creature into her cozy bed and hurried back outside to fetch the rest of her kittens. Soon she had five kittens in her little bed just as the storm revved up it's momentum and settled over the house. The old mother started to meow and ran back outside; one kitten was missing. I could hear her pitifully meowing outside, while looking all around for the last of her children. She searched everywhere, but it was no use, her kitten was gone. She came back into the house and together we looked in every nook and cranny. Lightning flashed and thunder shook the house. The mother cried and cried and continued her search, but I knew it was no use. It could have been anything out here, a fox, an eagle, cougar. I settled down into a meditation pose to listen to the storm. The mother cried and cried; the mother was in pain. Suddenly, in my mind's eye I was in another place. Inside a big room with many beds, little children were crying hysterically, they were running all over. Some of the children hiding in the in the corners of the room, were covered in blood, some were dead, others walked around in circles with terror in their faces. Through the windows I could see flashes and hear explosions. The feeling was gut wrenching—sickening terror and pain. I came out of the reverie feeling sick to my stomach with grief. In the cat mother's cries, I heard the pain of the world, and I shook with the terrifying feelings throughout the night.

The next day I left for Kerrville, but I couldn't get rid of the horrific images I had seen the night before; I was confused and scared at what I had seen. Two weeks later I was heading for Nashville, when about a half-an-hour away from town I started to get the same sickening feeling I had in Austin. Pulling my truck off the road, I noticed I was at Shiloh, the Civil War battlefield, which was now a national monument. I stepped out of my truck and sat with this feeling, thinking I was hearing voices around me. I can only describe it as very sad, as if ghosts were all around and could no longer speak; they could only express sadness in their silent sound, and I could feel a song starting to be born inside me; after so many years of writing I could recognize the feeling right away. That was all I knew; one moment I was empty, in the next moment I felt a seed inside my soul.

I moved on, and finally ended my tour in Boston and Martha's Vineyard. One evening, while staying at a friend's house, I happened to pick up an old newspaper to make a fire and noticed an article about the war in Bosnia. I shuddered as I slowly read the words. It described exactly what I had seen in my vision back in Texas with the mother cat. It was a story about a hospital for mentally retarded children, which had been abandoned by the staff when the Serbian Army was starting to pour into the area. For seventy-two hours the children had been left alone until UN Forces finally reached them. The article described everything I had seen. I looked at the date, it was two days before the vision I had in Austin. Not knowing what any of this meant, I stuck it in the back of my head and went on with my tour back across the states and eventually, completely forgot about it. About one year later I got this crazy idea in my head to go live and play music in Europe for a while. I packed up my instruments and headed for France and Holland. Meanwhile, the song had given birth to itself, and turned into a long epic about the absurdity of wars. Though it was not in a style that I had ever written before, people seemed to love this song and were often moved to tears. While in Holland I decided to supplement my income by teaching yoga classes. I rented a small space and told some friends. I had met a young Serbian refugee a few weeks earlier, and in a short time we became good friends, and soon my classes were filled with Serbian and Croatian refugees. These young people were very depressed, but had a real strength to them that I admired. We spent many late nights talking about the war and their situation now as refugees. Their Communist world was completely unknown to me, so I hungrily absorbed their words for the weeks that followed, when they finally asked if I would go to Belgrade to play some concerts for the peace groups. A Quaker friend gave me a round trip bus ticket, and with a few addresses to look up I made my descent into the unknown. Serbia!

It is hard for people in modern western countries to imagine what the Communist world is like unless you see and feel it for yourself. Karl

Marx had some good ideas, but what I saw was surely not what he intended. In the Sikh faith we were told that anybody who blindly followed other people would create hell for themselves, and this is exactly what I found. In my meditations I again saw the images I had seen many years earlier while living in the mountains— the giant lake of humanity now filled with strange creatures and bloodsuckers, because all the rivers and tributaries had been blocked and could not flow out naturally. The creativity and spontaneity of the human spirit was not able to move unobstructed, so it turned back on itself and became cannibalistic. Here, in former Yugoslavia I was seeing the living proof of my vision. Quite simply, fear had conquered love in this land. People were angry and rude to each other. The buildings were dark and crumbling, nothing was taken care of or treated with respect. When Karl Marx said that religion was the opiate of the masses, and it was decided to suppress them, they had created a dull, uncaring, fake world. Absolutely, the way in which religion was practiced, with all its political corruption, needed to be challenged, but these people had thrown out the baby with the bath water. Religion has certainly been corrupt, but in this place, it was not hard to understand that the basic ethics that religions tried to create in their earliest intentions were surely needed for happiness in society. Even if there were no loving God, still, ethics were needed to create some kind of civilization. But in this part of the world, there was an attitude of total disrespect for the individual. The State was everything— the individual nothing. The government agencies seemed to pick the rudest people to work for them, so the common person would always feel dominated, belittled and powerless. Embassies, post offices, police, water and power, anyone you had to deal with in some official way, were there to dominate you. Old women, burdened with heavy loads of wood or clothes, were sneered at; no one lifted a hand to help them on or off buses or through doors. "Why?" "Why should I help anybody?" "What will I get out of it?" This was the feeling that pervaded this hell world. The government was masterful at giving just enough for people to survive, but never could they get ahead so they might have time to think about something better. The people were ignorant of environmental pollution, no knowledge of modern nutritional science, nothing that would give the individual any hope for a better life in the future; all their dreams were stripped away or controlled by the government.

The TV stations in Communist countries were built like forts; if there was any kind of rebellion, everything was controlled from the stations and they were defended at all costs. These people were broken in spirit and filled with repressed anger, which spilled over into war. They were taught to mistrust each other and to tell the authorities if they thought their neighbors were doing anything wrong. The result was that even when communism officially ended, the people could not organize to start anything new because they were programmed not to trust each other. The old communist bosses still ran everything, merely changing the name of their fascist government, and much to my astonishment, my hip California New Age mentality was shattered; Ronald Reagan had been right— this was the "evil empire." As I walked through these old Communist countries, I became a better American and appreciated the promise of democracy like I had never done before. Democracy was not perfect, but at least we had the right to change something if we didn't like it, but this place was a political and spiritual black hole. Without any true core of self-esteem, people turned to intellectualism and shoddy art. The elite classes had an unbelievable arrogance and prejudice. Without any true core of self-trust, or feeling of connection with something bigger than oneself, humans puff themselves up with self-importance to try and cover over the fear and insecurity. In this stifling atmosphere nothing new was ever created; the worst of Western commercialism was stolen and amplified. Even the art was stolen; one could almost identify the textbooks from which the various styles had been copied. It seemed no one had the ability to think beyond official educational boundaries, all the real visionaries had been imprisoned or had left the country. The word democracy had been thrown around, but no one had the slightest understanding of what it meant. To think that an individual had the rights and the powers to make a change, or that an individual came before any organization or ideology, was a child's fantasy to these people, because the "government" did everything. Even the people who ran the fledging peace groups, neither had organizational skills, or the ability to envision new ideas, nor did they understand the concept that sometimes the individual should compromise and bend in order to work in a group for the good of all. Nothing here had really changed since the days of the kings and queens. The name of the form of government had changed, but now instead of royalty dominating the people, they had elite groups of criminal families running everything.

Over many years, I had learned the skill of talking directly to the soul of the person by-passing their programming and hypnotic trip words that set their programmed behavior off. Behind the filters of learned contrivance, the working people in Serbia were warm and generous, as I had found with the common working people all around the world, and I could only last in this place because I understood that these qualities were the true, natural qualities of humanity, not uncaring paranoia, artificially created by greedy criminals.

Into this environment, I, the California, biker, surfer, ex-fighter, mountain yogi, rockin' roller, who couldn't stand for anybody telling me what to do, plopped myself down for a long stay— a match made in Hell. I now began to see that God had made no mistakes in creating me a person who loved to fight. My long efforts at getting a grasp of my own volatile energies was a good one, but there is a time and place for everything, and there were moments in this land where all my years of meditative training flew out the window, discovering that in actuality I had only honed the energy to be much more formidable in the right circumstances. Every bit of my past training came into focus and now made absolute sense to me, as if pieces of a bizarre puzzle suddenly feel right into place. Every part of my being now became activated and focused, with vast reservoirs of energy and knowledge I had only felt on occasions, now becoming available to me. Miracles are not hard to do— show up in a place where they are needed, don't compromise with evil, even if it means trouble, and the impossible begins to look hap stance.

It is so very important for people with spiritual aspiration to understand the immense power available to them. In our Western world we are very spoiled, often taking for granted what we have, the spiritual technologies, the freedom to create, the many ways to explore consciousness, and we forget what can be accomplished with directed mind or prayer. Facing evil in the world is not what it looks like in the movies, books and TV. We see stories of powerful crime bosses and corrupt government hierarchies with unstoppable power; they seem to know your every move and can kill you at any time. This media illusion becomes a powerful programming in our minds. But in the real world these people are cowards with no power at all. The only way they stay in power is by isolation, and purposefully stay away from anyone with any focus of light. In this fear, they surround themselves with layers of defenses, deceptions and people who do not allow any reality into their leader's presence. As soon as a channel of Light confronts them, they crumble. In the outer appearance of things, it may take a little time, but in the inner spiritual world, their defeat is instantaneous. A person living in spirit does not attack or use force, one is simply there as a witness for a higher perception, a higher evolution. Evil destroys itself; a light worker merely shows up and names it as evil; the rest is automatic; nothing need even be said. And if you have the opportunity to meet that evil face-to-face, they see their defeat in your eyes, in your very presence; seeing with the eyes of spirit one can see them crumble in fear. Some are good at appearances of courage and power, but if the light worker stands firm in silent *knowing*, you can feel them crack. I met many corrupt politicians, and killers, and I witnessed this happening in every instance. And if you can't meet the person face-to-face, you only need walk near them. As a channel for Light, you merely put your feet on the ground where the named evil has walked; (where you stand is holy ground) it then becomes your kingdom, your ground, by spiritual right. The person filled with Spirit has more power than all the ambassadors and government officials of the largest countries, or all the armies in the world, because these people compromise with truth, but a person of Spirit never compromises and never stops. I met many public officials from the European Union, NATO, and United Nations— all the super powers were there. But secretly they all had their little deals going with the corrupt governments, endless intrigues and scheming for money, power and political advantage.

For four years, all the powers of the western world, religious and governmental, debated, negotiated and were 'outraged.' They twiddled their politically correct rhetoric and didn't lift a finger while tens of thousands were slaughtered. Concentration camps, rape, torture and everything that we now knew went on in WWII, it was all happening again, and our so-called leaders knew it and continued on— talking, talking, talking. I even met a wide variety of Jungian and New Age philosophers here. It was interesting to see how this philosophy had taken over so many Western Europeans. According to their philosophy, we were all killers, so actually the people who felt themselves to be of the spirit were really pushing down their killer-side and projecting it out on the "enemy," therefore, in some way causing them to act in this way. I was alerted and aware of how many times I had run into this philosophy and seen it misused, starting with my adventure in Greece so long ago. It seemed like a subtle dark cloud, hidden in fancy rhetoric that undermined people's trust in themselves to act in the face evil, something that evil relies upon so it can do it's work unchallenged. They were all here, people from all the religions and philosophies of the world, and while they debated their beliefs, thousands of old men and women and children were murdered. I could debate with the best of them about relativism and karma, but too many times I saw well-meaning people who wanted to sincerely look at and consider their own faults, fall into the mire of inaction. But the person of Spirit does not compromise with evil, and is no respecter of any government, religion, or people involved in murder. What the person of Spirit knows, and what all these others don't seem to know, is that once you have killed innocent men, women and children, once you have raped and dishonored the female, you have lost the right to rule, and eventually, the right to even participate in the world. Sooner or later they fall. Today, because of the increased power of individual Christ consciousness being born into the world, the destruction of these people happens much sooner. What I felt was not a soft Christ turning the other cheek, but a Christ with teeth and claws— the Christ who whipped the moneylenders out of the temple, an awesome power that overthrew entire governments in an instant. All it took were people to witness, people who wouldn't compromise with right and wrong, and I met many of them here; angels and beings of power, channeling God's wrath and harmony into this dark world; brave young men and women who came from all over the world to help the rape victims; rag-tag armies of young people who got the call to risk their lives and show up in the middle of a war to serve in a peaceful way. They brought food to refugees, cut firewood, repaired homes, they prayed and witnessed. Their very presence was the presence of a loving God in action. It is these little people who create real change, because they do not compromise.

I took a room in the center of Belgrade, across from the presidential building, and began my chanting, prayers and meditations. I gave concerts and taught yoga and meditation classes to the Serbian peace groups. To my astonishment, I found that these people had never experienced silence; this was the first time they had ever come together and shut their mouths, and turned off their overly intellectualized minds. New inner connections were being made. They had no name for "it" or even a belief in "it", but we all could feel new ideas and power starting to drop into the environment in these times of silence. Because they had never felt this, and because of the contrast of the darkness surrounding them, all who participated could feel a repelling effect against the darkness, moving out from the center of our silence, and rolling out into the environment in concentric circles of waves of energy. This is how they described it to me; I called it a "Vortex." In many ways these people were very spiritually innocent and were naturals at feeling the spirit when it was presented to them in a way that didn't bring up past associations with corrupt religions. The song that was given to me at the Shiloh Civil War monument became a huge success. I was asked to sing it everywhere I went; people wept and great healing took place. Grace and sacrament moved through this song, and did things to men and women that went way beyond my own conscious abilities to communicate. But after about thirty days I was noticed by the police and told to leave Serbia. In my last evening meditation I saw the President Milosevic and his wife, falling from power, and eventually the whole corrupt government collapsing. I saw it as clearly as watching a TV show. It was done. Amen.

✳ ✳ ✳

From Belgrade I took a bus to the Hungarian-Croatian border for a concert with high school kids, refugees from Croatia. They had lost their homes and families in the battles for the small towns on the Croatian- Serbian border. I was taken into an underground bomb shelter that they had turned into a nightclub. The club was loud, smoky and packed with curious teenagers. They had a set of loud speakers and were blasting the latest European disco music through the small room. I was supposed to play at a break in their party, but I only had acoustic instruments and felt a little intimidated because the volume and vibration in the room was one of "blow your mind anyway you can to forget the war." But they turned the music off and suddenly there was dead silence. I felt "spirit" take over the kids, they formed a semi-circle around me, standing wide-eyed and silent. I started off with my loudest and most intense spirit- rock Kundalini raising song. They had never heard this kind of spiritual music before. I was in love with every one of these young people; they were now my children and I was enraged with the forces that had killed their mothers and fathers, brothers and sisters. Again I felt God's healing come through the songs, and I wept when the concert was over and had to leave them. I wanted to stay and know them all, but I was just a one-night event in their lives. Whatever I was there to give, had to all come out in just a few hours. That's the way it is in a war zone. Everything moves fast and intensely. I could not be attached to what happened to them in that few hours, I only knew that something profound had taken place. I knew because it happened to me also.

I had no more invitations or connections to meet in this country, but knew I had to keep going, and spent my birthday on the daylong bus ride to Sarajevo. At first when seeing a few blown-up buildings, I made a few smug remarks to myself, "This is not so bad, I've seen worse than this in downtown LA or the Bronx." After a few hours I was silenced and humbled. The bus rolled along for the next nine hours through Southern Croatia and into Bosnia, and I was in shock. The

whole nine hours I saw nothing but destruction from the bus windows.
Every house, every village, every barn, church and Mosque were totally or partially destroyed. I had no understanding or frame of reference
for this kind of destruction; the Western news had not let out the truth
of the devastation in this war, and the further south we drove, the more
nightmarish it became. By the time we reached Sarajevo at sunset, my
sunny Southern California reality had been shattered. The city was in
shambles; giant modern office buildings completely gutted and burned
out, total destruction as far as the eye could see. Blown up trains and
trolleys, tanks and army trucks. The windows of all the homes had been
shot out. Armed soldiers nervously stared at me as I stepped off the bus.
Every nerve in my body screamed, "Get your butt back on the bus and
get the hell out of here." I didn't know anyone here, or even speak the
language. "God, what the fuck am I doing here?" But the bus drove off
and there I stood alone in Hell; I had one address of someone who may
or may not still be in Sarajevo, and that was it. I gave the address to a
taxi driver and we sped through the destroyed town, smashed into a
smoldering, hulking skeleton. We passed the Olympic Stadium, it was
completely destroyed, bomb craters everywhere. The armed soldiers
patrolled the streets, tense and grim. I struggled to grasp for any sem-
blance of my old reality, but the only thought I could pull up was, "Your
not in Kansas anymore, Dorothy", a last desperate stab at some kind of
humor.

    We pulled up in front of a crumbling building near the center of
the older section of Sarajevo. Everywhere my eyes turned, bomb
craters cut through the sidewalks and streets. The building was covered
with bullet holes, and in some places large chunks of the walls were
missing from the grenade blasts in the streets, windows were covered in
a grayish, bubbly plastic with the letters "UN" stamped in bright blue.
All the buildings had this UN plastic that moved back and forth in the
breeze, creating a hellish surrealistic scene, as if everything were alive
and breathing. The cab driver sped off, after overcharging me, leaving
me alone in the street. I nervously stepped up to the wooden door and
pushed the doorbell that said, "Bridge of Peace, Sarajevo." This organization had set up my concerts in Hungary and told me that they might
still have a branch office in Sarajevo, but because of the cutting off of
communications, they weren't sure what had happened to the people. I
waited for a few minutes then thought I should start looking for a hotel.
Then I heard a door slam and someone came running down the stairs
inside the building. The door opened, and I was in Love. *Damn!* The
most beautiful smiling young woman I had seen in months popped her

head out and sang, "Hello!" Ajla was a nineteen-year-old pre-med student with a smile that burned right through you. She had that vibration of light and humorous kindness that I had come to recognize as a person of spirit. I explained to her how I had come to be there, she gaily laughed and said, "Won't you come in, you look a little lost." These Balkan women certainly had a way about them, a subtlety of femininity that gently guides a man, even when you don't know it. Ajla walked me up the dark stairway where Nedim, her twenty-year old boyfriend, met me. *Damn!* Nedim was soft spoken and soulful, with not even a wisp of hair on his young face; I liked him immediately. He had been a soldier when only eighteen, and had fought on the front lines most of the war, seeing many of his friends killed and wounded. He was more subdued than Ajla, but I also saw in his smile that his spirit had not been broken. They spoke English well, so we chatted and laughed over Turkish coffee and bread. It was all they had to offer me and they gave it freely. That night they were going to have a birthday party for a friend, another young soldier. They were delighted when I told them that it was also my birthday. So on my first night we celebrated and played music, Nedim, being very good on the guitar and singing. I was amazed at how many old American rock and roll songs they knew. It was a happy first evening; in the middle of hell, I had found a haven of warm, giving people.

Later the 'little sister' came. Selma, Ajla's sister was seventeen and another strikingly beautiful young woman. She reminded me of a young colt let out of the corral in springtime; fiery and full of laughter. She had a tiny little body, a beautiful mature face, and wisdom beyond her years. Only twelve years old when the war started, and because of the food shortage during those formative growing years, her body was small and frail. But the war was almost over and she and her friends were out to party with a vengeance. These young women dressed impeccably and as I got to know them well, I often watched them as they prepared themselves to go out into their blown up city. They spent a long time putting on their make-up and making sure their clothes were perfectly neat. Yet, there did not seem to be any vanity in them. It was their way of showing defiance to the powers that hate beauty and life. It was their way of showing self-respect; even war was not going to break them. In this land where the individual was nothing, Ajla, Selma and her friends walked like young queens through the wreckage of their city. They seemed to have a powerful security in their femininity, and though all the women I met could be outrageously flirtatious, they had a solid core of morality that came from their Muslim upbringing. They all had wisdom beyond their years; they looked deep to see your soul and could not be fooled. In a world of liars, they no longer listened to what people said. They watched what you did and who you were.

I ended up moving in with Ajla and Nedim, paying them what little I could for the spare room. Bullet and bomb holes, paint peeling, water for only one hour a day, cockroaches; it was heaven. At times it was hard, but I came to accept that in the way I lived my life, there was never any clearly marked paths; it was all an experiment of faith and power. My nightly meditations were sometimes frightening. The images of the death and destruction I had seen and could feel all around, haunted me. I could no longer afford one slip, not one leak in my aura, feeling that much depended on my actions here, though I still didn't know exactly what I was to do. All I knew was that the buck stopped at Sarajevo; all the forces of dark and light hung in balance over this town. All the embassies of the major world powers were here, all the major western religions jockeyed for position. Bosnia had become a spiritual question mark for the whole world at this time in history. No one would help Bosnia during the war because there was nothing material to gain by it. They had no oil, no great resources and they were Muslim, and so they reluctantly turned to Iran for help. They were supplied with small arms and sent just a few hundred soldiers to help fight off the Serbs. That is when the west interfered. Bosnia is far different than the fundamentalist Muslim countries like Iran, they are modern European Muslims, proud of their heritage but by no means fanatic. They had existed within a Communist country for fifty years and really wanted nothing to do with Iran, but what were they to do, lay down and die? These brave people held off the vastly superior armies of the Serbs and Croats for the first years of the war, with almost no weapons. Genocide was being committed on them and all the western governments and religions new it. The UN estimated that the Serbs and Croats had systematically raped at least 50,000 young Muslim women. They felt that the Muslims would not "breed" with defiled women. So now the Iranians were here trying to spread their influence and even though Bosnia itself would never accept the Iranian's brand of Islam, the western powers were here to make sure of it. Iran's presence, so close to Western Europe alarmed everyone. The Catholic Croats, Orthodox Serbs and the Muslims all tried every means to gain influence in the region, and the town was filled with spies, from all the governments, secret police, and also, trained psychic manipulators, 'sorcerers' from the hidden dark sides of the religions. In meditation, the psychic planes were awash with plots and schemes, anger hatred and murder.

The question for the whole world that hung over this country was, "are we going to allow these kinds of things to continue into the twenty-first century?" "Are we going to continue to turn our backs when thousands of old people, men, women and children are starved, tortured and murdered." "Why not? The world population needs thinning out any way." "We have been living this way through our whole history, we have even made it very financially profitable to continue like this." I felt all these turbulent thought-forms and questions, churning, just outside my aura. Being new in this small town, the intelligence community started to take notice. I worked for no government, represented no organization, gave allegiance to no one religion, so who was I, what was I doing here? Just outside my conscious awareness, I constantly felt my aura being 'probed.' After a few weeks of this, psychically, I spread my *sound* out to meet them and answered:

*"I have come, to make sure you make the right decisions
and if you cannot... I will make them for you."*

That is why I had really come. This war was not just killing people here; it was killing people all over the world. It was killing our souls. I heard and felt the voices of myriads of beings inside me.

"I refuse to accept that I am powerless to make change in this world...
I will not live in a world where all I can do is sit helpless in front of the TV...
watching these atrocities, waiting for banana- spined leaders to do something."

This also is why I had really come, to save my own soul from dying. And I had come to represent all the good people who felt the same, but could not come. I blended my *sound* with theirs, sat down in the midst of the insanity and started the work of opening a "vortex" through the psychic cloud cover, a hole for Grace, so something new could drop into the world. I thought of my new friends. It was easy to read their thoughts when they thought of me. Behind their smiles, I saw the horrible pain they had suffered, the betrayal and lies that had shattered their world, the insecurity and fear of not knowing what was to come next; more war and betrayal by the Western powers? I knew about betrayal, it had saddened my heart for years. But the people here didn't have time to deal with their suffering; they had lived on the edge of survival for four years. Just staying alive took all their effort and time. I loved these young heroes and was humbled by their courage, and in my soul searching and asking what I could do for them, I saw what they needed most was simply to be someone they could trust, to let them know that there were people all over the world that still cared for them. I settled in and prepared for whatever would come. Evening meditation sometimes ended at about four am, when I would hear the beautiful call to prayer from the Mosque down the street. From the first week on, I stopped whatever I was doing when I heard the call, and joyously prayed five times a day with my Muslim brothers and sisters.

✳ ✳ ✳

After becoming comfortable with my immediate surroundings and dipping into the psychic atmosphere, I began daily walks through the city, talking to anyone who wanted to talk. The Bosnians are a very laid back race of people. Sitting around drinking strong coffee and talking is a national passion. A bartender told me an ethnic joke that very much captures the different personalities of the people in former Yugoslavia. The war divided the country between the three predominant cultures and religions, Serbs (Orthodox), Croats (Catholic), Bosnian (Muslim), though racially they were all pretty much the same. They were all once part of the great Austro-Hungarian Empire and had the features of northern Europeans. Bosnia became Muslim because they were taken over by the Turks in the fifteenth century and that was about the last time they existed as a true independent state. So the Joke goes:

God comes to the President of the Serbs and asks, "What do you want?" "I want to kill all the Croats and the Bosnians and take over all of Yugoslavia."

God then goes to the President of the Croatians. "What do you want?" "I want to kill all of the Serbs and Bosnians but we don't want any bad publicity."

God then goes to the President of the Bosnians. "What do you want?"

"Oh I just want some coffee." In my travels I found the joke to be surprisingly accurate.

After many weeks of daily talks with people of all ages, I was able to paste together a picture of what happened here, and also, the people came to know me. The Bosnians had been betrayed by the west, the news was slowly leaking out. The British, Germans, French, Dutch and Americans all knew about the concentration camps, there were 159 camps in Bosnia and 14 in Serbia and Montenegro. Some of the camps had been turned into "bordellos" where women were brutally raped and tortured. Of the estimated 50,000 women who were raped some 35,000 were thought to be pregnant. In other camps, men were forced to castrate and torture their fellow prisoners. The orders to rape and torture did not come from some unreasonable mad field commander; they came right from the top. A carefully planned policy of genocide following a five-point plan of ethnic cleansing:

Mass liquidations during the "take over" of villages and in concentration camps, to significantly reduce the population.

Rapes of women and castrations of men in order to make biological reproduction impossible.

Liquidations of the higher social layer, and intellectuals, to destroy the intellectual potential of the nation.

Expel the population in the cruelest ways, so that permanent fear of coming back stays forever.

Destroy all material trails, historical monuments, religious objects, national institutions and graves, as a final act of the people's eradication from the new territories.

Even after the UN came to create "safe havens," still thousands died. In the town of Srebenica, the Dutch commander given the promise that the prisoners would be fairly treated, turned over a UN "safe haven" to the Serb general. Some 7,000 unarmed young Muslims from that town alone are now "officially missing." The European press showed a picture of the Dutch commander toasting champagne with the Serb General Maladic. The story was quickly squashed by pressure from the Dutch government. Here in Sarajevo alone, 15,000 dead— mostly civilians, old men, women, and over 2,000 children. 50,000 wounded, many with permanent consequences. Sarajevo had become a turkey shoot. It is a small town in a valley completely surrounded by mountains. The Serbs surrounded the city with artillery, tanks and sniper units. All roads in or out were blocked and mined, the river was stopped and poisoned, the heat and power shut off. The UN sat well-fed in furnished bunkers while the people of Sarajevo got polished white rice and canned dog food spiced for the human palate. In 1993, 7,000 people alone were gunned down in the streets looking for water and trying to reach UN food sources. How could this happen in our modern day and age and no one move to stop it? Bosnia was never supposed to be. A secret deal had been hastily made at the beginning of the war to divide the country of Yugoslavia between Serbia and Croatia; everyone was disturbed by the prospect of a Muslim state in the middle of Europe. So the West turned its back on the slaughter and manipulated the news so public opinion could be controlled. I made friends with a British UN cameraman who had quit his job in protest when he was told to make propaganda films, actually fabricating evidence against the Bosnians. The order had come down when the British decided that their General Rose, then head of the UN troops was beginning to look bad in public opinion, because the UN did nothing to help the Bosnians. The scenes that were shown of Sarajevo in the western news were specially edited pictures of strange looking old toothless women in black robes, crying out in rage, trying to equate Bosnians with the more fanatic Shiite Iranians, thus alleviating the guilt of letting them die. Create the illusion that people are some how less human or intelligent, and no one cares what happens to them. But I saw no one like this anywhere in Sarajevo. These were modern Europeans, as well dressed as Parisians and also friendlier. The West also blocked arms from entering Bosnia so they could not even defend themselves. Bosnia is now trying to file a suit against England in the world court for leading this action, acting in complicity in genocide. The Croatian Catholics unofficially sanctioned the agreements between Croatia and Serbia by their age old 'say nothing, see nothing' tactic.

The beginning of the war was between Croatia and Serbia. Bosnia in the south really had nothing to do with it. But after the destruction of much Catholic property, it was decided to move the war south onto the Muslims, the historical enemy of both the Serbs and the Croats. After all, the war was really just a land grab by old communist criminal bosses after the break up of Yugoslavia. So together Serbia and Croatia attacked the peaceful Bosnian Muslims. Orthodox priest came to the battlefronts and 'blessed' tanks, cannons and rocket launchers. They created glorious ceremonies of thanks on the sights of mass graves where innocent Muslims had been hastily buried. The Orthodox and Catholic so-called "followers of Christ" had murdered, raped and tortured for the "righteous cause of ethnic purity" while Sarajevo had been a successful multi-ethnic, inter and multi-religious center for over 500 years. Rome did nothing. But in the world news, April 1997, we read "the Pope goes to Sarajevo — Bombs found under a bridge on his official route." We hear only this, and for the political powers that be, it serves many hidden interests to keep westerners from hearing the whole story. I am certainly not suggesting that killing the Pope in revenge is justified, but I can have compassion for, and understand why certain Muslims who lost their families and homes because of these 'Christians', might want to kill him.

Everyone I spoke with said they never believed the war would last more than six months. They thought that at least the Americans would stop it. But it went on for four years. For these people, all illusion about how the world works was stripped away, even the comfort of personal beliefs. Little Selma said it chillingly, "At first I prayed that the war would stop, but nothing happened. Now I don't know anything except my name is Selma and the world hates me because I am Muslim."

So this is the world we live in. In this town, every person from thirteen years up knew all these things. They are much better at facing reality and seeing through the political lies than the average person in western countries, asleep in their comfort. The hopelessness of being power-played by overwhelming forces is like a black cloud that hangs over this country, but also they had strength and a pride that they had survived. Why is Judeo-Christianity so afraid of the Muslims? Why do we hate them so much? The answer is hard for the old paradigm people to look at.

My one sided western view was expanded by an old Tibetan Buddhist who showed me how he saw the conflict between Jews, Christians and the Muslims. Having never been born into or influenced in any way by the "circumcised" religions, as he called them, he had a much clearer overview. Being a good Buddhist, he did not use the name God, but rather spoke of the "Balance and Harmony" of forces in the world. The Judeo-Christian faith spread through the world preaching the peace of Christ, but backed it with the sword. If you did not bow to the will of Rome your land was taken and you were slaughtered. The Christians mercilessly butchered millions in its zeal to spread the faith. Because of the power of intellectualism growing in the west, they could rationalize anything, and became blind to their own inconsistencies with the teachings of Jesus. But the forces of Balance and Harmony never allow this one sided energy. So the Muslims rose to squarely face and stop the Christian fanaticism. They became the shadow and mirror, so Christianity would see its own brutality. Everything the "political church" would not look at in itself, now got shoved back in their face. The West could never defeat the Muslim, and the Muslim could never defeat the West because they were mirrors of each other, born from the same seed of Abraham. The old monk saw the Jews, Christians and Muslims as a giant three-headed dragon trying to bite severely stressed out. Going outside to even take a walk was a ble on your life; the town was surrounded by hundreds of snipers. kind of emotions that come out while working hard in yoga was much for them, so for the first few months, the Bosnians came to tely 'visit' (smoke and drink coffee). There was an eleven o'clock ew, so we had many all night sleep over parties; this is what people here. There was no employment, so talking and drinking beer and ee was the big pastime. I was asked to sing the song that had come e at the Shiloh Civil War Monument over and over again. Nedim ught many friends, who I could see were very damaged from seeing much killing at so young an age. The song did things to their spir-at I had never seen before. A very old mystic woman heard me sing d said she saw hundreds of souls who had been killed in the bomb-being released into light, created by the song. She told me that n people die so fast without preparation, like in a bomb blast, they confused and become earth bound, not knowing where to go. They e coming to be released in the song. I didn't see this, but the song nitely had a powerful affect on people that couldn't be denied. No said anything, it was hard for them to speak of such things, but yone knew that healing was going on. Some people didn't even w why they came; they just wanted to hang around because it felt ceful in the house. I couldn't speak to them of God, because they e angry with God and wanted nothing more to do with any reli-as. I couldn't speak to them of healing in any form because they had n conditioned for the last fifty years not to trust the 'rich' western-But they could feel my love for them and they loved me, and that fused them, so we didn't speak of these things. I let them express r anger, and took many insults about America, and felt the pain of ng men who were forced to kill because the world turned it's back them. The Sound accepted it all without judgment and returned hing but Love. And the healing took place.

* * *

Nedim walked into my room one morning with a serious look on face. He sat quietly for a time as if trying to find some words that ldn't surface.

"Will you come with me today?" "I want you to see."

"See what?", I asked cautiously.

"Please just come."

Nedim was always sort of quite and mysterious but today was

itself. The West is so worried by the Muslims, but actually all they have to do is act ethically and morally, and they will have no problem with the Muslims as, they are a very pragmatic religion. What the Muslims hate about the West, is what the West hates about itself, and they are not going to roll-over and play dead just because Christians and Jews, lost in the momentum of their own self-righteous theologies, think they have divine rights. "Growing pains" is what the monk called it.

The tragedy of the conflict between Christianity and the Muslims is that the Prophet Mohammed had a true understanding and deep respect for Jesus. In the Koran He is recognized as "Logos." Mohammed did not have a full knowing of what that was, but neither did anybody, including the Church. At that time, the nature of Christ was still being debated in the Church also. It was only after many years and councils that the official theologies were created, and it is still growing and open to change. Mohammed intuitively knew the unique-ness of Jesus and understood His love and was greatly influenced by it. He knew as much as anybody else in the world, at that time, about Jesus. It was not with Jesus that the Muslims have a problem; the prob-lem was with the "political church." Muslims accepted the healing and forgiving nature of Christ, but they did not see it exemplified in the Church. The "political church" could not see its own corruption, but others did, and stood against it. Even the Protestant movement need not have happened if the "political church" had not been corrupt. Christ showed us that "all" humanity is Divine, but for this to become a reality on earth, we can't just speak the words and imagine we are fol-lowing Christ way, we must live it. We must actually act and treat each other in that way.

* * *

The answer to what exactly I was supposed to be doing in Sarajevo soon appeared. An Episcopal priest from America found out that I was here and showed up at Bridge of Peace carrying a Buddhist peace pole saying, "May peace prevail on earth" in all the languages of former Yugoslavia. A renowned Buddhist group centered in Japan created these poles and they have planted them in many places around the world. It turned out that the priest had mysteriously come from my own hometown in California; we actually lived only a mile from each other and now were meeting for the first time in sunny downtown Sarajevo. He was another brave soul who traveled into conflict areas, practicing his inter-religious ceremonies to pray for the dead and create peace. Reverend John had received permission, which was a miracle in itself, to plant the pole on a very particular bridge, and asked if I would assist in the ceremony. This bridge was where Archduke Ferdinand had been assassinated in 1912, which started WWI, which created the economic and political reasons for WWII, which created the hatreds, fears and conditions to start this Balkan War. After taking the pole around to get blessed by the Catholic Church and some of the Mosque', we had a big ceremony, with the news people present, as we stuck the pole in the ground. At the end of the ceremony, Mr. Jamakovic, then the city planner and a very holy and devout man, said a few words. He was a joyous, gentle man, loved and respected by many people, and his words had power in many dimensions. He spoke as we stuck the pole into the dirt, "May this be a stake in the heart of the vampire of war." That is when I saw what I must do here. I knew that I was here to deal with the psychic and mystical implication of his words. Everyone went home and into their own worlds, but now I understood that it was in my psyche that the words would live or die. Reverend John had come once before, in the middle of the war, to perform a ceremony on this bridge to clear the way for what we were doing now. He had done his job and continued on into other hostile spots in the world. Mr. Jamakovic' had done his job all through out the war, and continued to, his very presence was peace itself. Now it was my turn.

Before leaving Holland I had been working on a project with an interreligious group, to see the possibility of creating a forty day interreligious prayer event in Sarajevo, and told them I would look into the possibility. It was to be a continuous around the clock "sound temple" for forty days. I wanted to accomplish this, but knew that the timing might not be right, so I told myself that if it couldn't be done now, that at least I would stay to fast and pray for forty days. All events had to be cleared through NATO. I found the officers to be very fine people but saw that the temple, at this time, would cause more tension than peace, and opted to wait for a more auspicious time. For now, I was to be the "sound temple." Thinking of Mr. Jamakovic's words, I launched into the forty days of fasting and chants, with determination.

I jumped into the work with many expectations and ideas of how it should all turn out, but they were quickly stripped away. To put it simply, this "vampire of war" didn't want to die. Hatred had stalked this land for a long time and wasn't going to give up without a fight. Meditation in a war zone is an experience of excitement, passion and fear that stretches one beyond the fragile border of the unknown. It is definitely not for the faint at heart! I had always seen prayer as an acti-

vation of energy, and meditation as a passive, resting and rec[...] mode. Chanting, for me, was an experience of both at once. In Sa[...] it became the zone where danger clasps delight. In the late night[...] I would open my aura and enter into the psychic and emotional l[...] all the living creatures for many miles in all directions, taking in[...] thoughts and feelings into my circumference. Then with the ch[...] created a more harmonious and peaceful sound waves that would[...] mute the sorrowful energies that I encountered. The chan[...] changed according to whatever is encountered in the mo[...] Sometimes it is just a matter of finding words that the people [...] longer find, having faith when theirs is broken, crying tears whe[...] have no more to cry. The mistake that I saw many peace organiz[...] make here, was that they created a kind of a clinical "holier than[...] attitude. The key to success in this work is to enter into the life[...] people. Get your hands dirty, sleep on the cold floor in the[...] throw shoes at cockroaches in the middle of the night, starve[...] when there is no food, and most of all, laugh with them. Wh[...] become one with them, then they are lifted as you lift yoursel[...] "Sound" meditation and prayer. Speaking of God or theory of [...] mind does nothing. In a war zone it usually just irritates peopl[...] must live it oneself or fall on your face. It always works, because[...] defeated hearts, God's strength survives.

In a few days I was quickly propelled into chanting and me[...] up to nine hours a day. It had not been my intention to do thi[...] was all I could do to transmute the volatile energies around me.[...] more days, the Sound and meditation were continuous in me,[...] four hours a day. My body slept when it had to, but the Sound[...] on, forming an impenetrable ball of energy around me, that co[...] to expand and grow in strength. The original plan was to cont[...] forty days, but I quickly saw that all this had a life of it's own.[...] continue in this state, twenty-four hours a day for the nex[...] months.

As my fast continued, Ajla, Nedim and Selma started to[...] worried about me, and as my body continued to waste away, n[...] more people became curious. Soon the British press and A[...] press came to visit me and wrote a story, which appeared in[...] and Holland. More people came. The chanting was workin[...] many young war veterans and girl friends of Ajla and Selma, s[...] had been raped during the war. I tried to start teaching them[...] most of them were too weak to make it through even a sim[...] They had sat around, living on horrible diets for the last four [...]

something very different. We walked for about a mile down the street until coming to a bridge crossing the river at the end of town. There were fresh cut flowers and a memorial plaque on the railing. A burnt out Serbian tank silently stood at the end of the bridge. Nedim took a breath. "These flowers are for the men who died taking out that tank." We were on the front line; Grbavica. This is where Nedim and Ajla had lived before the fighting broke out. It was the newer part of town, with modern twenty story apartment buildings, that went on for miles. The Serbs and Muslims, Catholics and Jews had all lived here together before the war, but the Serbs took over this part of the town when the shooting started and threw everyone else out of their homes, murdering many of them. Now that the Dayton agreement had come into affect, the last of the Serb civilians now had to give up the homes they had tried to occupy for themselves. The moving and riots had been going on for the last two weeks and today was the first day that the Muslims could go back to their homes, the first time in four years. NATO forces had killed the last of the snipers just a few days before and wanted to spend more weeks sweeping for mines but the people wanted to come home now. Only former residents were allowed in, everyone else including the press were rudely turned away by the Italian troops stationed at the heavily guarded entrance. Nedim was sneaking me in the back way through the buildings where he had been stationed during the war. We turned up an alley, jumped through a hole in a rock fence and suddenly I was in another world. The modern buildings were torn to shreds, hulking burned out skeletons of death, and it went on for miles. We turned into a hole in the side of a building and I found myself in a maze of underground passages that weaved under, through and around almost all the buildings on this side of the town. On this side, the buildings were shredded by machine gun fire; on the other side the buildings were almost clean. I asked Nedim why this was.

"Because we had no big weapons or a lot of ammunition to fire back with."

Before Yugoslavia had split up, the Serbs made up most of the army, so they ended up with all the weapons. The Muslims had stood them off by sending groups of snipers through these underground passages and into the different buildings, always popping up in different places, making the Serbs think they were fighting many more men than were actually there. But hundreds of young Muslims had died in these buildings and Nedim walked with somber veneration for his fallen companions. He led me through the minefields and into the center of town near to his old apartment building. We came to a big four-story office building. Nedim pointed.

"This is where Ajla was during the war."

"You mean before the war."

Nedim turned to me slowly, no readable expression on his face.

"No, during the war. This was the prison where they kept the young girls. Her father was kept here too."

He touched my shoulder.

"Do not tell her that I have told you, she doesn't speak of these things."

He paused.

"I will tell you."

Ajla and her father, a respected doctor had been captured while trying to leave Grbavica. Selma and the mother some how escaped. Ajla was beaten many times, and God knows what else, no one knew because she would never speak of it. Her father also had been beaten many times then released after a few months. But Ajla remained. Her family was able to finally negotiate her release through the help of a Muslim officer who had been friends with the Serb commander before the war. Nedim and Ajla didn't meet till much later, but Nedim had been in this officer's regiment. The officer was later killed and Ajla and her family were deeply saddened that they never even had a chance to thank him for their lives. The father, once a loved and respected doctor now sits in painful depression unable to practice his medicine, and any spare bit of money that Ajla can find goes to support her father, mother and Selma.

Nedim finished speaking and let the feelings fill me as we continued to walk through this sad world. Nedim was truly a great young man. He didn't have a violent bone in his body. Before the war he had been a film student at the University and was truly a very sensitive artist. He had been thrown into the bloodiest fighting of the war until he finally cracked. One day he couldn't take it any longer and wanted to die. He jumped up out of his foxhole and raged at the enemy to kill him. His own comrades jumped on him and beat him up. He was sent to a mental hospital for a few weeks then put right back on the front lines. As a sniper and guard, many times he had enemy soldiers in the sights of his rifle, but didn't pull the trigger. He never let the rage consume him. He could kill when they were being attacked, but he could not kill someone standing alone not even knowing they were in his sights. To Nedim they were just like him, scared young men just wanting to survive. Before the war, they had been friends, gone to school together, drank in the same bars. Nedim, for now, was angry with Allah for what had happened, and didn't go to the Mosque. But in the eyes of Allah, surely, he was the truest of Muslims, and so humble, he didn't even know it.

We reached Nedim's old home in the center of town. They had lived on the fourteenth floor of a twenty-story building and we slowly began our descent up the dark stairway, cautiously checking for mines and booby-traps along the way. I had heard two loud explosions as we walked through the town and thought that it was the NATO soldiers clearing land mines. But no one really knew if all the Serb snipers were gone and we both knew the explosions could have been anything. We came to the fourteenth floor. Nedim's old apartment was the first door after exiting the stairwell, a corner apartment facing the main street below. We checked for traps then opened the door. The room was filled with trash and completely stripped. All the kitchen appliances and plumbing were pulled out of the wall. All the wood in the entire apartment was stripped, including the floor. Even the doorjambs and electrical sockets had been stolen. I later found out that every apartment in hundreds of these buildings looked the same. The Serbs had stolen everything. We moved towards Nedim's room, careful not to touch any of the piles of rubble. It was an old trick to plant bombs in the piles of the previous owner's old belongings. They would be blown apart while sifting through, trying to find some precious heirloom from their past.

As we entered the bedroom we noticed that a hole, about a foot square, had been carefully carved out through the cement wall facing the street. It had been carved in the old feudal castle style with the widened end on the inside, narrowing down to a small opening on the outside of the building. Spent rifle cartridges were all over the floor. A sniper had been living in Nedim's bedroom! It was easy to see his target was the tram and pedestrians down on the street. Who knows how many innocent people this 'brave' man had killed. We sat in the middle of Nedim's past in utter silence. I left him to his thoughts and took it all in, everything; the ghost, the thoughts and feelings that floated through these buildings like clouds. Anger, betrayal and heart break. After a long time, Nedim looked up. "Do you understand?" No, I didn't understand. But I was getting close. I knew that he needed to be alone for a while so I told him I would meet him back at our apartment. As I slowly moved down the stairs, there was another large explosion followed by two more. I kept walking. Now that I was in Grbavica, I could fit in with the hundreds of Bosnians in the streets so I headed for the main gate. When I reached the street, a truck raced by followed by panicked Italian soldiers and a large group of people. A military ambulance pulled up and the first vehicle moved up next to it. I was walking with a group of Bosnians when an Italian guard jumped in front of us, raised his automatic weapon and screamed at us to "stop"; panic in his eyes. I looked past him and saw the ambulance drivers pulling a beautiful young woman out of the first truck. Her left leg, from the knee down, had been blown off; the right leg was dangling by a few pieces of skin. What happened next shattered me. A young girl, about ten years old was pulled from the truck. The young woman was her mother. She ran over to her mother who was rolling her head back and forth, moaning and gasping for air. Everything started to move in slow motion and all I could see was the little girl standing there looking down at her mother. Her eyes slowly panning from left to right to the faces of all the people standing around; no one would look at her. She turned towards me, we looked in each other's eyes, and our souls met. Every empty space of cavernous groping human mind, every hidden fiber of dormant nerve asleep in human apathy, flashed white; I and the Universal Being became one, and I knew God's rage at the loss of innocence. You could take the Bible, the Koran, the Wailing Wall, Mecca, Rome and all the other things that are considered 'Holy' in this world, and in God's heart, together they did not match the worth of one innocent child, one human being. In her eyes, I saw that the whole world stood condemned and utterly powerless. Every religion or government who acted in complicity, every being who turned their back, crumbled in dust. I didn't know how, I didn't have to know how, but for these people, their time was over, and the "New" began. The Wheel of Dharma turned one more click, and the fabric of reality changed forever as the Universal Being came to look into the eyes of a child the moment she lost her innocence and faith in life, and that Being in me raged and wept.

The little girl and her mother were put into the ambulance. The door shut and I came back into time. What I saw in those few moments was going to take some time to fill our physical world, the fall of the principalities. But it was done — Amen. I heard more explosions as I walked home. It was not minesweepers. It was the sound of people being killed.

Westerners are good and caring people, but dulled into being mindless second-hand human beings by the endless violence in our media. Give war a face, a real live face, and your life is changed forever. But this one moment was something different, an event of cosmic dimensions caused by an ordinary young woman and her daughter, and someone, it could have been anyone, who was willing to let themselves see and feel without any filters.

Chapter 9

Love

I stayed in my room for the next few days and didn't receive any visitors. I told Nedim what I had seen. He was silent. Ajla and Selma brought me water but nobody spoke a word. They felt and shared my pain, and at the same time were happy that this had happened to me. They wanted me to know what they had lived through everyday for the past four years. It was their gift to me. What could be said? We wordlessly communed with each other, each soul's transfiguration a silent gift to one another. All my past meant nothing to me now, it died in the tears, and I began to feel my true lineage for the first time, a passionate fire that consumed my flesh. I felt the Jesus who would put a stone on someone's neck and cast them into the ocean if they hurt or corrupted a child, the Jesus who put the worth and sacredness of human beings before any temple, church, holy books or philosophy. I tumbled in the dark, as all that I had thought before to be 'spiritual' was stripped from me.

I could have stayed in this silent state for months, but little Selma would have none of it. Like the little birdman in India, she would always show up at the right moment. Knocking on my door in the middle of my chanting, always polite, but mischievously taunting, she would blurt out some ridiculous statement in her soft broken English. "George, how do I look?" standing there in my doorway with her hands on her tiny hips, dressed like some beauty queen, ready to go out and make her debut. Selma was a wonder of God; a raw, open nerve ending from the heart of Life Itself, with a smile that could make you shiver. At seventeen she was one of the wisest human beings I had ever met. Not one spare ounce of flesh, not one stray thought in her mind. Every emotion that moved through her could immediately be seen on her face and through her body. She told me she had become more 'grown up' because of the war— weeks, months, and years of nothing to do but think, no TV or distractions of any kind, just the stark reality of survival. I wondered what it was like for her sitting with her mother not knowing what was happening to her father and sister. Everyone knew of the atrocities that the Serbs committed. What ever she did to keep from going mad had turned her into mastery. She and Ajla both were the living proof that dark can never defeat goodness. It was Selma who convinced me to take food again. It was just too preposterous to be a silent fasting monk in the queendom of her laughter. Over the weeks she brought me back to this world in the gentlest way, and I made a vow to myself that I would not leave these people until I had seen some Divine sign, until I 'knew' that they were safe. No one really knew if the war was truly over, or if this were just a short reprieve. If the fighting started up again, I would stay with them until it was over or die with them.

It is the decision itself that changes reality, everything that happens after that is just a test of one's resolve, and without any words spoken, all my friends knew my decision. I could have run up the hill to attack the enemy and probably died in a flame of glory with my friends, I had been earned the trust of an underground group of Bosnian soldiers who constantly planned such things. They were frustrated with the UN commanders controlling the movements of the regular army. But in the new intensity of my prayer, I began to understand that this was not my destiny, no matter how strongly I wanted to fight at times. I had trained for many years to do something else with that rage, and now I was being put to the test. Yes, I could die for my friends, that would be quit easy and there was no fear, but could I live for them? Did I love them enough to sit there with those emotions and chew on them, swallow them, refine them and turn them into power to change the events around me? The pressure in my nervous system was almost unbearable, but my craft of yoga worked well, and in a matter of weeks of intensified practice I was able to take the resolve of a warrior under fire, sit perfectly still with it, and transmute it into a power of 'silent weapon' that moved out into the environment. Slowly the words like "enemy" and "fighting" fell away, and though I could not describe it in any kind of scientific way, with spiritual sight I was able to see the sound *turning chaos to order*. This became my weapon of choice and like other soldiers, I sometimes had to stay awake for many days at a time, releasing the maximum effort to win. But eventually even the word "win" held too much of the tinge of egotistical pride, that locked me into the past history of this planet. Winning was a short-term fix, "harmony" is the goal of the spiritual warrior, and though it was a harder goal to reach, it was far more lasting an accomplishment, for it is never static and finished, it is a living movement of the balance of forces requiring constant awareness to maintain. Constant decisions had to be made in the moment, sometimes relying on the wisdom of the past, sometimes breaking out into completely unknown territory.

For many years I had been a New Age dreamer. I dreamed of step three, the goal of Peace. I idealized it and felt some kind of self–worth because I believed myself to be a good man, because I dared dream of Peace in such an angry world. But like too many people of my genera-tion, I was not willing to do what it took to go through step one and two to get to step three. One and two were hard work; it was much eas-ier to dream. Because I had been programmed to believe in some kind of idealized world, a better world than this, I would not engage this world; I longed to go to that other place, and even felt that longing to be holy. But in my love for the new friends around me, I was beginning to experience Heaven on Earth, and began to truly understand for the first time what Jesus' way really was about. It was about loving people, loving God by loving people. I quit my subconscious whining, and came to understand that I had come to this planet by choice, for the purpose of doing this work; it was my ministry. Though I did not like the idea of only having 'the choice of the lesser of two evils', on this planet, sometimes that's all you had, and maturity required working with what one had, not what one dreamed about.

My relationship with Ajla started to change after this. She knew that now I knew what had happened to her, and in silence, her shame slowly unraveled in my unconditional love for her. It became clearer to me now why I had become celibate some seven years earlier because of the exorcism with Veena and Carissa. The Tantrik chants and com-munion with the Word had created a neutral aura around me. To me, I was just being myself and had not noticed how I had imperceptibly changed in those seven years. In this part of the world they had never seen a practitioner of Tantra who held both male and female polarity at once, except for some of the Franciscan priest, but the Bosnians didn't completely trust anyone aligned with the Catholic Church. The result of being celibate for that long, was that there was no over-dominant male energy to scare the women who had been brutalized by men, and without any conscious effort, healing took place. I could always tell when Ajla let herself open to healing. She still carried the stress of hav-ing to make it through med-school, but she walked around talking ani-matedly with her thumbs in her pockets, flapping her hands back and forth like some kind of junior angel trying to lift off. In the middle of this hell, I had landed in a nest of Angels.

✳ ✳ ✳

The big van pulled up in front of Bridge of Peace and "Hard Headed Soul" fell into the street. They were a dirty, Dutch punk-rock band from a very successful artist commune in the south of Holland. Most of them lived off of the Dutch welfare system so they had plenty of free time to be 'artistic.' And this particular group spent their time well. They had traveled into many of the post-communist countries, giving concerts, bringing literature about new ways of living, computers, alternative technology, etc. They were quite wild and crazy but very intelligent, with hearts of gold. On this trip they were making connections to bring special buses that could pick up wheel-chaired people, and of course playing concerts where and whenever they could. They also invited many Eastern Europeans back to Holland where they created huge cultural festivals granted by the Dutch government. We became fast friends and hooked up with "Serious Road Trip," a British peace group comprised of old rock and roll 'roadies' who had done a tremendous job all during the war bringing in food to some of the hospitals. They had found a mental hospital just outside of town and had helped them keep many of the people from starving during the war. They also brought out music 'therapists,' clowns, and performers to be with the patients. The Dutch were invited to play a concert there and I came along.

The director of the hospital was a wonderful Serbian man stuck alone in the middle of Moslem territory, trying to keep over two hundred severely retarded people alive. Over a hundred of them starved to death before any help found them. The local Bosnians tried to push him out and take what little food they had for themselves, but he refused to go and eventually saved the lives of many innocent people. We pulled up in the van and were greeted by a happy crowd of strange creatures of all shapes and sizes. These people had no means of hiding their negative or positive feelings. The most beautiful smiling faces, many toothless and Mongoloid surrounded us; handshakes and hugs from dirty hands and arms, pure unbounded, unpretentious love. We opened the van, and in minutes all the amps and equipment were carried up the stairs and set up in all sorts of hilarious ways. They had never seen a rock band, and the fact that outsiders had found and come to see them was a great miracle in their simple minds. Normal people have many ways to push down their feelings in stressful times, but the mentally retarded, or 'challenged' as they say in America, have no defenses. They become the 'psychic sponge' for the whole area and take on what others discard and don't want to feel. They didn't have much understanding but felt intensely the horror going on around them, and they had watched many of their friends starve to death during the war. Simon, the leader of Serious Road Trip, told me that when they first found these people, many were in shock, crying and smashing their heads against the wall until they bled or went unconscious. These were the forgotten of the forgotten.

The band cranked up their guitars. They let the people themselves become the center of the concert and come up and scream into the microphone, and the hospital went 'crazy.' It sounded like the old Grateful Dead, a mass of sound and confusion that slowly wove itself into hypnotic music. Good, loud screaming rock and roll. The wonderful staff and head doctor came in and danced, they had never seen a punk band either. We yelled, screamed and danced for two hours. The people released their pain in the joy, and because the band's intention was to *give*, we all experienced the best healing ceremony any of us had ever seen. No exaggeration! A vortex opened up and the Spirit dropped in. This punk band had created some of the best 'Sound Temple' work I had ever witnessed.

It is the way of our culture to package things in new and interesting ways. But methods and techniques are useless without love. It is not a popular subject these days; it's not 'hip' anymore to even speak of it; it's so 'unscientific.' I knew that the only reason for being there was to *see* the beauty in these people. Imagine the tragedy of a child that grows up with no one to watch them. They use the parent as a reference point to know they are OK; they need someone to watch with loving attention so they feel confident to continue on their unique journey of growth. These people have never had that. In their part of the world it is thought that they are deformed because they are the "Devil's Children." So when someone looks at them with love and no judgment, they grow in leaps and bounds. They grow in intelligence and confidence. And this is the same for everyone. It makes no difference if they are children, war veterans or war criminals. Love is the only catalyst of evolution. This is the job of the healer and peace worker—to look past the 'appearance' of things, to look past the judgment of society or even the judgment that people have of themselves, and to see the perfection of their unique Soul. There is an overabundance in the world of people who will judge and condemn, but you may be the only person in that someone's life who sees goodness in them, which allows them to let it out and gives them a chance to grow. This is the only technique that a healer and peace worker need really know.

The next day Paul and Marsa from the punk band, asked me to go into Serb-held territory to take pictures for their newspaper back home. Paul was a tall, handsome and very well mannered photographer with a Mohawk haircut. Marsa was the girl driver of the band and she was short, squat and 'skank.' Marsa was a true hippie artist who lived in her car in Amsterdam, even in wintertime. She wore a big 'O' on her back, signifying that she didn't really exist; some kind of Amsterdamian Zen flag. And it worked. No one talked to her, but probably more because she hadn't washed in 'who knows how long.' To the Bosnian women, who dressed impeccably, she was a real enigma. But once our eyes met and we smiled at each other, I saw she was definitely more than yesterday's news; this was a formidable spiritual giant.

I was worried about going with them; they were nice people but dangerously unaware and arrogant in a war zone. The Dutch can tell a policeman to go take a hike if they want; they are a country that has won many interesting civil rights. But they always seem to make the innocent mistake of thinking that everyone else is as rational as they are. I told them to cool out a little, but they even saw that as an infringement of their rights. The kind of carnage and killing that had gone on here was so far from their reality that they might as well have been on the moon. But what the heck! Paul's birthday was the same day as mine, that was good enough reason to go.

We crossed the border and rolled into Pale with the stereo blasting. Pale is a mountain town currently in the international news because it is the hideout of the war criminal and head of the Bosnian Serbs, Karadzic, and the General Maladic. The town is called "Twin Peaks" in the western news (after the bizarre TV show) because of the somber, paranoid atmosphere. And we drive in and sit down like 'Pale's first tourists'! We were promptly arrested and taken to police headquarters. I'd had experience with the Serb police in Belgrade, so I knew what to expect. They watch a lot of western TV and mimic perfectly. Good cop—bad cop, accusations of being CIA, threats of how much trouble you are in, etc. They usually have two or three crews of questioners, and will take turns up to twelve hours grilling you. I sat calmly and prepared myself for the long haul. Paul and Marsa didn't fare so well. They were chain smoking, fidgeting, demanding their 'rights.' Marsa started to cry, which only made the police angry. The policeman yelled, "Why are you crying? We are not rapist." That only set her off more. I knew that according to the Dayton agreement, we had freedom of movement in their part of the country, so they were just going to play their game and then have to let us go. Inside I was laughing that the Dutch rockers were getting a good reality sandwich, but I was worried about Marsa's antics, and felt we would all end up in big trouble if we had to go the whole twelve hours. So I folded up my legs and went into meditation with my eyes open. I started the ancient Kundalini chants down in my belly and returned to the Sound that was now going on inside me, around the clock. I never know what is going to happen with these chants. They can invoke a strange supernatural atmosphere, but whether or not they become the horrifying destructive power of Durga or the soft compassionate power of Lakshmi, I never know. The first thing that happened was that the Sound dissolved the images that I had of the destruction I had seen created by the Serbs. Then the anger at what had happened to Ajla fell away. Now these were not 'Serbs' they were 'individuals,' no matter what they thought themselves to be. They seemed to become more agitated and confused the calmer I became. Paul and Marsa rallied in some silent understanding passing between them, and started grinning like fools. One of the policemen took Paul's film canister and told him that he was going to confiscate it. Paul calmly said, "No, it is blank film, there are no pictures on it." The officer shot back, "I am taking it from you!" Paul again, calmly and simply, answered, "You cannot have that." The policeman looked confused and put the film down. They started to ask me questions and I answered back in a monotone chanting sound. The police started looking at each other like, "Who are these crazy people?" If we were spies we certainly didn't act like anything they had seen before. The silent chanting started to lighten up the atmosphere. They bantered back and forth in their own language, laughing, rolling their eyes back, and raising their shoulders as if to say, "I don't know!" The finale came. They picked up Marsa's passport and began to look through it. Like all good hippies, she had pressed flowers and little mementos in all of her books, and they started to fall out of her passport. Suddenly, a very big, squashed cockroach dropped to the desk. Eight police gathered around to look, like shocked little children. One blessed himself with the sign of the cross, and the interrogator rolled his eyes up and said, "God save us." They all shook their heads in agreement and hurried through their paperwork as fast as the old typewriter would churn. One of the policemen started to joke with me, "As an American, have you come to take away our Karadzic and our General?" I spoke from my heart, without thinking. "My first allegiance is to God, which makes me care equally about all people." There was a genuine moment of knowing and spiritual touching each other with respect. We laughed and joked some more, and were out of the building in another fifteen minutes. I asked for permission to come back to their town and was invited back. They walked us to our van and stood in the parking lot waving goodbye as we pulled away. They didn't learn *that* from western TV!

God has great humor and wisdom. Three very different and odd 'missionaries' had been stuck together for a most dangerous mission. We landed amid the most brutal murderers of the whole war, and had laughed. I felt the "vortex" open in Pale, and in my spiritual eye I saw Karadzic falling from power and ending in ruin. It was done — Amen.

Actually, I had liked all these Serb policemen. They were in their late 20's and early 30's, and had an innocent, child-like curiosity that was charming. I knew they were just doing their jobs. They had been taught and programmed from the time they were children to hate the Muslim. And the Croats had sided with the Nazis in WWII and killed thousands of Serbs. So the old fear of the "Nazi-Croats" was invoked in this war. But underneath their programming they were like anyone else in the world. They loved life, they loved their children, they wanted to be free and feel secure. So why do nice people kill nice people? We always think of bullets as doing the killing, but rarely do we consider that it is *ideas* that launch the bullets.

When I was confronted with the kind of brutality that goes on here, all I could think of were the words of Jesus on the cross, "Father forgive them, they know not what they do." Seeing the destruction in this country, the point really hits home, they really "don't know what they do," and it would be impossible to point blame to any one people. Though it appears that the Bosnian Muslims are the victims, I could point out reasons why this happened to them. The world news would have us believe that all of a sudden perfectly normal next-door neighbors woke up and started shooting at each other. This creates the illusion that terrible events just happen, that we are victims to the whims of fate and anything can happen to us. But I do not believe in victimology and, again in the words of Christ, we are given a clear statement of how the world works. He says that even if you have done something in your mind, you are still responsible, as if you had done it in the physical world. And, of course, there will be repercussions. "As you sow, so shall you reap." "Every action has an equal reaction." Mr. Jamakovic, a very honest man, put things in perspective for me. He said, "In this part of the world we are very lazy, we have too much time to think. And what we usually think about is our neighbor. And what we usually think about is what is wrong with them. So if you think bad thoughts about your neighbor, it won't be long before he is thinking bad thoughts about you. When we are better people, we will have better conditions." Besides the Communist system needing to be destroyed here, this is a very accurate picture of the inner mental world and the root cause of the bloodshed, here and anywhere. The Moslems, Jews and Christians all have this not so endearing trait of thinking they are "the Chosen Ones," and openly or silently wish that the 'other' would disappear. Sarajevo has always been thought of as a place where the religions and ethnic groups have been able to live harmoniously, and they have. But look a little deeper and you could see that they have just developed good manners and have learned to successfully ignore each other. Compared to the religious battles that have gone on around here, this is a great accomplishment. But perhaps in Sarajevo we are seeing that evolution is asking us to evolve further—to actually caring for each other—if we wish to survive as the Human species.

I knew I could not share any of this with any of my friends in Sarajevo. It would take many years before they could see the world in this way, and that saddened me. I was in an atmosphere that had so much hatred for the Serbs, and it was hard to keep myself neutral after I saw what they did, and I began to think maybe I'd done all I could do here for now. From that day on, my evening meditation started to become a deep churning for more understanding. New 'realities' came as I opened myself more to the clashing thought forms of the world, and worked to balance them. Some huge event had happened to me personally, when I looked into the eyes of that young girl and her mother with her legs blown to shreds. What I could barely stand to think of in the weeks following that horrible moment, now I wanted to bring into clear focus, see exactly what this was.

Chapter 10

Meditations from the Frontline

An eagle flew out of the dark void and sat in front of me, perfectly still and staring. In the late evening meditations, this formidable being appeared again and again, watching me with earnestness, looking for an opening in my mind. I knew some new awareness was trying to make itself known to me. All the religious symbols of the world swirled in front of my spiritual eye, dancing together, clashing, enmeshing themselves into one another, then morphing into other symbols I had never encountered. I pondered the words of St. Paul, about how God had one day become tired of His old covenant with the Jews, because the people no longer followed it. So God created the new "everlasting" covenant between Christ and mankind; a covenant of forgiveness and redemption. But I could no longer accept anything on faith. I pushed and pulled, rolled and tumbled with the changing symbols. I questioned everything:

> *"If God one day gets fed up and ends the first covenant, it seems that he could just as easily do the same with the second." I'm sure the people of the old covenant thought it was going to be everlasting too. We have practiced turning the other cheek and forgiveness for 2000 years, and the world is still dammed by spineless tyrants and killers who spit on our holy forgiveness, and would take your life with no remorse, thinking they have the perfect right to do so."*

I had often tried to forgive people who had not asked for forgiveness, because I thought this was what I was supposed to do. I knew how to forgive to a fault! Jesus said forgive seventy times seven, and on the

cross he said "Father forgive them, for they know not what they do."
But that was His triumph of compassion and mercy, His magnificence.
But for those who had no change of heart, God did not forgive. Shortly
afterwards the corrupt priest and their temple were destroyed, and
eventually the corrupt Roman society fell too. It seems that God does
not ever break a covenant to create a new one, but rather that they both
now stand together. Jesus sowed the action of forgiveness in to the fabric of reality, by His words and actions while dying on the cross, and
that doorway is always open, but one must ask for that forgiveness. So
there is still the old covenant of the "Law" and the old justice for those
who are still to hate-dominated to live in a compassionate way towards
people, and also the covenant of "forgiveness and salvation" for those
who have made mistakes and are truly sorry for them. I contemplated
these things for many days as I worked to balance the thoughts and
feelings of all the many cultures that passed through my mind here in
Sarajevo. These covenants had been around for a long time, but still,
mankind did not seem to be learning. The carnage all around me was a
constant prod that forced me to wrestle with God and all I knew about
God. I reasoned with Him:

> "God...we need a new covenant, a free flowing and compassion-
> ate balance of the two...whatever has been in the past...it is not work-
> ing...this killing must stop... God, if something doesn't work, throw
> it our and come up with something new...It's just common sense
> man."

Then the "ah Ha" moment came. Of course! It had been in me the
whole time.

Sarajevo had been caught in the middle of the clashing eastern and
western cultures for centuries, and had been destroyed many times. But
one thing was different this time. Something that had never happened
before— the Americans were now here. One morning I took my daily
stroll through the middle of town, passing near my favorite Mosque in
the central square. Turning the corner into the grand square I was confronted by two heavily armed jeeps and a group of American officers.
My spirit just about leaped out of my body, I was so proud to be
American at this moment. One could quite literally feel the fear and
tension in the city dry up and crawl away when the troops started landing. Forgetting how strange a tall man wearing a black cowboy hat in
the middle of Sarajevo must have looked to the soldiers, I walked
straight up to the head colonel, stuck out my hand and said, "How the

hell are ya, man am I glad to see you guys." The officers were on edge in this new war zone, looking a little startled, they looked at each other in confusion. Finally the colonel stuck out his hand and with a thick southern accent said,

"Who the hell are you?!"

"Who the hell am I?" I stared back.

"Hell, I'm in charge of the whole damn operation!"

The officers looked at each other in astonishment. Then from our hearts and guts, a belly laugh roared out and filled the square, the Bosnians watching us with amusement. You could feel their tension start to lift, and this became the beginning of my relationship with one of the most wonderful, spirit filled, and positive group of men and women I had ever had the honor of working with. I assigned myself as "official greeter" and walked all over the city meeting and talking to soldiers in their many post and assignments. These soldiers moved me deeply, and this was not a superficial, nostalgic judgment. I had many long conversations, and got to see the American soldiers side by side with British, Italian, German, French, Russian, Dutch and Turks. Maybe it was the long history of war between European nations that contributed to this attitude, but the European soldiers were not very friendly to each other, or the Bosnians. In contrast, the Americans were very polite and calm. They did not strut around with macho dark faces like the Italians and the Turks. The Americans had that 'fun first' light attitude that we don't see about our culture until seeing it in contrast to other cultures, and yet there was an assurance in their demeanor that only comes from a place of secure power. They knew that America carries the 'big stick' in the world, so they forgot all the posturing and came across with a childlike curiosity and purity in contrast to these older cultures. What impressed me most was how polite they were to the Bosnians, every single soldier that I met, and that was many. I felt very at one with them in attitude and spirit and actually, for the first time as an adult, I was very proud of my country. There was nothing for us to gain in a material sense by being here; it was just the right thing to do. What a concept! At the same time there was also a feeling of no nonsense in their aura. One could feel the intensity of their superb training and warrior spirit. As I had seen in my meditations in Serbia, when people begin to murder innocent men, women and children, no matter where they were in the world, even their own countries, they had lost the right to govern themselves. These NATO forces were an awesome, physical and spiritual force to see and feel, and if these Balkan people were going to act like mad dogs, then the more intelligent of the species had the right and the duty to take control, for killing is the ultimate stupidity.

After setting up yoga classes with the help of a nurse captain, I began to meditate and engage with the spirit of these people. Never did I feel a sense of violence from them, but to my astonishment, what I felt was a genuine caring for human life, not only in the men and women, but also in the high ranking officers and the forces that controlled them. The caring of human life was not only for our own soldiers but even more so for the people of former Yugoslavia. Life was precious to these men and women, and I had never seen it so clearly until seeing it in contrast with other races of people who did not have this caring and respect for the individual. The West had money, and they were more than willing to take more time and throw more money into the conflict, to slowly change the feelings of the people, rather than jump in with a traumatic iron hand. The NATO commanders were relying more on the psychological warfare units rather than the heavy armor, though it's overwhelming presence was there assuring the people that the war had really stopped. But the American troops especially had a deep impact on the Bosnian people. The Americans were made up of Whites, African Americans, Oriental Americans, (the Admiral and commander of this area was a Mexican American), and Women, lots of Women. No other troops from any of the other European countries had such a racially integrated army. For people who had just torn themselves to shreds in a race war, the psychological impact of seeing the Americans was the most powerful instrument of peace in the world. And they all knew that NATO wouldn't have even come unless the Americans came.

In my pondering all this, I began to understand the awesome spiritual destiny of America, the gift that it was to the world, and would even more so become. America had been a cry for justice and freedom from tyranny in the collective hearts of the masses for many hundreds of years. The longing for freedom from tyrant kings and corrupt religions throughout the ages had to finally be created in the physical world, so that God's work of "E Pluribus Unum" could take place. Even the founding fathers couldn't see the spiritual vehicle that Democracy truly was to become. For evolution and intelligence can only unfurl when humans become self-aware enough to desire to be self-governing; America had opened this floodgate for the whole world. Also, Intelligence, and thus compassion for our fellow beings, can only increase when the problems of having "choice" are encountered. Without choices, there can be no challenge for intelligence to grow, and humans remain spiritual infants. America had many problems to work out, but the "intention" of America was pure, and in line with evolution— to give the most amount of freedom of creativity to the most amount of people. This is the natural way, because the Universe itself continues to evolve through the freedom of creativity of It's creations. While the religions and governments of old were systems created to control people, spawned from a mis-trust of the human, a belief that they were separate from Universal Intelligence, and in many cases, a belief that humans were downright evil— in contrast, Democracy was the ultimate affirmation and belief in the intelligence and goodness of people. A belief that if the human was given freedom, they would work out their destiny in line with "Divine Providence", as stated in the Declaration of Independence, our first statement of who we are as a Nation. Things had not always gone well, but the genius of democracy was that if it didn't work, one could always work to change it; it is always a work in progress. Sometimes I wished that all Americans could live in a Communist country, so they could see what it was like for people who had no rights or means to change anything, for the greatest tragedy of democracy was that people also had the choice to not use it. It was the ultimate dare that humans would work it out and do the right thing, and eventually live by Universal values, or not. I especially had a great reverence for Democracy because of my time with the Sikhs, who believed that Democracy was now at this time in evolution, God's tool for the furtherance of our human destiny. That is why they made it a cornerstone of their religion.

As the ambiance of the NATO forces continued to pervade the land, it created a feeling of safety for all people and allowed a letting go of the symbols and security blankets that kept us all tied to the past. Though I sometimes floundered and grasped for handholds while moving into the insecurity of the "new", a new way of being began to come into focus, a way that allowed a feeling of balance, peace and security to face the future. The emblem of the American eagle became a living symbol with a new spiritual significance for me; it became a representation of what I was personally feeling, and the way in which I now used my own energy. In one talon was the olive branch of peace— I offer you all this. But if you will not accept, for whatever reason, in the other talon, I have all these sharp arrows. Though most people try to feel secure by holding onto set rules for meeting new challenges, I felt on the deepest levels of my being how this behavior caused instead, the deepest insecurity. The feeling of a true security comes only when we rest in a Self trust in our own abilities to meet the challenges of the new with a fresh mind, that operates like the Universe itself—extravagant experimentation and unquestionable and unqualified trust that the core our Being, the very core of our actions is generosity and compassion for all Life. This was a radical stance to rest in, while in the middle of the carnage and insanity which was all around me; a formidable wraith that constantly whispered in one's ear, "See! This is your true nature, behold yourself." To hold a fortress of peace in the middle of this onslaught took considerable skill, it was truly a matter of 'being in the world but not of it.' Sarajevo became for myself, and for the soul of all society, a place and world event, where faith turned to knowledge and skill. This was the choice we were going to have to make to consciously take control of the destiny of this planet and stop this ancient human miasma of murder. Take control of the planet?! Was I still lost in a New Age dream? In moments of doubt, I merely walked over to the soldiers and communed. If I had doubts, these people had none. They were trained and absolutely ready to take control. They, without a doubt in anyone's minds, even the proud warlike Slavs, took control of this part of the planet, and it was done gently but firmly, without any trauma or loss of life. (Ye know a tree by its fruit). What was a new and marvelous experience for me, was to commune with these people and discover that the spiritual core that controlled them was benevolent, aligned, and all compassion. Also, anyone aligned with that frequency, by the right of Democracy, had the ability and right to be part of the governing forces behind these world powers. While practicing the Tantrik chants, many times I became a being whose arms and legs were these NATO forces. All had the right to participate on the spiritual plane. Because of the pure intention of America, by declaring it's own unique nature (a firm reliance on Divine Providence) and not a whining 'oh God save us' kind of self-pity, the doorway for all to be royal kings and queens stood wide open. All that was required was the passion, desire and Love to do so.

The quality of human being that I had been looking for in the ashrams and monasteries, I now found all around me in these dedicated soldiers. They were strong, brave, aware, protectors of human life, and lived by a code of honor, and being so disciplined, they took to yoga and meditation instructions with great attention. I felt deeply honored to be teaching them, and felt a great smile for being given the opportunity to serve my country in a way I never would have dreamed of.

America was the only place in history, where all the religions and races co-existed in peace. America was an umbrella to them all; she would bring peace to the world, not them. America was as sacred as any religion.

* * *

My nightly meditations were becoming much more visual and fantastic. I took part in discussions in fantastic counsel chambers, with incorporeal beings that debated the future of humanity. The consensus was that the time of suffering to help others was over. The time of martyrs was over. The wheel of "Dharma" or human destiny had turned to a pure Democracy, meaning that the individual had to become more self-reliant and take more responsibility for their own destiny and connection with God, without the 'middle men.' The path of 'taking on the suffering of the world' had served its purpose; it had created a compassionate, giving human species— at least the souls who took this path. But the Universe evolves by experimenting on itself and this experiment had only been partially successful. It was time for a new refinement of the path in which the Human species would evolve to a more Universal consciousness, or as St. Paul said, "to have the mind of Christ." This did not mean that we no longer helped suffering humanity. On the contrary, in this age, the path to Universal consciousness is service, no longer asceticism or scholarship. But it did mean that we could be even more effective by *not taking on the suffering*. It is very possible to help someone and not take on their pain. There is no more reason to martyr oneself to help others, and I was experiencing this myself; though in the midst of such suffering, my daily meditative practice kept me in perfect peace and health. I saw the people of Sarajevo collectively coming to this new decision also. After many months of running scared through their own city, hiding and moving in back alleys to avoid the snipers, at some point in the war it seemed they collectively decided they had enough of living like rats, and decided to just go on with normal life, they were not going to run and hide any longer; thousands were gunned down, but they seemed fearless of death. Also, hundreds of people committed suicide during this war. At first, there was great effort to stop them, but after a few years, the helpers were just too busy with people who wanted help. Eventually suicide was looked at as a reasonable personal choice, and under these circumstances, no one had the ability or right to tell an individual what was right or wrong for them; and this was done more out of respect, rather than frustrated resignation. Self-healing, self-choice, and self-responsibility was becoming the first rule. There was no other way for God's compassion and power to reach all.

The nightly interior council meetings were a philosopher's dream.

Ideas that had been set in motion, meant to last for hundreds of years in earth time, now no longer made sense. The Human species was evolved enough to learn to have to think on the run, nothing was set in stone. But what about the energy of pain and suffering, what would happen if all the light workers stopped taking it on and transmuting it for everyone else, praying for the salvation of the souls who caused suffering in the world. It looked like Heaven's new policy was going to be 'tough love', though it always had been, it was going to get tougher. The energy of pain and suffering was now going to fall on those who caused it, like a ton of bricks; let those who create the pain take it on. Who are those that cause the suffering? There was no great debate about the nuances of what was right or wrong, it seemed like most things were allowed on this planet and that freedom was necessary for humans to evolve by the lessons of discernment. But the murder and rape of innocents, this was clearly not allowed. It was as if human evolution ran between two tracks. It had to run freely so that intelligence could evolve, everything had consequences but was looked on as learning. But murder of any species was crossing the line, going over the track. The time of 'father forgive them, they know not what they do', for murders, was passing; now it is time in evolution in which the collective and the individual 'do know what they do'— and if they don't, they will learn very fast, because evolution now speeds up the process of feeling the consequences of ones own actions. It is actually not compassion to indiscriminately pray for to shield people from the consequences of their actions, for how else will they grow and change? In the West, we have a very limited idea of compassion. The Buddhist names it "grandmothers" compassion. But there is another kind, called "crazy wisdom" compassion, meaning if someone really needs a punch in the nose, it is a very compassionate act, to give it to them. Of course this philosophy can be abused, so it takes a Universally aware being to know when to use which kind of compassion. From what I saw and felt, these soldiers and the forces of America that controlled them, had that enlightened wisdom and balance.

To participate in this powerful, grace filled wave, the requirement was to stop whining about the past abuses of judgment that America had gone through, and instead know that Democracy was a living plant that was alive right now, needed water and caring right now. It gave power to, and belonged only to those who participated. There was no more time for judgment of what went before. I was riding on the spear tip of evolution of the planet, and there was just too much to deal with in the moment to be bogged down with something as cumbersome as

judgments of the past. We were evolving beyond being murders, by
Universal will and by the will of the people of this planet; there was
nothing philosophical or personal about it, it just is. This was the question that was up for everyone at the Battle of Sarajevo.

The past religions had taught obedience to authority outside of
oneself, in the form of a person or an unquestionable dogma. But as the
heat of continuous combat in the mental planes burned away what was
no longer useful, the experience of 'having the Mind of Christ' was free
to surface. For myself, it was a feeling of restful 'knowing' and a
grounded whole body feeling of being in alignment with Universal
Will. That all parts of myself, all attitudes were created for a reason,
and in the right place and time, were used to further the Universal
Cause. I no longer needed to know what the Universal Cause would
look like in its completed form on earth; I couldn't possibly know how
everything was going to work out. Instead, there was an understanding
that as long as I could feel and commune with my core intentions,
'Peace on earth, good will to all beings,' then my actions in the now
were Universal Will. In the expanse of time I was just one small cog on
the wheel, but at the same time, so much for the past and future
depended on my actions. That kind of confidence comes only with a
mind unfettered by the passing currents of civilization, un-afraid to set
sail into the unknown. However, to stay in that mindscape takes manual labor in this world, and in my personal life I was soon to learn that
the only thing that can conquer us, comes from our own weaknesses. It
was time for me to get my butt kicked. *Damn!*

* * *

I had been going to the old Catholic cathedral every other day for
the last seven months. It was clear that the priest did not like me there
because the younger people seemed overly curious about who I was and
what I was doing there. Most of them knew that I was welcomed at the
Sufi Mosque, and also prayed with them. This kind of thing wasn't
done in this part of the world. You were supposed to be one or the
other, and that was that. I did not cower to the priests, did not call them
"Father" and they were furious. These priests acted as if Vatican II had
never happened, and still tried to control the people by scare tactics and
separation of the priesthood and the lay people. But two miles across
town was an old Franciscan Monastery, and here I was warmly welcomed and had met many new friends. This is where I came on alter-
nate days. One day at the cathedral I met a striking young nun, and we

slowly started up a silent 'energetic' relationship. I would always sit no more than one row away from her so we could shake hands when the part of the ceremony came to wish each other peace. It had been very hard to keep my sexual energy in balance, being around Selma and her outrageous friends. Even though I wasn't eating much, chanting gave me tremendous energy, one slip and who knew what would happen. There were many beautiful young women around that I could have made love to, and was encouraged to do so by my friends, but in the circumstances it didn't feel appropriate. My decision to stay celibate after Veena, had always been a day-to-day decision, I never thought I would go more than a year. But it felt right so I kept going, and before I noticed, seven years had gone by. Truthfully I was becoming very lonely for a woman. It was not my intention to stay celibate for my whole life and I knew that some day I wanted to find a mate. So I was happy to be exchanging 'energy' with this nun because I knew the only way I could have a relationship with her was to have one of absolute purity, and that's more of what was required of me in my current situation. As the months went by, I started to love her, and that more than anything helped me keep my thoughts pure; using a little discipline, it was a very fulfilling relationship. It became obvious to others that we liked each other, especially the two young priests who said most of the masses here; I definitely pushed their buttons. I'm sure it was hard for them; they couldn't even look me in the eyes. One night at the end of my meditation, I remembered thinking, "I wonder if she would leave the convent and learn to know the worship of Marriage with me." I fell asleep. I awoke in a waking dream, and a priest was standing in front of me holding the Chalice and Host, the most potent symbol, the very essence of the Catholic faith. The priest said,

"Leave here and go work in Mexico." I answered,

"What?"

His words just didn't feel right to me! I closed my eyes and said to myself,

"I'm in a waking dream."

I opened my eyes and he was still there holding the Host and Chalice in front of me. He spoke again,

"It is the Lord telling you to go work in Mexico, and if you won't listen I don't know what to tell you."

I woke in the morning feeling violated and angry. One of the ways one knows they have had contact with an authentic spiritual source is that you feel up, joyous and energetic. I was angry. This is a common trick of advanced sorcery. Sorcerers will use a potent symbol to hide behind, picking one that they know you are already conditioned by, and plant their promptings in your mind while ones reactions to the symbol play out in the nervous system. Religions and governments all through human history, and now in modern day advertising have used this technique successfully. But years earlier, Jesus had revealed Himself to me directly, I did not need symbols. In the Catholic mass, the Host and Chalice become the body and blood, or the very essence of Christ that feeds you in a physical way, but only because of one's faith. The symbols have no power of their own unless there is someone there to give them power, by their faith. There has to be willingness. In the mass, my own "I Am" *chooses* to make it real. In this waking dream, "I Am" had not given my permission to be approached and participate. I was happy that I had caught it right away, showing me that I could no longer be conditioned, even on the deepest psychic planes, and I could even muster up a sense of humor about it. Hey, I was playing around with his girl friend, he had a right to try and put the 'whammy' on me. But it was too late. Like a computer virus, it had been planted and now had to run its course; the anger threw me out of balance. My aura leaked open, and the negative depression that stalked this land pounced on me. Then, to make things worse, every night for the next two weeks, "they" came. Every woman I had ever had sex with— without love, every girl I had ever fantasized about, every picture of every girl in Playboy magazine I had masturbated to as a kid. The sexual energy was excruciating; I knew if I slipped, I would be carried away on a runaway train for weeks. I could not collapse like this here in Sarajevo. I held it all in, and burned in my own interior Purgatory; depression hit hard:

> *"What was I doing here?" "Who the fuck do I think I am, trying to help these people?" "I'm nobody, what can I do?" "Hell, I don't even know if prayer works anyway, I just came all the way over here on a big ego trip, just trying to find myself, I don't care about these people."*

All the thought forms that the dark powers want us to believe had their way with me. Ajla, Nedim and Selma became scared as they watched me transform over a few days. Watching them became so painful; I finally came to them and told them it was time for me to leave. They were heartbroken, and had no idea what to say or do for me, and I fell into shame knowing I had hurt them. This was one of the greatest fears of people in war. So many people leave and never come back, they would just rather not get attached to anyone, it hurts so much to keep losing people. They had trusted and loved me, and now I was leaving. And like this! I sadly walked over to the Franciscan Monastery for the afternoon mass. I asked for guidance and help, and participated in the Communion that I did give my faith to, then came back to my room and sat. A few days passed and the phone rang. Nedim knocked on my door.

"It is the phone for you, it is a girl".

I felt a breath move through my body as I picked up the receiver.

"Jeorge, qu'est-ce qui se passe?"

It was Veena! She had called my mother in California to find me and wanted to talk to me. She said she was happy, now and in her first normal relationship with a man who loved her. I could hear in her voice that she was a different human being with a center of strength and joy, and we chatted away like no time had past. She said she was thankful for our time together, and would I please stay in touch with her. I had kept my celibacy and prayed for her and her family every day for seven years. When I put down the phone, I was smiling. Everyone in the room changed with me. Selma taunted me,

"Who was *thaaat*, George?"

I smiled and said,

"You know I'm coming back, don't you", and I began to laugh. Selma shook her head,

"You're not normal, George." I laughed more.

Faith is not a matter of hoping something will happen or being worried about what is the right way to proceed. It is about deciding to take a stand, no matter what the cost, never giving an inch until one sees the result. But there are things we do to ourselves that cause us to waver and miss our mark. I do not like the word "sin" and never use it. I never felt guilty for my past, even though I knew I would have changed some things if I had a chance, but I never saw it as sin. But I will say this, for every person we have ever hurt, including ourselves, we will get to feel that pain again someday. For all waste of our energy, we must one day pull it back and grow our nerves to what they should have been had we not wasted it. We are responsible for what we do with our life force, and whatever we cast out into the world must some day be retrieved. This is the real Purgatory, and it's about as much fun as teething.

✳ ✳ ✳

That night I had another dream. I was in an underground cavern with Ajla, Nedin and some other friends. Two old women approached me, one was all white and pudgy like the Pillsbury Dough Boy, and her eyes were dark and scary. She would not speak or look at me. I knew she was part vampire. She was also the goddess of the region. All the religions in this part of the world were sky God religions, and "She" was not respected. The religions dominated women and had no real respect for them; there was not even a caring for the Earth. So out of frustration, she drank the blood of the people here. She caused the centuries of war and carnage, but she was not happy and received no nourishment from it; though she was fat on the gluttony of war, her skin was pale and dead. The other woman spoke to me,

"You cannot do what you came to do here because of the law of," she started to list a barrage of names.

I stopped her and said, "I have earned my right to be here." They both looked at me.

"I am building a Sound Temple where everyone will make the *Sound of God*, and you are invited." She simply said "Yes," and was happy.

The next evening, we had our last party, and on this night, a ferocious thunderstorm rolled over the hills. Late in the evening, Nedim picked up the guitar and started singing wonderful old Bosnian tunes; everyone raucously and loudly joined in. Selma sat next to me, her tiny body shaking with spirit, pushing her soft voice into the crowd. Suddenly, a crack of lightning and thunder, and the power was out. We went right on singing louder. They had spent many months just like this in the past four years, singing and partying in the dark. Nothing could break these people. In that darkness that I had been blessed to share with them, all power and light was being born.

We tumbled out into the street to catch the new morning rays. We all looked up at once, and there over old Sarajevo, from mountaintop to mountaintop, was the most magnificent, giant, double rainbow, brighter than any I had ever seen, even in Hawaii. To the Muslim, Noah was one of the great prophets, and they all knew the story in the Bible of how God sent the rainbow as a sign after the flood. Nedim said they had seen rainbows, but no one here had ever seen a double rainbow. People all over town came out of their shops to look. They were still cautious with their hearts, it would take awhile before they let in any kind of feeling of hope. But Nedim finally turned to me, the words came out quietly, "It's a good sign."

I know I am a very dramatic fellow, and have worked in Hollywood and all that, but I swear it's the truth—that's the way this ends! — Amen!

Epilogue

The Way

Out of the living Void we came, the very ground of our being, the
ultimate generosity. So generous that it poured it's ALL into creation,
and that is why it is empty, void. The first photons of light boiled into
existence and created incalculable complex operations to create the first
elements. The same attraction called Love that pulls humans together,
formed complex combinations in the heat of giant furnaces called stars.
The Life evolved into more and more complex combinations until the
worlds were created— Colors, sounds, power and beauty. Then it
evolved further through countless experiments until it created an organ
out of ITSELF, whereby IT could look back at ITSELF and feel a
sense of wonder and gratitude. It was called the Human Being. How
did this all come to be? How did it harmoniously lead to the Word
made Flesh, the template ideal that all humanity must become? Who
can speak of and explain this holy chronicle? None. In ancient times
it was simply called "the Way."

The Truth

In Jesus' times, as in our own, there were hundreds of advanced
philosophies, systems of religion and mystery, all saying "we are the
truth." Priests, magicians, philosophers and scientists filled with power
and authority to tell you and convince you what the truth is. The systems, then as today, became more important than the person.
"What truth should I listen to? Which one is the right one?", we
ask. Jesus cut through it all and answered for all of us, "I AM the
Truth." What pours out of Me is the Truth. From the very Source,
every cell of My Body poured forth. Every photon of light that was
there in the beginning is now present in our own nervous systems, ani-
mating our thoughts and movements. From the generosity of the Way,
we poured forth and are Truth. What the Way now continues to pour

forth through those who love, is the Truth.

The Life

Endless vitality, alive in myriads of countless galaxies— every form of life, from the smallest cell, to the largest galaxies, filled with Life, in constant motion.

G-generating, O-organizing, D-destroying. Every cell of our bodies, one with the endless process of birth, death, and rebirth—moving through and in the life of the Way—in eternal motion— spinning on the wheel of Love.

* * *

Throughout the many months in Europe I fasted and prayed as I had done for many years earlier. But this time it was not for the purpose of chasing enlightenment, or to attain God or salvation, but rather out of love for my friends. I grew to love and respect these people so much that I would have laid down my life for them with no question. In that willingness of giving, I found my true Life and everything that passed before was as if a dream. I understood the unique salvatory nature of the Christ mind, as the whole history of the world passed thru my body and dissolved into the Sacred WORD. Now every cell of my being sings the Word with all of creation, "Hosanna in the Highest!" With no more philosophy, thinking or argument, I now am effortlessly and erotically breathed by the Universe. I know nothing more or less than I knew that day in Alaska standing on the plateau with my friend, the moose. But now I can appreciate the fullness of what I knew. Now, the physical world is to me the Spiritual world.

Because it is what I was made to do, what we are all made to do, I became aligned and one with

The Way
　　The Truth
　　　　The Life.

* * *

In looking back over just the last ten years, we can see the speed with which world changes are beginning to happen. As we inch our way toward a more mature species of Human, there is great alarm in the world at the upheaval and blood shed that change sometimes brings. But consider this — if an alien from some other world were to come and see a woman giving birth, they would probably be just as alarmed. There is moaning and screaming, there is blood and trauma. But behind the appearance, there is a great miracle about to happen. It is just so with the transition that we pass through on earth. Many new miracles await us if we can traverse this historical birthing channel and embrace our magnificent, true human design. How should it be done? —With great care and love. With great respect and thankfulness for what has gone before, the people and the institutions. Many millions of beings made great sacrifice, many gave their lives so that we would know the fullness of our lives. There is much that is good in the old religions and institutions, and it is the privilege and duty of our generation to distill from them what is good, forgiving the rest, knowing that all was necessary for us to awaken in any moment. For though the debate goes on about dates and times of the Second Coming, still, many heard Jesus say it loud and clear — "the Kingdom is Hear and Now", and it always will be Hear and Now. There will be those that resist this realization and try to hold on to what is familiar. But in my own journey, I found my happiness and spiritual maturity grew in direct proportion to how patient and compassionate I could be with those whose transition was (in appearance) slower and more filled with fear than mine. If in dealing with the 'old hierarchies', we turn it into a contest of 'us against them', then we have lost the Christ. And if we lose the Christ, we have lost ourselves and will go the way of the dinosaur. As a member of the human family, I have an interest in seeing that this doesn't happen.

Over three decades I studied the many advanced spiritual technologies, but they did not 'fill my cup.' In the end, it was the simple Human love for my fellow beings, and them for me, that spurred me on to find Truth. It is in this spirit that I offer my memoirs, in hope that it will inspire others to try more, dare more, believe more in yourselves and your talents. The common person has immense power to make change in the world, power that is given, as we are willing to let it spill out into the world.

"To him that hath, it is given; to him that hath not, it is taken away."

It is effortless, all we need do is 'suit up and show up' and the Universal creates the miracles all around us. Let each person now do their part to opening the doorway to "Heaven on Earth." Let each person know the joyful truth of themSelves———Amen!

About the Author

George Craig McMillian {Kirantana} began his formal spiritual research with the Catholic Brothers of the Holy Cross of Notre Dame. While beginning pre-seminary studies, his mother and father divorced. His mother was unfairly shunned by the Church, causing his whole family to leave the Catholic faith. George continued his search in eastern religions and mysticism. He had already mastered two styles of Kundalini yoga in over 20 years of practice in ashram and monastic life before meeting Tenzin Gyatso, the 14th Dalai Lama, who taught and initiated him into the Kalachakra Tantra. Many years later he became a teacher and heir in the Shambala lineage while performing the Kalachakra ritual for World Peace, continuously for eight months, while serving as a peace worker in Sarajevo in the closing months of the Bosnian war. After having received a vision of the Universal Christ, he gave up all titles and compiled the knowledge of his three decades of spiritual search into the "Peace Yoga" classes and seminars.

George has been a dish washer, waiter, cook, store manager, film laboratory technician, welder, carpenter, bus and truck driver, yoga and martial arts teacher, club bouncer, body-guard, drug rehab councilor, recording artist and peace worker. Today he is a musician, Naturopathic Medical Doctor, and teacher of peace studies.

Join us at
www.DemocracyByTelepathy.com